International Comparative Research

Also by Linda Hantrais

* CONTEMPORARY FRENCH SOCIETY

CROSS-NATIONAL RESEARCH METHODS IN THE SOCIAL
SCIENCES
(*co-editor with Steen Mangen*)

FAMILIES AND FAMILY POLICIES IN EUROPE (*with Marie-Thérèse
Letablier*)

FAMILY POLICY MATTERS: Responding to Family Change in Europe

* GENDERED POLICIES IN EUROPE: Reconciling Employment and
Family Life (*editor*)

MANAGING PROFESSIONAL AND FAMILY LIFE: A Comparative
Study of British and French Women

POUR UNE MEILLEURE ÉVALUATION DE LA RECHERCHE
PUBLIQUE EN SCIENCES HUMAINES ET SOCIALES (vol. 2)

* SOCIAL POLICY IN THE EUROPEAN UNION (*third edition*)

THE UNDERGRADUATE'S GUIDE TO STUDYING LANGUAGES

LE VOCABULAIRE DE GEORGES BRASSENS
Vol. 1: Une étude statistique et stylistique
Vol. 2: Concordance et index des rimes

* *From the same publishers*

International Comparative Research

Theory, Methods and Practice

Linda Hantrais

First published 2009 by
PALGRAVE MACMILLAN

Palgrave Macmillan in the UK is an imprint of Macmillan Publishers Limited, registered in England, company number 785998, of Houndmills, Basingstoke, Hampshire RG21 6XS.

Palgrave Macmillan in the US is a division of St Martin's Press LLC, 175 Fifth Avenue, New York, NY 10010.

Palgrave Macmillan is the global academic imprint of the above companies and has companies and representatives throughout the world.

Palgrave® and Macmillan® are registered trademarks in the United States, the United Kingdom, Europe and other countries.

ISBN-13: 978–0–230–21768–3 hardback
ISBN-10: 0–230–21768–0 hardback
ISBN-13: 978–0–230–21769–0 paperback
ISBN-10: 0–230–21769–9 paperback

This book is printed on paper suitable for recycling and made from fully managed and sustained forest sources. Logging, pulping and manufacturing processes are expected to conform to the environmental regulations of the country of origin.

A catalogue record for this book is available from the British Library.

A catalog record for this book is available from the Library of Congress.

10 9 8 7 6 5 4 3 2 1
18 17 16 15 14 13 12 11 10 09

Printed and bound in China

Contents

List of Figures

Preface

For centuries, comparative approaches have been used to observe and analyse social phenomena and, more recently, to develop and test theory in the social sciences and humanities. Despite their long history, the debate continues about the fundamental questions raised by comparisons, more especially when they cross national, cultural and linguistic boundaries. Since the late 1980s, interest in international research projects and networking has grown exponentially, particularly within the European Union. Governments have called for researchers to be internationally active and to cooperate at international level. Within Europe, such cooperation is seen as essential in making the Union 'the most competitive and dynamic knowledge-based economy in the world, capable of sustainable economic growth...and social cohesion' (Lisbon European Council, Presidency Conclusions, 23–24 March 2000). Efforts to strengthen the European Research Area, combined with European enlargement to the East, and the rapid development of the data collection capacity of international organizations with worldwide reach have created a niche for a book designed to help equip new generations of students and researchers with the skills and knowledge required to make a meaningful contribution to the understanding of global research markets in the social sciences and humanities.

Within such a context, the present volume aims to fill gaps in a major body of hitherto largely disconnected and disparate literature by responding to the needs of researchers, funders and users of comparative research from a wide range of disciplines, different epistemologies, research cultures and national backgrounds. In recent decades, efforts have been made to prepare comparative researchers more adequately for their task. For example, the occasional series of *Cross-National Research Papers* (see www.xnat.org.uk), launched in 1985 and co-edited by the author of the present volume, set out to inform researchers engaged in, or contemplating embarking on, international comparative studies about the experience of others working in the field. Five years later, Else Øyen's (1990: viii) edited collection of papers sought 'to make visible some of the important choices' faced by researchers engaging in cross-national rather than single-nation studies, 'thereby displaying pitfalls to be avoided and improving…awareness of available strategies and their limitations'. An edited collection published in 1996 by the present author and Steen Mangen aimed to provide an accessible resource book for cross-national comparative researchers in the social sciences. It remains, however, that researchers embarking on international comparative research across national, societal and cultural boundaries, as well as experienced researchers, funders and users of research findings wanting to enhance existing skills, often lack the knowledge, competencies and tools needed to conduct effective comparisons or evaluate outcomes.

The International Comparative Research Process

The task of contributing to a greater understanding of the research process is central to the present book. The objective is to provide researchers, practitioners, policy advisers and organizations commissioning international comparative research with a sound theoretical, methodological and practical resource covering the design, management and delivery of reliable comparisons. The book sets out to guide readers through the research process using illustrations from a variety of comparative studies, many of them with a strong focus on European societies, the knowledge base and the policy dimension. The chapters draw on real-life experience of managing and conducting international comparative research projects and studies, acquired over more than 20 years from personal involvement and from accounts provided by researchers at varying stages in their careers, to analyse and document the theory, methods and practice of international comparative research.

Mutual policy learning and transfer across national borders has become an important offshoot from comparative research at a time when international interest in policy evaluation and evidence-based policy is being developed far beyond the Anglo-American policy and research communities. Much of the work referred to in this volume is relevant to policy and concerns the contribution of comparative research to well-informed policy formulation, development and implementation.

The scope of the book is designed to be broad yet specific. It is broad both in its disciplinary coverage and in the approaches described. Examples are drawn from political science, economics, history, linguistics, anthropology, ethnology, psychology, sociology and public/social policy, ranging over quantitative and qualitative strategies. Reference is also made to innovative methodological approaches and the issues raised by combined methods. The book is specific in that it narrows the focus to questions relating to the theory, methods, management and practice of international comparisons insofar as they add an extra dimension to comparative research and require additional skills when crossing linguistic and cultural boundaries.

The volume adopts a topic-based approach, covering the definition and mapping of international comparative research, the selection of units of observation, disciplinary variants, concepts in relation to contexts, combined methods, the research–policy interface, evidence-based policy, policy evaluation, learning and transfer, and the issues raised by international project management. The chapters address the various stages in the research process and the impact of the international comparative dimension, from research design and data collection through to the analysis and interpretation of findings. The concluding chapter on research management devotes attention to the acquisition of team and networking skills, access to funding, the impact of funding bodies on the nature and conduct of research, and the contribution made by international comparative research to the development of theory, methods and practice in the social sciences and humanities.

Chapter Outline

The first two chapters provide a state-of-the-art review for readers who are less familiar with international comparative research across a range of disciplines. The introductory chapter sets out to define what is meant by international comparative research. It does so by seeking answers to two key questions: What are the defining characteristics of international comparative research across nations, societies and cultures, and what are the benefits to be gained from undertaking comparative studies in international settings? The chapter goes on to track the development of comparative research, particularly since the 1980s at European and national level, in response to the call for a coherent international engagement strategy in research and development to underpin a Europe of knowledge and the European Research Area.

Individual disciplines have developed their own distinct theoretical traditions, which are reflected in the research design and data collection methods they adopt in comparative work. These differences are often presented in terms of a dichotomy. At the one extreme are large-scale quantitative approaches such as those used by political scientists, for example to compare voting patterns or electoral systems, with the aim of identifying universalistic trends from which generalizations can be made. At the other are the fine-grained detailed qualitative studies undertaken by ethnographers interested in understanding how different cultures have evolved. Drawing on a wide variety of examples, the second chapter examines how the whole spectrum of comparative approaches has developed and is applied within and across disciplines.

Chapters 3–5 will be of particular interest to those seeking to gain a fuller understanding of the international comparative research process. The aim in the third chapter is to explore the many components of research design in international comparative research projects, and to show how choices made at the outset can influence the research process and outcomes, and how the many pitfalls can be avoided or countered. The likely outcome of any international comparative project is largely determined at a very early stage in a research project. The selection of the object of inquiry, units and levels of analysis, the formulation of research questions, the theoretical and methodological approaches adopted, and the analysis and interpretation of findings are closely interrelated factors that need to be taken fully into account in project design. The rationale for selecting particular topics, comparators or units of analysis can often be explained by non-scientific factors. Yet the scientific rationale is critical in determining not only the inputs in terms of the methods and materials but also the outputs in terms of findings and dissemination strategies. The difficulties involved in reaching consensus over the epistemology of comparisons, the selection of comparators and the variables used within different disciplines and research cultures justify an analysis of the effects that these choices can have on research findings and, ultimately, on those who use them.

The lack of a common understanding of central concepts and the societal contexts within which phenomena are located and where national policies are formulated and implemented can undermine international comparisons. The purpose of the fourth chapter is, therefore, to examine how some of the key concepts in the social sciences and humanities are understood and interpreted in different national settings, and to look at issues of equivalence of concepts, procedures and interpretation. The chapter provides researchers involved in international comparative projects with a rationale and practical guidance for analysing socioeconomic and political phenomena in relation to their institutional and sociocultural settings. It tracks the shift in international comparisons in the social sciences and humanities away from universalistic culture-free approaches to culture-boundedness, and offers guidance on the selection of contexts, in recognition of the centrality of contextualization for the theory and practice of comparative studies.

The fifth chapter explores the advantages, but also the problems, of combining and integrating different research strategies within and across paradigms in comparative research. It reviews the reasons for the supposed incompatibility between epistemological approaches and the methods that have come to be associated with them. It then examines the various ways in which methodological pluralism or multi-strategy research can be exploited to extend the scope of comparative studies, test and reinforce their validity, develop new insights and offer concordant or discordant explanations for observed similarities and differences. The concluding section acknowledges the limitations of multi-strategy comparative research while also reiterating its advantages.

The sixth chapter will be of particular interest to researchers, policy advisers and practitioners involved in policy-oriented research, since it examines how international comparative research in the social sciences and humanities can assist policy development. It asks what can be gained from studying the research–policy interface, what policy actors can learn from international comparative research into social phenomena, and how such research can inform policy. In seeking to answer these questions, the chapter begins by analysing the relationship between research and policy with reference to a number of theories about the utilization of social science and humanities research by policy makers and practitioners. It explores the differing nature of research and policy making, the limitations of social science knowledge, the capacity of research governance to integrate research and policy, and the attempts made to bridge the communications gap. The growing interest in evidence-based policy, policy evaluation, learning and transfer at national level, particularly in Anglo-American research communities, has further extended the scope of international comparisons. The success of policy-oriented studies depends on an in-depth understanding of the policy process in different environments. Such work raises a number of important methodological issues about the conditions that need to be met if lesson drawing and the transportability of policies across national boundaries are to be effective. In conclusion, the chapter reviews mechanisms for enhancing the synergy between research and policy.

The final chapter revisits the issues raised throughout the book to provide guidance for the effective management of projects that cross national, societal and cultural boundaries. It examines how the composition and coordination of research teams across disciplines and countries impact on research design and implementation. In addressing issues of funding for international comparative research, the chapter explores the implications of disciplinary classifications for access to funding, project management and cooperation. The conclusion offers a tentative assessment of the contribution that international comparative social sciences and humanities research can make to scientific inquiry, international understanding and the global socioeconomic knowledge base.

Linda Hantrais

1

Defining and Mapping International Comparative Research

Not all international research is comparative, and not all comparative research is international or cross-national. The social science and humanities literature has engaged in a long-running debate about terminology and substance. If agreement is relatively widespread regarding the meaning of 'comparative research', the same cannot be said of 'international', 'cross-national' or the other terms used to describe research that crosses national, cultural or societal boundaries.

In this chapter, an attempt is made, firstly, to reach a working definition of international comparative research, the preferred term in this volume, by addressing the 'what' and why' questions. The chapter goes on to map the development of international comparative research from its origins to the present day, with particular reference to the changes over the past century associated with globalization. The growing interest in international comparisons can also be seen as a response, at international and national level, to the call for a more coherent regional engagement strategy to support research and development, epitomized in Europe by the launch of the European Research Area in 2000.

Defining International Comparative Research

Attempts to define international comparative research raise two clusters of key questions that are the focus of the first section in this introductory chapter. The first cluster concerns our understanding of the term 'international comparative research'. What is international comparative research? What, if any, distinction can be made between comparisons across nations, societies and cultures and within-country, within-society or within-culture comparative studies? Is it justifiable, accordingly, to talk about a distinct method and/or methodology in comparative studies that cross national, societal or cultural boundaries? The second cluster of questions involves discussion of the benefits to be gained from undertaking international comparisons. Why should, and do, researchers devote time and effort to the immensely complex task of designing, managing and conducting systematic comparative research projects? The 'when' and 'how' to compare questions are addressed in subsequent chapters.

WHAT IS INTERNATIONAL COMPARATIVE RESEARCH?

In the social sciences and humanities, 'comparative research' is the term widely employed to describe studies of societies, countries, cultures, systems, institutions, social structures and change over time and space, when they are carried out with the intention of using the same research tools to compare systematically the manifestations of phenomena in more than one temporal or spatial sociocultural setting.

Social scientists in general agree that international comparative studies require individuals or teams to compare specific issues or phenomena in two or more countries, societies or cultures, without expressly excluding the possibility of comparison over time. More specifically, in their definitions of comparative studies, political scientists tend to adhere to what has become conventional usage in their discipline, namely that comparison should be between countries or cross-national, thereby largely discounting intra-country comparisons and the temporal dimension as defining properties (Mackie and Marsh, 1995: 173).

Consensus is less widespread across other disciplines about the appropriateness of both the prefix 'cross-' and the adjective 'national' to describe the process, which is why the term is deliberately avoided in its generic sense in this volume. The prefix has been criticized for its functionalist connotations: 'cross', it is argued, implies that the phenomena under study in different settings are assumed to be functionally equivalent (Maurice, 1989: 178–9; Dupré et al., 2003: 10). In addition, the value and interest of 'cross-national' research is said to be limited because such research does not go beyond juxtaposition of data. Although this assessment may have been justified with reference to the macrolevel research carried out in the 1950s and 1960s, it is manifestly not necessarily the case in many of the cross-national comparative studies undertaken in later years. In further mitigation, it can be countered that this shortcoming is not inherent within the term 'cross-national'; the same criticism could clearly be levelled against any purportedly comparative study that is not conducted using a rigorous comparative approach, as exemplified by much of the benchmarking activity, however designated, of the 1990s (Barbier, 2005b: 49).

In the absence of a direct translation for 'cross', researchers in continental Europe tend to prefer the prefix 'inter', as in 'international' or 'intercultural research', since it introduces the notion of context, now widely recognized as being crucial in comparative research, especially in studies that cross national or cultural boundaries (Schultheis, 1991: 8; Hantrais, 2007a). In this case, it can be argued that the prefix 'inter' conveys a similar meaning to the English 'cross', while 'international' is frequently used by Anglophones with another meaning, as noted below.

Commenting on the situation in the 1980s, Peter Grootings (1986: 285–7) drew a clear distinction between what he termed 'cross-national research' (CNR) and 'international comparative research' (ICR). He advocated ICR as the most effective approach on the grounds that it systematically analyses the relationship between the social phenomenon under study and relevant characteristics of the country. He contended that, in CNR, by contrast, contextual details appear only as descriptive background information in the final analysis, if at all. It could be argued that the key term in Grootings' labelling is not 'cross' or 'inter' but 'comparative'. Its omission from the first label is assumed to imply that the approach is not intended to be comparative and, as he explains in the same chapter, it is not sufficient for more than one country to be involved in a study for it to be comparative (Grootings, 1986: 285–6).

Another possible prefix, 'trans', is less often found in the comparative literature. The term is applied in 'studies that treat nations as components of larger international systems', involve 'transnational analysis' (Kohn, 1989: 23 and part VI), or describe 'tendencies in social policy which operate to transcend and/or bypass the nation state' (Jones Finer, 1999: 1). Melvin Kohn (1989: 99) goes so far as to append 'trans' to 'historical', arguing that interpretations must be historically informed and that sociological interpretations of cross-national differences are 'quintessentially transhistorical'. 'Trans' is also found as an alternative to 'global' in the context of 'transnational governance', suggesting 'interdependence', 'entanglement and blurred boundaries' to a degree that 'global' cannot. Organizations, activities and individuals, it is suggested, constantly span multiple levels, thereby 'rendering obsolete older lines of demarcation' and 'fostering the need for systematic comparisons and benchmarks' (Djelic and Sahlin-Andersson, 2006: 4).

When the term 'cross-national' is chosen to qualify comparative research, it raises the issue of whether 'nation' is an identifiable and appropriate unit of observation and analysis, or can be considered 'as context' (Kohn, 1989, parts III and IV). The same can be said of 'cross-cultural', which is, in addition, considered by its critics to be too particularistic (see Chapter 5 in this volume).

Another option is 'cross-societal', used in the 1960s and 1970s by Robert M. Marsh (1967) in the title of a book that attempts to codify societies as units of sociological comparison, and appearing elsewhere as an alternative to 'cross-cultural' (Przeworski and Teune, 1970: 4; Warwick and Osherson, 1973: 5–6; Ragin, 1987: 4, 6–7). Since the 1980s, organizational studies have used 'societal' without the prefix (for example Maurice, 1989). 'Cross-country' is rarely employed to describe comparative studies; notable exceptions are Edmond Lisle (1985: 20), Else Øyen (1990: 7) and Henry Teune (1990). Writing about comparative research after the Second World War, Teune (1990: 38–40) expressed his preference for 'country' as the unit of analysis on the grounds that it provides an appropriate point of departure for comparative studies.

In an analysis of the variables used in comparative studies of nations in the early 1980s, Johan Galtung (1982: 17) retained two of the three possible meanings that he attributed to 'nation': as a 'country' or 'state', defined as an autonomous political entity in territorial space; and as a sociocultural entity in non-territorial space, characterized by a shared culture. He rejected the use of 'nation' meaning 'nation-state', qualified as a country 'populated (almost) only by members of the same "nation" (ethnic group)'. When used in this volume, 'nation' is defined essentially as a geopolitical and sociocultural entity. As in the European context, from which many of the illustrative examples are drawn, the term 'cross-national comparative research' is, thus, understood to mean comparisons across legally delimited and administratively implemented national boundaries, recognizing that different countries, societies or cultures are contained within increasingly fluid borders (see also Chapter 3).

Again in the European context, 'international comparative research' has come to be used more loosely to refer to comparative research projects carried out by international teams. For Øyen (2004: 287), with particular reference to poverty studies, 'international' implies that large numbers of countries are being examined, opening up 'pathways to an internationalization of research'. As suggested in the introduction to this chapter, not all international projects are comparative, as would be implied if the descriptor 'comparative' was removed from Grootings' (1986) ICR label. Many international projects result in the production of series of parallel studies that may, or may not, have applied the same methods, and that may, or may not, have been conducted using a comparative research design. Throughout this volume, 'international comparative research' is used as a catch-all term to indicate comparisons across national, societal and cultural boundaries conducted within international settings, most often by international teams. As explained in the next section, much of the comparative work carried out in the 1950s and 1960s was under the control of a single-nation team. Although this project design has become less common, the comparative projects undertaken by postgraduate research students frequently involve a single researcher conducting a case study with only two comparators, making the research more tractable than in most large international projects. These smaller scale studies still qualify as international comparisons, but the approach raises a somewhat different set of issues and challenges. Ultimately, whatever the descriptor chosen and the composition of the research team, the conceptual and practical questions remain of how to define and select the nations, countries, cultures and societies to be compared (see Chapters 3 and 4).

THE SPECIFICITY OF INTERNATIONAL COMPARATIVE RESEARCH

Following on from definitional issues, the related question has also long been debated of whether a distinct 'cross-national', 'cross-societal', 'cross-cultural' or 'international' comparative research method and/or methodology exist, setting the approach apart from that adopted in single-nation comparative studies. In the 1960s and 1970s, many sociologists, economists and political scientists rejected the claim that 'comparative studies' had specific attributes that singled them out as a distinct field of inquiry, justifying the development of a distinct method. The claim was based on the conviction that all social science and humanities research is, by definition, comparative, thereby removing the need for perspectives that are any different from those adopted in the analysis of a single unit of observation at a given point in time or space.

Proponents of comparative – and more especially international or cross-national comparative – studies as a distinct field of inquiry, and of the comparative approach as a sociological method in its own right are usually less concerned with the choice of the unit of analysis than with the way in which the data are analysed and interpreted with reference to an explicitly comparative frame of reference. For Nicole Samuel (1985: 7), 'Comparative sociology is a distinct branch of research in that it introduces time and space as controlling variables in generalisations concerned with the behaviour of social groups.' Even opponents of a distinct comparative method argue that a specific task of comparative sociology is *'to distinguish between those regularities in social behavior that are system-specific and those that are universal'* (Grimshaw, 1973: 5, original emphasis). Accordingly, two conditions need to be met: the frame of reference has to be comparative, and time and/or space must be

controlling variables. It then follows that an important defining characteristic of a distinct comparative method is that the comparative
approach should be applied throughout the process: from the research
design stage through to the interpretation of findings (see Chapter 3).

Presented in these terms, comparative approaches can be seen not
only as methods but also as strategies (Kohn, 1989: 77–102; Vigour, 2005:
17), to the extent that the term 'strategies' appears in the titles of
comparative methods books as a deliberate substitute for 'method', or as
a complement to it (Armer and Grimshaw, 1973: Ragin, 1987; Dogan and
Pelassy, 1990; Dogan and Kazancigil, 1994; Lallement and Spurk, 2003).

Rather than being seen simply as a technique or method, some analysts consider comparative approaches to be epistemologies or 'intellectual postures' with an ethical dimension (Dupré et al., 2003: 7, 9, 14). This
line of argument, which emphasizes the distinctiveness of comparative
approaches, has been varyingly accepted in political science and social
science research methods books. Following Arend Lijphart (1971: 683–5),
who places the comparative method alongside experimental and
statistical methods, some political and social scientists argue that the
comparative and experimental methods operate according to the same
logic (Burnham et al., 2004: 61), or that a fine line separates comparative
and statistical methods (Smelser, 1973: 53). Since the comparative
method is said by some analysts to merge with the statistical method
when sufficiently large numbers of cases are being compared, the term
has been used in a narrow sense to refer to the comparison of large
macrosocial units, as noted by Charles C. Ragin (1987: 1).

In general, however, social scientists recognize that the experimental
(or 'scientific') method is almost impossible to apply rigorously in their
disciplines. Rather, the comparative method may be better described as
'quasi-experimental'. For Lijphart (1971: 685), it is 'not the equivalent of
the experimental method, but only a very imperfect substitute'. By
contrast, Lisle (1985: 16) argues more confidently that, when they set out
'to control, and correct for, the cultural environment in which a particular phenomenon occurs', cross-national or cross-cultural studies in the
social sciences are 'the equivalent of the controlled experiment of the
natural sciences'. Because disciplines such as sociology were less
constrained by statistical frameworks, they began earlier than political
science to borrow and try out a wide range of methods from other
disciplines, and applied them in comparative research, albeit not without
provoking fierce debates over the relative merits of quantitative *versus*
qualitative approaches (see Chapters 2, 3 and 5).

Between the 1960s and 1980s, whole volumes were dedicated to the
description and classification of what was depicted as the comparative
method, although very few authors ventured to use the term in their

titles, especially in the singular. Many chose instead to refer to a specific disciplinary approach, thereby indicating their reluctance to identify with a single comparative method. The most widely cited works from the period are listed below (dates refer to first editions), together with an indication of how the relevant terms are used in their titles. A number of these publications were to become classics in the comparative literature, and they continue to be cited as authoritative reference works in the twenty-first century:

- sociology and the social sciences in general – Marsh, 1967 (comparative sociology), Rokkan, 1968 (comparative research across cultures and nations), Rokkan et al., 1969 (comparative survey analysis), Przeworski and Teune, 1970 (comparative social inquiry), Vallier, 1971 (comparative methods in sociology), Armer and Grimshaw, 1973 (comparative social research), Warwick and Osherson, 1973 (comparative research methods), Smelser, 1976 (comparative methods in the social sciences), Szalai and Petrella, 1977 (cross-national comparative survey research), Ragin, 1987 (the comparative method), and Kohn, 1989 (cross-national research in sociology);
- political science – Macridis and Brown, 1961 (comparative politics), Scarrow, 1969 (comparative political analysis), Groth, 1971 (comparative politics), Almond, 1974 (comparative politics), Dogan and Pelassy, 1984 (comparing nations);
- social policy and administration – Rodgers et al., 1968 (comparative social administration), Liske et al., 1975 (comparative public policy), Rodgers et al., 1979 (a comparative approach), Jones, 1985 (comparative analysis), Wilensky et al., 1985 (comparative social policy);
- anthropology – Holy, 1987 (comparative anthropology);
- law – Hall, 1963 (comparative law); Zweigert and Kötz, 1969–71 (comparative law)
- education – Bereday, 1964 (comparative method in education), Noah and Eckstein, 1969 (science of comparative education), Holmes, 1981 (comparative education).

The uncertainty, characteristic of the 1960s to 1980s, about the existence of a distinct comparative method is still found in the chapter headings of more recent research methods books, where the terms 'method', 'methods' and 'methodology' are used almost interchangeably. For example, the relevant chapter in the political science research methods book edited by David Marsh and Gerry Stoker is entitled 'The comparative method' in the 1995 edition (Mackie and Marsh, 1995), and 'Comparative methods' in the 2002 edition (Hopkin, 2002). Chapters in other political science methods books refer to 'The comparative method'

(Collier, 1993), 'The logic of comparison' (Peters, 1998) and 'Comparative methodology' (Burnham et al., 2004). In social research, Patrick McNeill and Steve Chapman (2005) include a chapter that covers 'Experiments and the comparative method'. Relevant chapters in psychology methods books are entitled: 'Comparison studies' (Coolican, 1999) and 'Cross-cultural research methods' (Lyons and Chryssochoou, 2000).

Some edited volumes purposefully emphasize the essentially interdisciplinary nature of comparative research (for example Hantrais and Mangen, 1996, 2007; Lallement and Spurk, 2003). In social policy, consensus remains difficult to achieve in determining whether social policy is itself a distinct discipline or a multidisciplinary, cross-fertilizing field of study, since it habitually brings together sociology, political science, economics and history. Agreement is similarly difficult to reach about whether comparative social policy can be considered as a distinct methodology (Clasen, 2004: 94–6). In parallel with comparative public policy, it has become an important field of social inquiry, justifying book-length publications on the methods and practice of comparative studies (Clasen, 1999; Kennett, 2001, 2004; Barbier and Letablier, 2005).

The large number of specialist journals brings further confirmation of the academic legitimacy of comparative research as a distinct field of inquiry in a variety of disciplines, but not as a distinct method:

- *Comparative Anthropology;*
- *Comparative Economics, Comparative Economic Studies;*
- *Comparative Education, Comparative Education Review; Compare;*
- *Comparative Family Law, Comparative Labour Law, International Journal of Comparative Labour Law and Industrial Relations;*
- *Comparative European Politics, Comparative Political Studies, Comparative Politics, Revue internationale de politique comparée;*
- *Comparative Research, Comparative Social Research, Comparative Sociology, Comparative Studies in Society and History, Cross-Cultural Research, International Journal of Comparative Sociology, Journal of Comparative Social Welfare.*

As argued in Chapter 2, the existence of journals bearing the 'comparative' title may not necessarily indicate an interest in methods. Scrutiny of the articles published in many of the above journals suggests that they attach more importance to practice and findings than methods.

Faced with the growing plurality of methods, defined as the tools and techniques employed by different disciplines to acquire, manipulate and interpret data, it has become difficult to sustain the argument that comparative studies require a distinct method. Clearly, individually and severally, comparativists today use, adapt and refine the whole panoply of instruments available to social scientists, irrespective of their ontological and epistemological bent (see Chapter 5). Rather than attempting to engage with the longstanding debate over competing methods, it may be more fruitful, from this perspective, to look for a distinct overarching comparative methodology defined as a set of principles and theories guiding the choice of methods in the comparative study of societies.

The debate will undoubtedly continue as to whether a distinct comparative method and/or methodology can be said to exist. The standard definitions of comparative research reviewed in this chapter apply equally to studies over time and space, within and across countries. Arguably, and this is the line taken in the present volume, comparisons designed to cross national, cultural, linguistic or societal boundaries introduce an extra dimension, making the process more complicated and more expensive of time and effort than within-country, within-culture or within-society comparisons. The problems involved may be no different in kind, but, it is claimed, 'they are of such great magnitude as to constitute an almost qualitative difference for comparative, as compared to noncomparative research' (Grimshaw, 1973: 4).

WHY DO INTERNATIONAL COMPARATIVE RESEARCH?

In response to the question of how to capture the essence of the comparative method or methodology, researchers often couch their definitions in terms of objectives and outcomes. To account for the wide variety of situations in which cross-national, cross-societal or cross-cultural comparisons are undertaken, the 'why' question is explored here in three stages: firstly, by looking at the more personal reasons for conducting international projects; then by examining why researchers embark on systematic comparative research in international settings; thirdly, by reviewing the reasons for carrying out international comparative policy-relevant research.

When early career researchers from across Europe are asked why they participate in international projects, their responses generally include personal reasons, such as the desire to find out more about other cultures, broaden perspectives and extend knowledge about other systems (Hantrais, 2003: 8). Almost equally important is the interest among researchers in gaining a better understanding of their own cultures and systems, and in questioning their own assumptions and perceptions, thereby guarding against ethnocentrism. The opportunity to develop international contacts and visit other countries can provide a further incentive, as do the institutional pressures exerted to encourage participation in international research teams for financial reasons, and to ensure that researchers bring their findings to the attention of an international readership through publications. European Commission funding, in particular, has undoubtedly provided an important incentive for gaining experience in international research cooperation.

Although it is clear that not all European funded projects require comparisons or are conducted using the most rigorous comparative methods, scientific justifications for becoming involved in international research include developing new insights, advancing the knowledge base by testing theory against practice, promoting understanding of how processes operate, heightening awareness of cultural diversity, and learning from the exchange of information and experience. Far from resulting in cultural levelling, international cooperation thereby provides a means of contributing to the development of a richer international research environment.

None of these reasons alone would justify undertaking complicated, costly, time-consuming, systematic comparative studies. At the theoretical level, comparisons, and more especially systematic comparisons in international settings are, as noted in the previous section, deemed to come closest to the experimental method of the natural sciences, insofar as they enable researchers to control the variables making up a theoretical relationship, and identify necessary and sufficient conditions under which relationships occur in reality. In political science, the aim in carrying out cross-national comparative studies has long been to establish scientific explanations on the basis of a specified empirical relationship between variables (Burnham et al., 2004: 59).

Systematic comparative case studies within and across disciplines can be used, inductively or deductively, as an instrument to generate, interrogate, test or support hypotheses and theory (Glaser and Strauss, 1967: 21–43; Mackie and Marsh, 1995: 175–6; Landman, 2000: xviii). Alternatively, existing theory may be utilized to illuminate, confirm or validate cases, and to identify deviant cases, on the grounds that theory development in one country is more valid if it applies to others (Lijphart, 1971: 692). For Paul Pennings et al. (1999: 8), validation of explanations by comparison is a primary aim of a comparative approach on the grounds that 'theory always precedes comparative analysis'. A similar argument can be made for combining different research methods to study a particular case, thereby enabling triangulation and validation (see Chapter 5).

Drawing on the main scientific justifications provided in the methods literature for undertaking comparative research, the relationship between comparative theory and method can be summarized in the following terms:

- provide an empirical basis for theory;
- generate hypotheses using case studies;
- identify, explain and interpret multilevel variations;
- search for constant factors or general laws capable of explaining phenomena;
- test the transferability or generalizability, and robustness of a theory or hypothesis;
- verify or falsify relationships between variables;
- establish scientific explanation from relationships between variables enabling predictions to be made;
- develop sets of concepts that travel;
- validate by comparing units of analysis.

Researchers interested in policy analysis have additional reasons for adopting a comparative approach. International and national research funding agencies (for example the European Commission's framework programmes, policy reviews and joint reports on social protection and social exclusion) require 'value for money', which in turn places the onus on researchers to demonstrate the policy relevance of their work. Although international evidence-based policy evaluation has not become a routine procedure, and some observers would argue that policy evaluation is not research, comparisons are used increasingly in assessing the effects and effectiveness of policies (see Chapter 6). International comparisons with a policy dimension are expected to:

- inform policy;
- identify common policy objectives;
- evaluate the solutions proposed to deal with common problems;
- draw lessons about best practice;
- assess the transferability of policies between societies.

The attempt made in this section to answer the what and why questions illustrates the great diversity in both understandings of what is meant by a comparative approach, method or strategy, and the personal and scientific reasons for embarking on comparative research across time and space. Although the main emphasis here and in subsequent chapters is on comparisons that cross national, cultural and societal boundaries, many of the issues raised are also relevant to comparisons within countries and over time designed to capture and analyse social differentiation and change. Both temporal and spatial dimensions are taken into account in this volume when observing how the comparative research process has developed and in identifying the needs of new generations of comparative researchers, as discussed in the remainder of this chapter.

Mapping International Comparative Research

Comparative inquiry has a long and distinguished history dating back to Antiquity. Many of the influential figures and founding fathers of what are known today as the social sciences exploited the comparative method in their path-breaking work. The intention in this section is not to provide a detailed account of the extensive literature on the theory and practice of international comparisons, and, even less so, to attempt to compile an inventory of the innumerable studies carried out under the banner of comparative research. Rather, the aim is to track the early development of international comparative research and take stock of the situation reached at the turn of the twenty-first century.

By reviewing developments during previous decades and locating them in relation to the changing international scene, the objective is to gain a better understanding of the reasons for the fluctuating interest in international comparative research, as well as the persistent shortcomings in the available literature on the subject, particularly with regard to the training needs of researchers engaging in international comparisons in the social sciences and humanities.

THE LONG VIEW OF COMPARATIVE RESEARCH

Already in Ancient Greece, Aristotle and his followers combined reason with empiricism in analysing the constitutions of more than 150 Greek towns to determine the optimal form of political organization. In more recent times, the eighteenth century sociological thinker and social commentator Charles de Montesquieu first examined French customs through the eyes of a cultural outsider. He then embarked on an extensive exploration of different forms of government, institutions and the legal apparatus, setting them in relation to contextual factors including value systems, climate, population and religion.

Comparative approaches were developed from the nineteenth century across the social sciences and humanities in disciplines ranging from law, history, political science, economics and sociology to human geography, linguistics, anthropology, education, psychology and religion. The internationally renowned French political scientist Alexis de Tocqueville, the French sociologist Émile Durkheim and the German philosophers, cum economists and sociologists, Karl Marx and Max Weber were among the influential figures who adopted a comparative perspective to identify and explain the specificity of social phenomena. The nineteenth century English philosopher John Stuart Mill is, in turn, remembered for his early systematization of what came to be known as 'the comparative method' (see Chapters 2 and 3).

After a period of decline in the interwar years, the twentieth century postwar period brought renewed interest in comparative approaches, particularly in the United States. This surge of activity was fuelled by the data needs of the newly created international organizations: the United Nations (UN, 1945) and its first specialized agencies, including the United Nations Educational, Scientific and Cultural Organization (Unesco, 1945), the International Labour Organization (ILO, 1946) and the World Health Organization (WHO, 1946); followed by the Council of Europe (1949), the European Economic Community (EEC, 1957) and the Organization for Economic Cooperation and Development (OECD, 1961). The emergence of new self-aware societies and the increasingly rapid development of innovative technological tools and techniques enabled researchers to undertake systematic sociological investigation on an unprecedented global scale.

The sharp increase in the number of international cooperative research programmes from the 1980s can be attributed in no small measure to the deliberate efforts of national governments to promote international exchanges between researchers and to support multinational cooperative networking, not only in the natural sciences but also in the social sciences and humanities. Within Europe, the activities of institutions like the European Commission through its framework programmes for research and development, or the European Science Foundation, which was established in 1974 to act as a catalyst for pan-European scientific and science policy initiatives, provided strong incentives to develop cooperation through multilateral research programmes, projects and networks.

THE SHIFTING LOCATION OF COMPARATIVE RESEARCH

Efforts from the 1950s to record and classify the many thousands of comparative studies are testimony not only to the immensity of the task, but also to the growing interest that social and political scientists were showing during the postwar period, especially in the United States, in comparisons within the international arena. The first major survey, commissioned in the 1950s by the Unesco Division of Applied Social Science, of journal articles on cross-cultural research published between 1925 and 1955 yielded 1103 entries worldwide (reported by Scheuch, 1989: 149). Elina Almasy's (1969) annotated bibliography and indexes of comparative survey analyses covering the period up to 1965 were based on twelve and a half years of record keeping. In an edited volume of essays on comparative methods in sociology, Susan Bettelheim Garfin (1971) provided a classified, annotated bibliography of items published between 1950 and 1970 (mostly in the United States during the 1960s), selected 'on the basis of their quality, general sociological interest and unique contribution to the comparative field' (Bettelheim Garfin, 1971: 423). Over 100 of the monographs and articles selected treated the theoretical, methodological and technical problems of comparative research. In the mid-1990s, Joseph W. Elder (1976: 209) found that the bibliographies of cross-national sociological studies were running into hundreds, if not thousands, of citations. After this period of intense production and recording, the interest in comparative studies waned in the United States. By the late 1970s, the main focus for cross-cultural methodology had shifted to Europe.

The European dimension of international comparative research was given a major boost in the 1960s, when Unesco set up the European Centre for the Coordination of Research and Documentation in the Social Sciences in Vienna in 1963. The Centre was established as an autonomous body of the International Social Science Council with the status of an international non-governmental organization or agency. Funding was provided by ministries, academies of science and research councils in 21 countries. The objective was to promote closer cooperation between European researchers in East and West by acting as a forum for the meeting of different research traditions, schools of thought and disciplines, by facilitating the exchange of social science information and documentation. The Centre coordinated projects, conferences and training seminars in all areas of the social sciences, extending to the theory and methodology of comparative research.

Having organized a round table with the International Social Science Council in 1972 on the experience gained from conducting international comparative research, in 1979 the Vienna Centre began planning a series of international seminars on cross-national comparative and cooperative research, with a view to sharing accumulated expertise and transmitting experience to 'young researchers from Eastern and Western Europe' (Nießen, 1984: xiii). The 1972 event reflected the state of the art in international comparative research at a time when it was confined almost exclusively to a single approach: survey techniques. During the 1970s, the theory, methodology and practical problems of the research process were monitored and analysed. The Centre was acutely aware of the need for tailor-made training to be based on firsthand knowledge and experience of the practical everyday problems faced in international collaborative and comparative research (Nießen and Peschar, 1982: xiii).

Through its various activities, the Vienna Centre can be credited with having acquainted large numbers of early career social scientists with knowledge about not only the specific theoretical, methodological and organizational features of East–West comparative research, but also the implications of practical issues in the conduct of that research. The Centre rejected the 'asymmetrical', 'imperialist' or 'colonialist' model that had hitherto been dominant in international research in favour of a more 'symmetrical' approach, which was subsequently to be almost routinely adopted in the management of research projects and networks funded by the European Commission. The earlier model had been based on a team of researchers from one country, usually the United States, who prepared a research programme. The team used established concepts and technical procedures that it dispatched to other participating countries with a view to collecting, analysing and interpreting data, without necessarily seeking the cooperation of researchers in the countries concerned (see Chapter 7).

Viewed from a critical perspective (for example Dupré et al., 2003: 8), the implicit objective of much of the 'Anglo-Saxon' research in the 1960s and 1970s, at a time when European social scientists were 'rediscovering' the founding fathers of sociology, was to use comparisons to demonstrate the superiority of the Western model of economic and political development. By contrast, according to the Vienna Centre's symmetrical' model, all national groups were expected to be equally represented and involved throughout the research process.

The Vienna Centre's projects were cross-national in that they covered several nation states in Eastern and Western Europe. They were international since they were conducted by researchers located in different countries. The projects were designed to be comparative in that the research teams set out to study social phenomena in several countries, adopting comparative approaches to formulate empirically verifiable propositions. They used a number of controlled variables and based their observations on what were considered to be universal concepts, at least insofar as they applied to the countries in the confined geographical area concerned.

Research managers at the Vienna Centre worked tirelessly to find solutions to what often proved to be intractable problems, as recorded by researchers who participated in the Centre's activities. Issues raised by East–West research, which were also present in other combinations of countries, included how to deal with ideological and cultural differences in research practices, understandings of concepts and interpretations of findings, and how to overcome problems of cooperation and reliability of sources (Deacon, 1987: 15; Kinnear, 1987: 9; Lesage, 1987: 1).

Jan Berting (1987: 2, 5, 8) criticizes the cultural bias created by the self-selection of participants in the Centre's project, and comments on the clash of intellectual styles and the implications of differences in national institutional settings. Despite their best efforts and increasing openness to new approaches, in the 1980s many of the Centre's projects still suffered from the limited availability of reliable comparable data, resulting in reports that were often descriptive and confined to information, and based on juxtaposition of data rather than systematic comparison (Berting, 1987: 10). Another criticism levelled at the comparative research being carried out by European organizations like the Vienna Centre in the 1980s was that such work was not widely disseminated: it remained largely unknown in the United States (Scheuch, 1989: 148).

With the collapse of the Soviet Union at the end of the 1980s, and the enlargement of the European Union to the East in 2004 and 2007, the need diminished for a designated East–West European coordinating centre for research across the ideological divide. The interest the Vienna Centre had stimulated in comparative research across political and cultural boundaries and the substantial contribution made to methodological refinement in the social sciences are not, however, to be forgotten or underestimated. Several generations of early career researchers gained their first experience of working in international teams through the Vienna Centre's training and research activities.

THE EUROPEAN FOCUS ON INTERNATIONAL COOPERATION

Many of the researchers associated with the Vienna Centre made lasting contacts on which they would later build to take advantage of the opportunities offered by international research funding agencies, such as the activities organized by the European Science Foundation's two Standing Committees for the Social Sciences and the Humanities. Like the Vienna Centre in the postwar period, national research councils and academies support the Foundation's activities. As a result, the institution is less directly dependent on national governments and the European Union, although it has received funding from the European Commission's framework programme budget. The Foundation differs from the European Commission not only in its funding mechanisms but also in its country coverage and procedures for selecting and managing research in the social sciences and humanities. For example, the Foundation's EUROpean COllaborative RESearch (EUROCORES) scheme allows the research community to take the initiative in proposing topics for scientific investigation and activities to encourage international co-operation. This instrument was launched in 1998 as a networking tool to support research projects funded nationally. Subsequently, it was opened to associate partners from anywhere in the world. The aim is to create the critical mass necessary for scientific excellence by developing collaboration and scientific synergy. The scheme provides a flexible framework, which allows national basic research funding organizations to support top class European research in and across all scientific areas.

In the early 2000s, the Foundation funded a major multinational and multidisciplinary EUROCORES programme in the humanities, containing a strong comparative component, designed to study the 'Origins of Man, Language and Languages'. The Foundation was also one of 14 original partners in a European Union ERA-Net scheme under Framework Programme 6. Research councils in the Humanities in the European Research Area (HERA) formed a network with the objective of developing funding opportunities for collaborative research, in preparation for the launch of a major transnational research programme in the humanities in 2009, and in parallel with new funding opportunities for the humanities under Framework Programme 7.

Although the Foundation does not explicitly set out to promote international comparative methods, it has funded work on quantitative comparative methods in the social sciences. In 1995, it provided a launch pad for the European Social Survey, which went on to be the first social science project to win the prestigious Descartes Prize in 2005, awarded by a Grand Jury of eminent scientists on behalf of the European Commission to outstanding transnational research teams from any field of science (Jowell et al., 2007b).

The acceleration of the European enlargement process and the need for applicant states to meet the economic, social and political criteria laid down for membership provoked criticism of narrowly focused evidence, and created an incentive to extend the knowledge and methodological skills base. Enlargement also gave governments in East and West a fresh stimulus to take advantage of opportunities for cross-border learning and transfer, requiring a discriminating and contextualized analysis of the relationship between macro- and microlevel structures in the exporting and importing countries (see Chapter 6). The European Commission's Targeted Socio-Economic Research stream under Framework Programme 4 and the key action for 'Improving the Socioeconomic Knowledge Base' in Framework Programme 5 opened up new opportunities for social scientists to cooperate across both national and epistemological boundaries.

The official launch of the European Commission's open method of coordination in 2000 generated the need for more sensitive social indicators to measure trends in employment, social inclusion, pensions, health and social care. Coinciding with enlargement to the East, the European Commission closed most of the observatories that it had set up in the 1990s to monitor and compare sociodemographic trends and policy responses and replaced them by a social situation observatory in

2004. This composite observatory was renamed in 2007 as the European Observatory on Demography and the Social Situation, reflecting the growing concern in Europe with demographic issues. During the same period, the Directorate-General for Research and Development progressively intensified contact with the policy directorates-general, thereby reinforcing the linkages between research and policy (see Chapter 6).

In addition to the momentous change in East–West relations, several other factors stimulated renewed interest in comparative approaches in the social sciences and humanities within Europe and beyond in the late twentieth century. Among the most significant advances for the research community were the impact of globalization on the forms and effectiveness of national systems of governance and the political economy, and the diffusion on a global scale of new information technologies and cultural practices. Cooperation between international agencies was also intensified in the collection and exchange of data in an effort to reduce duplication and increase reliability and consistency. New large-scale survey instruments were established, with input from social scientists, and the data were made available to the research community for enhancement and secondary analysis (Dale et al., 2008: 522–6). In response to the need for comparable data created by the open method of coordination, the European Commission called for extensive research on common indicators that could be used to inform policy within the enlarged Union, notably in the area of poverty and social exclusion (Marlier et al., 2007).

REINFORCING THE RATIONALE FOR COMPARATIVE RESEARCH

European research programmes may have helped to raise awareness among some researchers of the work going on in neighbouring countries and the conditions under which comparative research is being carried out. However, parochialism and ethnocentrism still tend to be the hallmarks of research communities in many member states in the European Union and elsewhere in the world (Dupré et al., 2003: 16). Attention is often devoted primarily to encouraging cooperation rather than promoting theoretical and methodological refinement in comparative research. In an edited collection on comparative methodology, including contributions by Erwin K. Scheuch and Teune, Øyen (1990) entitled her own chapter, 'The imperfections of comparisons'. Symbolically, she went on to call her contribution to Patricia Kennett's (2004) edited book on comparative social policy: 'Living with imperfect comparisons', implying that many of the problems identified by comparative researchers in the 1980s had not yet found satisfactory solutions. In her chapter, Øyen bemoaned the fact that 'comparative methodology has not developed at the same speed as new information and information technology' (Øyen, 2004: 276). Without wishing to dismiss the considerable gains that have been made, her assessment of the situation in the early years of the twenty-first century is that the progress made does not compensate for 'the methodological, practical, ethical and political barriers that have to be overcome' (Øyen, 2004: 285).

In a similar vein, in a book promoted as a guide to the practice and methods of comparisons in the social sciences in France, Cécile Vigour (2005: 5) underlines a paradox that is not peculiar to French researchers: the stark contrast between the abundance of comparative studies and the lack of reflection on the use and development of comparisons, resulting in what she portrays as a multitude of false comparisons.

Chapters in research methods books and whole volumes devoted to comparative approaches routinely highlight the limitations of the techniques used in comparisons. All too often, however, accounts by authors of comparative studies tend to gloss over the problems that they had to confront when they were carrying out the research, focusing instead on key findings and success stories. Yet, as demonstrated in this volume, findings are inevitably affected by methods. Innumerable cases can be quoted of studies where the results are invalidated due to insufficient attention being devoted to methodological rigour at the research design stage. Pennings et al. (1999: 3–4) begin their introduction to a volume on comparative methods and statistics in political science by presenting examples of simple types of comparison, as often found in the media or in pronouncements by politicians, where unsystematic and non-rigorous studies have resulted in biased views, flawed conclusions and misleading perceptions of reality. Giovanni Sartori (1991, 1994: 27) talks of 'miscomparing', underachieving and loss of focus, and Mattei Dogan (1994) of 'use and misuse of statistics in comparative research'. Misuse and abuse of comparison, like those of statistics, make the task of committed comparativists even more difficult to realize, undermining confidence in their painstaking work and reinforcing the need for more attention to be devoted to dissemination of good practice.

These assessments by critical observers of developments in comparative methods are not very different from our own. When in the mid-1980s, the Cross-National Research Group was launched in the United Kingdom, with support from the Economic and Social Research Council, the initial modest aim was to encourage the exchange of information and experience among researchers engaged in, or contemplating embarking on, cross-national comparative studies. Researchers came together to discuss the theoretical, methodological, managerial and practical problems involved in research that crosses national boundaries. Ten years after the first meeting of the group, in an edited book that was able to draw on four series of seminars and some 20 published papers, the editors expressed their concern that few social scientists were receiving the training needed to equip them to conduct studies that cross national boundaries and compare different cultures (Hantrais and Mangen, 1996: xvi). Echoing and elaborating on the comments quoted above, in the preface to a special issue of the *International Journal of Social Research Methodology* in 1999, subsequently published in book format, the same editors felt justified in claiming that '[t]he growing interest in cross-national comparisons within the social sciences since the 1970s has not...been matched by commensurate advances at the theoretical and practical level' (Hantrais and Mangen, 2007: 1).

Similar comments resurfaced in 2006 when the British Economic and Social Research Council was considering launching a new initiative on methods and resources for cross-national comparative social science research. Due to the lack of appropriate training, it could still be argued that researchers participating in international projects often had to learn 'on the job' how to deal with the many theoretical, conceptual, managerial and practical issues raised by comparative research in international contexts. The steady increase in the number of substantive programmes and projects enabling social scientists to work together internationally had not, it could be claimed, been matched by similar developments in capacity building to equip researchers with the tools needed to conduct effective comparative studies. The heavy investment in data mining and the attempts at *post hoc* harmonization of national data by international organizations were not accompanied by a similar level of attention to methodology, methods training, research design and the research process among funders. Far from becoming obsolete, the Vienna Centre's justification for organizing dedicated training events to equip researchers new to the field with the tools required for cooperating in an international environment and carrying out effective international comparative studies remained apposite in the early twenty-first century, since such training had not become standard practice.

The advisory group established in 2006 by the Economic and Social Research Council to reflect on the shortcomings identified in the cross-national comparative research process in the United Kingdom noted a number of outstanding problems. These included not only insufficient general research training in comparative methods and/or its systematic provision, but also the lack of specialist resources and methods development, involving protocols for data access, harmonization, analysis, management and the ethics of data handling. A strong case could still be made for developing communication across disciplines, domains, topic areas and research communities. The heavy investment of time and expertise required to attain the highest standards of cross-national comparative work was recognized, together with the acknowledgement that the additional effort involved deserved to be taken more fully into account in research assessment.

Keeping International Comparative Research on the Agenda

Despite its long and distinguished history and the large body of material addressing the theoretical, methodological, managerial and practical issues that arise in international comparative research in the social science and humanities, there is no room for complacency. The renewed interest in international comparisons at the turn of the twenty-first century was not matched by an adequate supply of appropriately trained multidisciplinary researchers with the necessary skills, knowledge and understanding of the comparative research process. The chapters in this volume seek to address the shortfall. Drawing on the large body of available material, they set out to:

- explore ways of contributing to theoretical and methodological advancement in comparative research with a view to developing robust theoretical frameworks for comparative analysis of socio-cultural phenomena;
- review the tools needed for the analysis of social constructions of concepts, and identify the factors affecting the comparability of quantitative and qualitative data, and indicators;
- promote understanding of regional diversity and develop synergy and more effective cooperation between researchers from different scientific and cultural traditions;
- identify the conditions necessary for successful policy transfer and learning and make the case for greater sharing and dissemination of knowledge between researchers, funders, policy actors and other stakeholders;
- encourage reflexivity about method and process among researchers engaged in international comparative research;
- foster good practice in international comparative research and contribute to the development of training material for researchers preparing to embark on international projects.

2

Disciplinary Approaches to Comparative Research in International Settings

While some research methods books are intended for social and human scientists from a wide range of disciplines, others target readers specializing in a single methodological approach. A similar distinction is found in comparative research methods books between texts designed for social and human scientists in general and works that are discipline specific, which is perhaps most evident in the case of law and politics. As argued in the first chapter of the present volume, social and human scientists are far from agreeing that a distinct comparative method and/or methodology exist, setting comparative approaches apart from other research methods and methodologies. Nonetheless, it is clear that individual social science and humanities disciplines have developed their own distinct theoretical traditions and schools of thought, which are reflected in the research design and data collection strategies they adopt in comparative research. These differences are often expressed in terms of a dichotomy between universalist and culturalist, or particularistic, approaches. At the one extreme are the large-scale quantitative studies, as exploited in the 1960s and 1970s by social scientists, especially in political science, almost to the exclusion of other methods, for example to compare electoral systems or voting patterns, with the aim of identifying universalistic trends from which to make generalizations. At the other extreme are the fine-grained, detailed qualitative studies, as undertaken in the humanities, for example by anthropologists interested in using comparisons to gain a better understanding of how different cultures have evolved and adapted to their environment over time and space. Some countries or regions have come to be identified with particular epistemologies or intellectual styles and research paradigms, which determine preferences for specific approaches and, consequently, the extent to which researchers from different regions might be expected to cooperate effectively in international teams (see Chapters 3 and 7 in this volume). Between the two paradigmatic extremes, a variety of intermediate approaches have progressively come to the fore. By the early years of the twenty-first century, in most fields, methodological extremism in comparative research was thus being replaced or tempered by pluralism, mixed or combined methods (see Chapter 5).

Another factor counteracting extreme positions is the tradition in comparative research of drawing on different disciplinary approaches, to the extent that studies can frequently be considered as multidisciplinary or interdisciplinary. Comparative social policy is a prominent example of the meeting of disciplines and their mutual reinforcement through comparison (Clasen, 2004). Insofar as international comparisons cross or breach disciplinary boundaries, they raise many of the same issues of language, culture and method as interdisciplinary research.

This chapter builds on the information and arguments presented in Chapter 1 when defining and mapping international comparative research. The primary aim is to examine how different disciplines have adopted comparative approaches, and to explore how these approaches evolved, were appropriated by particular disciplines, and came to be associated with distinct epistemologies. The concluding section of the chapter considers the implications of disciplinary preferences for methodological advancement in international comparative research. The chapter thus prepares the ground for the discussion in the remainder of the volume of research design and management, data collection techniques, analysis and interpretation of findings.

Tracking Disciplinary Interest in Comparative Research

Although comparisons were used in Ancient Greece by Aristotle and Plato, among others, and by social thinkers in the seventeenth and eighteenth centuries, methodological considerations did not become a focus of scholarly attention until the nineteenth century, when serious attempts were made to legitimize the social sciences as academically respectable fields of scientific inquiry. In the postwar period, discrete disciplines momentarily came to be associated with specific comparative approaches amid controversy over theory and method. This section tracks the shifting emphasis in comparative research from discipline-free through discipline-bound to contested and competing approaches within and across disciplines.

DISCIPLINE-FREE COMPARATIVE RESEARCH

Early interest in comparative approaches was not identified with individual disciplines as we know them today. Although eighteenth century French social thinkers such as Charles de Montesquieu (1689–1755) and Henri de Saint-Simon (1760–1825), or Scottish enlightenment philosophers, including Adam Smith (1723–90) and David Hume (1711–76), used comparisons in their seminal work, they did not label themselves as sociologists. They did, however, have a strong influence on their followers and can thus be seen as precursors of modern sociological thought.

August Comte (1798–1857), who is held to have coined the term 'sociology', came under the influence of Saint-Simon when working as his secretary. Comte went on to undertake comparative and historical studies in his own observation of society. Comte's influence can, in turn, be traced in the writings of Émile Durkheim (1858–1917) at the end of the nineteenth century. Durkheim's analysis built on a wide-ranging academic background encompassing economics, history, philosophy, law and sociology. The path-breaking work of Alexis de Tocqueville (1805–59) later in the nineteenth century led to him being widely recognized as one of the first comparative political and historical sociologists. The writings of the English philosopher John Stuart Mill (1806–73) on the scientific method were influenced by both Comte and Tocqueville, while the social theorist Herbert Spencer (1820–1903), another follower of Comte, extended an early interest in geography and biology to psychology and sociology in an attempt to demonstrate the universal applicability of the evolutionary principle.

Like Durkheim, Max Weber (1864–1920) had a multidisciplinary background, spanning philosophy, law, economics and history. He held chairs in Germany and Austria, successively in law, political economy, economics and sociology. Karl Marx (1818–83) had also been a student of law and philosophy but was strongly influenced by French socialist thought, Hegelian philosophy and proponents in England of political economy, the name given at that time to the academic study of economic processes, which was a core component in Marx's work.

Durkheim, Marx and Weber, who have long been recognized as the three leading classical sociologists, cannot therefore be located in relation to a narrowly defined and delimited disciplinary base. Their shared concern, most fully articulated by Durkheim and Weber, was to ensure that the social sciences were placed on a sound methodological footing. This common objective led them to look for ways of establishing sociology as an autonomous 'scientific' discipline. It was Mill, however, who, in *A System of Logic* (first published in 1843), attempted to systematize the comparative method, which was subsequently critiqued and developed in Durkheim's *The Rules of Sociological Method* (first published in 1895) and *Suicide* (first published in 1897), and in Weber's *The Methodology of the Social Sciences* (first published in 1903–17) and *The Protestant Ethic and the Spirit of Capitalism* (first published in 1904–05). Mill's comparative method was intended to provide a basis for establishing universal general laws and explanations of phenomena through empirical research by applying the scientific method in social as well as natural sciences. Both he and many of his critics, including Durkheim, recognized, however, that the rigorous application of the comparative method to social phenomena was an ideal rather than an attainable objective (see Chapter 3).

Arguably, if the juxtaposition of 'social' and 'science' is not to be considered as a contradiction in terms, disciplines concerned with the study of society must be underpinned by systematic research methods that are meticulously applied. Interest in comparative approaches, understood to imply studies carried out with the intention of using the same research tools to make systematic comparisons (see Chapter 1), thus mirrors closely efforts to lend legitimacy to the academic study of social and human, as distinct from natural, phenomena.

THE SCIENCE OF COMPARATIVE SOCIOLOGY

Following common usage, the umbrella term 'social science' is taken in this book to encompass all disciplines concerned with the systematic study of social phenomena in the broadest sense. As coined by Comte and developed by Durkheim and Weber, 'sociology' referred essentially to the scientific and positivistic study of society, in practice removing any defining characteristics that might distinguish it from social science in general. In effect, for much of the twentieth century, sociology and social science were, demonstrably, almost synonymous.

Whereas, by the postwar period, other disciplines were becoming more specialized and were tightening their boundaries, because of its wide reach, sociology continued to harbour competing paradigms and approaches. The term 'sociology' came to be connoted with a whole range of disciplines, including many that are more usually classified as 'humanities', such as fine arts, cultural and religious studies. Used as a prefix, 'socio' extends the fields of inquiry covered by sociology, among others, to biology, linguistics, economic and legal studies (see entries in Jary and Jary, 1991). In a much quoted statement, Durkheim (1938: 139) claimed that: 'Comparative sociology is not a particular branch of sociology; it is sociology itself, in so far as it ceases to be purely descriptive and aspires to account for facts.' This view by no means commanded consensus, as demonstrated by the major epistemological debates that ensued about comparative sociology as a distinct field of inquiry.

The waxing and waning of comparative sociology

The promotion by the founding fathers of sociology as a generalist social science was based on the shared emphasis they placed on the careful observation of society through comparative and historical study. In their efforts to apply scientific methods to the social sciences, the comparative method was the closest they could come to the experimental method of the natural sciences, although just how close it could and should come remained a contentious issue (see Chapter 1).

After the surge of enthusiasm for comparative studies that had been generated at the turn of the century, academic interest in 'comparative sociology' waned in the interwar years. It then developed unevenly in the postwar period in a variety of disciplinary fields within the social sciences and humanities, as researchers sought to establish their scientific credentials by displaying methodological rigour.

During the 1930s and 1940s, the technical initiative had shifted to commercial companies, who launched large-scale public opinion surveys, using panel and interviewing techniques. Their work prepared the ground for the development of government sponsored institutes and international services, and provided an impetus for social scientists, firstly in the United States in the 1950s and then in Europe in the 1960s, to rediscover the value of large-scale international comparative research.

The founding of the International Social Science Council in 1952 under the auspices of Unesco 'as an administrative and intellectual base for continuous interdisciplinary and internationally comparative work' did not initially have much impact (Scheuch, 1990: 24). Then, under the leadership of Stein Rokkan in the 1960s, the Council established networks of researchers interested in organizing international conferences and creating data archives on comparative research. In parallel with the growth in the number of comparative studies, the methodological literature in sociology, especially on comparative survey methods, increased exponentially during this period and throughout the 1980s, much of it published in edited collections in English, with contributions often from the same group of authors (exemplified by Rokkan, 1968; Rokkan et al., 1969; Vallier, 1971; Warwick and Osherson, 1973; Kohn, 1989; Øyen, 1990). Like the monographs (for example Marsh, 1967; Przeworski and Teune, 1970; Smelser, 1976; Ragin, 1987; Dogan and Pelassy, 1990), the edited methods books cite large numbers of studies, sometimes running into the thousands, from a wide range of disciplines bearing the comparative label (see also Chapter 1).

Significantly, the description 'comparative sociology' was only rarely used during this period to denote a discrete field of sociological inquiry. For example, despite its title, the *International Journal of Comparative Sociology* was established in 1960 by Sage to publish research from a variety of disciplines, including political science, geography, economics, anthropology and business sciences, provided that the work was international in scope and comparative in method, the explicit aim being to encourage competing perspectives from different disciplines (see http://cos.sagepub.com/).

Robert M. Marsh (1967) stands as something of an exception in entitling his methods book *Comparative Sociology*. Marsh (1967: 20) was an ardent defender of comparative sociology as 'a field in its own right'. The subtitle 'a codification of cross-societal analysis' referred to the need that he perceived to develop theoretical and methodological frameworks for systematizing findings from empirical studies. He selected 90 cross-societal studies published between 1950 and 1963 from a possible 1000 in his annotated bibliography. The studies, which each covered at least two societies, had been carried out mainly by sociologists, social anthropologists and social psychologists, but he was also interested in ecology, urban sociology and demography. He used the studies to construct a series of codified propositions based on cumulative knowledge with the aim of identifying generalizations that could be universally applied.

Most of the major proponents of comparative methods in the 1960s and 1970s seemed, almost deliberately, to be avoiding references to comparative sociology, preferring titles such as 'comparative research across cultures and nations' (Rokkan, 1968), 'comparative social inquiry' (Przeworski and Teune, 1970), 'comparative social research' (Armer and Grimshaw, 1973), 'comparative research methods' (Warwick and Osherson, 1973), and 'comparative methods in the social sciences' (Smelser, 1976). When they referred to sociology, the term was used to locate studies within sociology as a discipline: 'comparative methods in sociology' (Vallier, 1971), or 'cross-national research in sociology' (Kohn, 1989).

In their much cited work, which has become a classic in the comparative research literature, Adam Przeworski and Henry Teune (1970) set out to provide a research methods book based essentially on the technical and epistemological problems arising in comparative research across systems from an area studies perspective. Although individual disciplines might be interested in different phenomena, they argue, unlike Marsh (1967), that comparative methods constitute a 'logic of inquiry' and serve as a heuristic tool applicable in all the social sciences (Przeworski and Teune, 1970: 86).

In the introductory chapter to their edited collection on comparative research methods, Donald Warwick and Samuel Osherson (1973: 6–8) claim that comparative sociology does not constitute a distinct method and that comparative studies in the 1970s were increasingly combining variables drawn from disciplines such as sociology, economics and psychology. While Neil J. Smelser (1976), who was one of the contributors to the Warwick and Osherson collection, chose not to use the term in the title of his monograph, he devotes three of the seven chapters in his volume to the 'comparative sociology' of Durkheim and Weber. He examines critically a variety of comparative studies to illustrate methodological issues that have been addressed in anthropology, political science, economics and psychology. His primary concern, like many of his contemporaries, was to improve the body of comparative knowledge.

In the context of the ongoing debate about the justification for identifying a discrete comparative sociological method, Smelser (1976: 2–3) also rejects the notion that comparative studies require an approach that is different from sociological analysis more generally. He maintains that the problems with which comparativists have to contend are the same as those facing all social science investigators. However, he makes a distinction that is found in some of the writings of his contemporaries on comparative politics (for example Lijphart, 1971: 684) between statistical and comparative methods, determined by the number of cases (Smelser, 1973: 53).

The limits to methodological refinement in comparative sociology

A major focus of attention in the comparative sociological literature, and the social science literature on comparative approaches more generally, through to the 1980s, was methodological refinement in data collection and analysis in large-scale surveys. In line with the aims of the founding fathers of sociology, the purpose was to establish the scientific credentials of the social sciences and demonstrate the universality of social phenomena. The assumption seemed to be that sociology was acting on behalf of all the social sciences in seeking methodological improvement in a context where technological and statistical advances had provided the tools that made possible large-scale data collection and analysis. By the early 1980s, however, against the background of the work of the European Centre for the Coordination of Research and Documentation in the Social Sciences in Vienna (see Chapter 1), it was being argued that the emphasis on large-scale research in the social sciences was diminishing and that other paradigms were coming to the fore (Nießen and Peschar, 1982: xiv). Attention was said to be shifting away from the technical issues arising in comparative studies to the more practical problems of international collaborative and comparative research.

In 1986, the International Sociological Association established a Research Committee on Comparative Sociology, with the primary objective of advancing comparative research in the field of sociology and facilitating scholarly communication relevant to international comparisons (see www.isa-sociology.org/rc20.htm). By the late 1980s, however, with reference to comparative survey research, Erwin K. Scheuch (1989: 148) was warning that, 'in terms of methodology *in abstracto* and on issues of research technology, most of all that needed to be said has already been published'. Provocatively, Scheuch subtitled his article: 'why the wheel of cross-cultural methodology keeps on being reinvented'; in his view, the central problem was no longer technical but theoretical.

During the 1990s, the focus on comparative research methods in sociology *per se* was losing its prominence. The official journal launched in 1961 by the International Social Science Council's Standing Committee (ISSC) on Data and its Standing Committee for Comparative Research, *Social Science Information sur les sciences sociales*, based at the Maison des Sciences de l'Homme in Paris, featured a regular specialized section on comparative research until the mid-1990s. In the early twenty-first century, the journal continued to publish articles in English and French, with the stated aim of focusing on theoretical debates, methodology and comparative and cross-cultural research, but without the specialized comparative section (see http://ssi.sagepub.com/).

By the late 1990s and early 2000s, other journals and book-length publications on comparative sociology were also devoting much less attention to methodological issues than to reporting the findings of comparative studies. When the International Social Science Council revised its mission statement in 2007, no reference was made to comparative studies (see www.unesco.org/ngo/issc/index.htm). The policies of other journals further illustrate both the continued openness of comparative sociology to other disciplines and the relatively low level of interest in methods *per se*. When Brill took over publication of the journal of *Comparative Sociology* in 2001, the aim was to advance comparative sociology by presenting detailed scholarly accounts of studies made in different cultures on a comparative basis, ranging from macro to micro, and from quantitative to qualitative approaches. Brill also published an occasional book series of 'International Comparative Social Studies' (see www.brill.nl/). The primary interest lay in the findings from broadly sociological studies rather than in methodological development as a specific issue central to the concerns of comparativists, providing a further indication of the fading importance for editors and contributors of comparative methods *per se*.

In an authored book with 'comparative sociology' in the title, Graham Crow (1997: 6) argued that comparisons continue to have relevance in the age of globalization. Rather than contributing to the development of comparative methods, however, he suggested that comparative sociology provides a useful analytical framework, on the condition that societies are not seen as completely self-contained units, and that analysis is not restricted to the level of national societies. Writing a few years later, Sharot Stephen (2001) included 'comparative sociology' in the title of a monograph on world religions. He was interested in comparative case studies and not in methodological advancement. Drawing on the work of anthropologists and historians rather than sociologists, Stephen adopted a Weberian model in the search for interpretative understanding and causal explanation for religious action.

At least in the field of comparative sociology, it would seem that Scheuch's (1989) warning in the late 1980s to avoid reinventing the wheel of cross-cultural methodology was being heeded. These trends can also be seen as confirmation that the proponents of comparative sociology as a distinct field of inquiry, method or methodology had either lost the argument, or felt the debate had, for the time, being lost its salience.

THE DISCIPLINARY BASE FOR COMPARATIVE POLITICS AND LAW

Just as the term 'political economy' went into temporary eclipse at the end of the nineteenth century with the recognition of economics as a freestanding discipline, political science emerged in the early twentieth century as an autonomous discipline, although the 'science' label was less readily accepted in the United Kingdom than in the United States (Marsh and Stoker, 1995: 3). Academics in political studies, the preferred term in the United Kingdom, and law, or legal studies, were less reluctant to establish comparative studies as a subdiscipline or field of inquiry, as testified by the methods books, journals and reference works that proliferated in the postwar period, unashamedly entitled 'comparative politics' or 'comparative law'. Opinion has, however, long been divided within these disciplines over the extent to which the comparative approach could be considered merely as one method among many or as a distinct method lending them legitimacy as disciplines (for example De Cruz, 2007: 3; Penning et al., 1999: 23–6).

The reason why politics and law went furthest in distinguishing comparative research as a legitimate field for disciplinary inquiry may, at least partly, be attributed to their illustrious precursors. Aristotle, Plato and Montesquieu had all used comparisons to classify legal systems and forms of governance in an effort to identify best practice, and this tradition developed into a major plank in comparative political studies and comparative law or legal studies. Weber provided a more scientific basis for an approach that was to come to full fruition in political studies with the development of large-scale data collection made possible by the technological advances of the 1950s and 1960s.

Comparative politics as a field of scientific inquiry

Within political studies, and indeed within comparative politics, two schools of thought can be identified. The one has been concerned to describe and compare patterns of government and politics, drawing on the work of philosophers, historians and constitutional theorists, without any pretensions at being scientific. The other has been more interested in setting political studies on a scientific footing, to the extent that 'political sociology' has come to be recognized as a distinct approach, characterized by its insistence that the investigation of political institutions must be treated as embedded in society and not studied in isolation. In political sociology, comparative analysis of types of political systems and their relative effectiveness and stability have thus been accepted as legitimate fields of inquiry. The systems approach that came to the fore in the 1950s and 1960s in the United States, when the study of political culture and comparative approaches were also being developed (for example Almond and Verba, 1963), could be seen as a third school of thought, possibly bridging the other two. Later, it was extended to development studies and world systems theory, thereby melding together interdisciplinary inputs from sociology, economics, politics and history (Wallerstein, 1979).

In a seminal article, referring to political studies, Arend Lijphart (1971: 682) defines the comparative method as 'one of the basic methods – the others being the experimental, statistical, and case study methods – of establishing general empirical propositions'. He parts company with many other political scientists in affirming that the comparative approach is definitely a method, and in stating that it is does not equate with the scientific method. Unlike many earlier writers on the subject, he also insists that he regards the comparative method 'as a *method of* _discovering empirical relationships among variables_, not as a method of measurement' (Lijphart, 1971: 683, original emphasis); measurement is only the first stage in a two-stage process. Furthermore, method is to be distinguished from technique. It follows that, for the purposes of the article, the comparative method is taken to be 'a broad-gauge, general method, not a narrow, specialized technique'. Thus defined, the comparative method can also be described as a basic research strategy. According to Lijphart (1971: 684), although the comparative method closely resembles the statistical method, it remains distinct from it because the number of cases involved is too small to allow 'systematic control by means of partial correlations'. From this perspective, the main problem facing comparativists has been identified as too many variables and not enough cases, which became a major issue in research design (Lijphart, 1971: 685) (see Chapter 3).

Many commentators do not follow Lijphart's (1971) distinction between statistical and comparative methods. Consequently, political scientists often refer to three main types of comparative analysis: 'case studies of individual countries within a comparative framework; systematic studies of a limited number of countries; and global comparisons based on statistical analysis' (Mackie and Marsh, 1995: 176). Although the first two types of comparative analysis were undoubtedly being extensively used in the 1960s and 1970s, it was the third type that came to be most closely associated with comparative politics. Social survey techniques, structured interviewing and self-administered questionnaires were widely accepted as satisfying the need for a rigorous, reliable and systematic scientific approach, capable of producing trend data with predictive value. According to Giovanni Sartori, (1994: 22), researchers are seeking to use these methods to achieve 'law-like generalizations endowed with explanatory power' about the patterning of variables, leading on to statements about convergence or divergence and providing support for normative theory. Quantitative methods became the bedrock of comparative politics, justifying whole volumes exploring the research designs and statistical tools needed for analysing the huge amounts of data assembled by researchers (Rokkan et al., 1969; Dogan and Pelassy, 1990; Pennings et al., 1999; Landman, 2000).

The abundant literature devoted to large-scale surveys deflected attention away from the development of more qualitative approaches, interested in examining the ways in which complex sets of variables interact. As in the other disciplines that are reviewed in this section, divisions arose between political scientists. On the one hand, the proponents of universally applicable laws governing political behaviour based their work on studies of large numbers of cases. On the other, the detractors argued that 'social phenomena are too unpredictable and contingent to be explained in terms of such laws, or too complex and immeasurable for such laws to be identified' (Hopkin, 2002: 251–2).

Borrowing from historical comparativists, in the 1960s political scientists became interested in studying phenomena in their contexts (see Chapter 4). Historical institutionalists in comparative political economy used qualitative comparative approaches to identify and analyse the specificity of individual cases. By combining a number of factors, they were able to produce findings capable of challenging the results of statistical analysis (Ragin, 1987). In their review of historical institutionalism in comparative politics in the late 1970s and during the 1980s, Kathleen Thelen and Sven Steinmo (1992: 6) highlight the 'partial shift, away from general theorizing toward a more midlevel Weberian project that explored diversity within classes of the same phenomenon' in the search for explanations for systematic differences. Despite considerable epistemological and methodological diversity, by the early twenty-first century the comparative approach in politics could still be described as 'an essentially positivistic methodology' (Hopkin, 2002: 265).

Comparative public and social policy as an interdisciplinary field

Comparative public policy developed in the 1970s as a field of study within comparative politics. Comparative social policy, which is sometimes regarded as a subset of comparative public policy (Clasen, 2004: 93), gained academic status after the Second World War, but was still not fully recognized as an area of academic study in some countries in the early 2000s (May, 2003: 17).

The growing importance of public and social policy within comparative studies can be located in the postwar period of expansion of welfare provision in advanced societies, when reformers were interested in learning from the experience of other countries. At macrolevel, using quantitative aggregate data and ideal-type taxonomies, attempts were made to classify welfare systems across industrialized societies and detect signs of convergence and diffusion (Wilensky et al., 1985: 9–15). Detailed comparative studies of developments within welfare states were conducted in the 1970s and 1980s (for example Flora and Heidenheimer, 1982), although the focus was not primarily on methodology. The most widely cited and much critiqued of these studies by Gøsta Esping-Andersen (1990) was based on an empirical investigation of similarities and differences in a number of developed industrialized societies around the world. Renewed interest in classificatory schemes from the 1980s can be explained by a number of factors, including the impact of globalized economies on public welfare systems, the pressures on governments to benchmark their performance and the development of mixed economies of welfare (May, 2003: 18–19).

While comparative public policy lacked the necessary unity to be seen as a distinct field within political science, it had developed a number of policy theories and was productive in generating new data, explanations of social change and analytical insights (Hancock, 1983: 298–9) (see also Chapter 6). The large-scale analysis of Western European welfare states combined a configurational analysis of institutional variations, where countries were considered as cases, with an analysis of empirical data, the aim being to test specific hypotheses. Jochen Clasen (2004: 97) sees the extension of analysis from a single nation to a cross-national perspective as a method for 'testing and advancing the robustness of theoretical propositions', concurring with its description as a 'methodological device'. While macrolevel studies benefited from the methodological refinement developed in sociology, political science, history and economics, more qualitative methods were progressively used to track the dynamics and impact of welfare systems. The different perspectives and approaches exploited in comparative social policy studies should not, however, be seen as competing with one another. Rather, the various strands of analysis and approaches would seem to be mutually challenging and supportive (Clasen, 2004: 100).

Comparative law in search of a method

In terms of methodological and theoretical advancement, comparative law followed a very different trajectory from comparative politics. Despite its early antecedents in Antiquity and then in the eighteenth century with Montesquieu, seen by some as the probable founder of comparative law (Gutteridge, 1946: 12), its development as a field of scientific inquiry and an academic discipline was not recognized until well into the nineteenth century. The first chair in the general history of comparative law was founded at the Collège de France in 1832; the first chair in historical and comparative jurisprudence at Oxford University was established more than 35 years later in 1869. The main interest in comparative law at that time was to identify and classify legal systems and to look for models of laws and legal codes. The delay in developing comparative law as an area of scientific study is attributed, in large part, to the long-held conviction that law is universal (Vigour, 2005: 37–8).

In what has become a classic introductory text to comparative law worldwide, Konrad Zweigert and Hein Kötz (1998, first published in German in 1969–71) identify the founding of an International Congress for Comparative Law in Paris in 1900 as a turning point. Already by the mid-1940s, comparative law had become firmly established as a distinct area of inquiry, if not a distinct discipline, denoting 'a method of study and research and not a distinct branch or department of the law' (Gutteridge, 1946: 1). The importance of comparative law as a major field of inquiry internationally was recognized in the early 1950s in publications such as the *Traité de droit comparé* (Arminjon et al., 1950, 1952), and from the early 1970s in the *International Encyclopedia of Comparative Law*. A significant stimulus for its development in the late twentieth century was the establishment of the European Economic Community in 1957 with its European Court of Justice, bringing together different legal traditions and creating a large body of supranational legislation.

At the turn of the twenty-first century, Peter De Cruz (2007: 3, original emphasis) defines comparative law straightforwardly as 'the *systematic study of particular legal traditions and legal rules on a comparative basis*', as applied in two or more legal systems. The terms 'vertical comparative law' and 'horizontal comparative law' were coined to distinguish between comparative legal history and the comparison of modern systems of law (De Cruz, 2007: 10). Comparative legal studies focus on three types of objects: rules and institutions; decisions on cases (or jurisprudence); and legal systems constructed at national level according to a logical and homogeneous structure, often involving description and classification. However, many of the works bearing the title of 'comparative law' would not, strictly speaking, be recognized as comparisons, since they are confined to the presentation of meticulously detailed parallel descriptions of national legal codes and systems. By contrast, sociolegal comparative studies draw on the sociological approaches of Weber, Durkheim and Marx to challenge utilitarian, individualistic and positivistic views of legal systems and law making. For Zweigert and Kötz (1998: 10), importantly, the value of the contribution that the sociology of law brought to comparative law was to provide a means of discovering causal relationships.

In his reflections on the development of international law as a distinct strand, De Cruz (2007: 9) makes explicit reference to the roots of its principles in 'the comparative law method'. However, unlike comparative politics, comparative law has paid scant attention to methodology. Zweigert and Kötz (1998: 33), who devote a chapter to the study of concepts, functions, aims, methods and history of comparative law, claim that very little systematic writing exists about methods. For the same two authors (1998: 34, original emphasis), '[t]he basic methodological principle of all comparative law is that of *functionality*', on grounds that 'in law the only things which are comparable are those which fulfil the same function'. Their proposition is supported by the observation that the legal system in every society has to deal with the same problems and does so by using different means. Recognition of this principle provides the starting point for research design (see Chapter 3).

For his part, De Cruz (2007: 219–49) sets outs to fill the gap that he identifies in the literature by offering a theoretical and practical framework, and a range of comparative techniques designed for comparisons at both macro- (systemic) and microlevel (analysing specific institutions or issues within legal systems). His focus is primarily the series of problems that comparativists need to resolve, encompassing linguistic and cultural issues, the selection of comparators and the viability of theory, before examining purpose and subject matter. Only a few pages in his lengthy monograph are devoted to a discussion of techniques, providing what he describes as a blueprint for an approach or method of comparison (De Cruz, 2007: 242), presenting eight steps in comparative research projects, together with guidelines for their application.

The relative lack of interest in methods in comparative law contrasts sharply with the debates and detailed accounts provided in comparative sociology and politics, suggesting that the disciplines examined in this section could be characterized as much by the extent to which they have been concerned with methodological advancement and refinement as by the actual methods, techniques and theoretical positions that they adopt in comparative studies.

COMPETING EPISTEMOLOGIES BETWEEN AND WITHIN DISCIPLINES

The diversity of approaches not only between disciplines but also within them makes it necessary to consider comparative research as both a meeting point and a source of competition for researchers seeking to advance knowledge within their fields of inquiry. The preceding sections illustrate how disciplinary boundaries develop and change over time and how dominant epistemologies emerge. The distinction made at the beginning of the chapter between universalist and culturalist approaches is pursued below with reference to a range of disciplines, all of which draw on a number of comparative approaches, in some instances resulting in fragmentation of the disciplinary base.

From macro- to microeconomic comparative approaches

When the academic discipline of economics was known in the nineteenth century as political economy, interest lay in studying economic processes, focusing on the relationship between economic theory and political action. The separation of economics from politics at the end of the century coincided with the recognition of economics as a science in its own right. Despite the contribution of the major economic theorists, including Smith and Mill, or the interest of Marxian economists in the sociopolitical analysis of world economies and the allocation of resources at a global level, comparative economics did not go on to develop into a subdiscipline to the same extent as comparative politics. Competing perspectives have long divided researchers in economics, most notably between macro- and microlevel theorists, as reflected in the approaches adopted by economists engaging in comparative studies.

The universalist approach, which is widely recognized as characterizing macroeconomics, became a central tenet in econometric studies aimed at modelling behaviour. Richard Rose (1991: 452) describes macroeconomics as 'landless economics' insofar as a single generic model is assumed to fit all countries. Rather than developing as a distinct disciplinary field of inquiry, in many of the large-scale comparative studies carried out in the 1950s and 1960s, economics was often one of several disciplines contributing to the analysis of the relationship between the economy and various social institutions. Building on the earlier interest in political economy, many of the studies bearing the politics label were, for example, interested in establishing linkages between economic development, as measured by *per capita* gross domestic product, and political systems (for instance Lipset, 1960).

In an edited volume, Kirsten S. Wever and Lowell Turner (1995: 1–2) examine 'the comparative political economy of industrial relations', in an attempt to capture the many linkages between the 'economic' and the 'political' and 'between actors, events and dynamics at the micro (company or local), meso (industry and regional) and macro (national or economy-wide) levels of analysis and activity'. They were seeking to elevate the status of comparative industrial relations, reaffirming its centrality in relation to other comparative fields, contributing to knowledge about advanced industrial economies and moving forward theory (Wever and Turner, 1995: 6). In his retrospective of comparative political economy, Charles P. Kindleberger (2000) included case studies in finance, foreign exchange, international trade and economic policy, but without devoting attention to methodology.

Economics was one of the many disciplines contributing to organizational theory, which had been largely confined to monosocietal studies in the postwar period (Lammers and Hickson, 1979). The economic and social process of industrialization, which had long been an important focus of comparative analysis among classical sociologists, was revisited in studies of the relationship between industrial society and welfare in the 1950s and 1960s (for example by Wilensky and Lebeaux, 1958). When the economists' notion of culture-free contexts was applied in the study of organizations in the 1970s, the aim in developing normative models from which generalizations could be made involved searching for a scientifically determined 'one best way' in organizational management (critiqued by Rose, 1985: 66).

Again building on the concerns of classical sociology, the interests of economic and industrial sociology and the sociology of work focused primarily on the workplace, often involving microlevel studies of firms. During the 1970s, economic and industrial sociologists were looking for alternatives to universalist and culturalist approaches. The Aix Group led by Marc Maurice (1989: 177) was interested in analysing 'l'effet sociétal', without claiming the approach as a method. Although much criticized (for example by Rose, 1985; Iribarne, 1991) for falling between two stools, the societal approach, as defined and applied by the Aix Group, was adopted during the 1980s in multinational projects on new technologies and work organization supported by the Vienna Centre (Grootings, 1986). Its proponents combined macro-, meso- and micro-level analysis in an attempt to identify societal coherence within each of the countries under study, emphasizing the interdependency of phenomena and the forms of mediation needed to achieve coherence. By demonstrating the effect of the national context on the object of study, the aim was to determine the extent to which generalizations could be made from the theoretical models and hypotheses that the researcher is seeking to test empirically. According to this line of argument, comparisons are made possible by the fact that each unit of observation has a systemic coherence rooted in national specificity.

Although the societal method could be seen as presenting a middle way between the extremes of universalism and culturalism, it did not mark the end of the controversy among economists over the status of comparative studies. Nor did it herald a new era of interest in comparative approaches as a specific field of inquiry and methodological development. The debate did, however, give researchers an opportunity to argue for alternatives to technological determinism, taking account of the 'complicated interplay of political, social, economic and even unexpected factors' influencing technological change and shaping work organization (Grootings, 1986: 278).

Reconciling approaches in comparative history

As in many other disciplines analysed in this chapter, recognition of comparative history as a distinct field of inquiry has long been contested. The application of comparative approaches to historical topics remains problematic. Epistemological divisions were apparent from an early stage among comparative historians, but little effort was made until the 1980s 'to explore the methodological aspects of comparative history as such in any systematic fashion' (Skocpol and Somers, 1980: 174).

Conventional historians interested in social change were reluctant to embark on cross-national studies because, like many anthropologists, they were resolutely opposed to any attempt at generalization or model building. In France, the threat of sociological imperialism made historians wary of abandoning their studies of historically anchored events in the search for more universalizing trends. Interest was not confined to comparisons over time or to evolutionary theory. The Annales School, founded by Lucien Febvre and Marc Bloch in 1929, sought to bring historical studies closer to social science by distinguishing their work from traditional national, political, chronological and narrative history, which had hitherto been characteristic of the discipline. Their comparative historical research involved extensive exploration of geophysical, demographic, cultural and social structural factors, drawing on approaches developed in the social sciences to focus on similarities and, more especially, differences. Bloch's (1939, 1940) study of feudal society and Fernand Braudel's (1979) account of civilization and capitalism 40 years later served as models for comparative sociological historians wanting to analyse social change in whole societies, by situating them in relation to worldwide trends over the longer term (exemplified by Wallerstein, 1979).

Reviewing the discipline in the late 1970s, Theda Skocpol and Margaret Somers (1980: 175) identify what they call three 'distinct logics-in-use of comparative history', each with its own purposes and characteristics: macrocausal analysis, which is close to multivariate hypothesis testing, and sets out to make causal inferences about macrolevel phenomena, possibly leading to generalizations; parallel demonstration of theory, aimed at determining the relevance of theoretical arguments for certain cases across historical trajectories; and contrast of contexts, whereby contrasting cases are juxtaposed. Each approach is shown to have strengths and limitations. However, rather than presenting them as competitors and as mutually exclusive, Skocpol and Somers (1980: 188) advocate using the different approaches in combination in a triangle of comparative history (see also Chapter 5).

Contrasting approaches to the scientific study of cultural phenomena

Until the 1980s, comparative research in the social sciences, *qua* sociology, and in political studies as a major social science discipline, was dominated by large-scale quantitative analysis, which was recognized as an essential component in establishing their scientific credentials. Unsurprisingly, particularly given the broad reach of sociology as a discipline, this did not mean that other comparative approaches were not being developed in parallel as alternatives and competitors to studies based on large-scale social surveys. Constructivists undertook participant observation, semi- and unstructured interviewing, and applied techniques such as focus groups and discourse analysis in comparative studies (see Chapter 5). Culturalist, phenomenological, constructivist or interpretive positions, most characteristic of the humanities, contrast sharply with the universalist or positivist stance, more typical of the social sciences. While these approaches could be mutually enhancing, they could also result in competition within and between disciplines.

Since sociologists generally investigated their own societies, in comparative studies they often had to rely on data collected by other disciplines, especially by anthropologists, whose work was considered to be more intrinsically comparative. 'Social' anthropologists as they were called in the United Kingdom, and 'cultural' anthropologists as they were known in the United States, had long drawn on ethnographic accounts of geographically remote societies to conduct cross-cultural comparisons. Their collection of information relied heavily on participant observation, and required an in-depth analysis and understanding of social behaviour in other cultures. The classical writings of Alfred Radcliffe-Brown (1881–1955) and Bronisław Kaspar Malinowski (1884–1942) were instrumental in shaping structural–functionalist anthropology and in establishing the preference in the United Kingdom for analysing social structure rather than culture, as in the United States. Malinowski can be credited with bringing to an end the separation between ethnographers working in the field and anthropologists based in academic departments. Radcliffe-Brown is recognized as having promoted a form of anthropology that he called 'comparative sociology' (Jary and Jary, 1991: 366, 517).

Even within anthropology, divisions arose and were still salient in the 1960s between researchers who stressed the need to establish universal characteristics under the banner of comparative sociology (see the analysis by Marsh, 1967), and those who were more interested in differences, such as Edward Evans-Pritchard (1902–73). Despite being trained by Malinowski and succeeding Radcliffe-Brown at Oxford University, Evans-Pritchard and his followers saw anthropology as being closer to history than to science. Their interest was in differentiation and diversity between and within countries, taking account of the complexity of the factors involved. Generalizations as understood by sociologists became difficult to apply within a cross-cultural comparative framework, as exemplified in the work of ethnomethodologists (Garfinkel, 1967) and interpretive analysts, who were searching for meaning rather than laws, using 'thick description', and looking for generalizations within rather than across cases (Geertz, 1973: 5–6, 26–7).

With his more restrictive definition of comparative research, Lijphart (1971: 690) claimed that '[i]t is no accident that the most fruitful applications of the comparative method have been in anthropological research', on the grounds that the number of variables is 'not as bewilderingly large as in more advanced societies', making them easier to control and analyse. He therefore agreed with Siegfried Nadel (1951: 228) that anthropology afforded 'almost a laboratory for the quasi-experimental approach to social phenomena'.

By the late 1980s, however, Ladislav Holy (1987: 1) had identified the main recurrent problem in comparative anthropology as 'the relation between description and generalization and…the role of comparison in describing particular cultures and societies, and in generalizing about culture and society'. He argued that it was no longer valid to refer to a 'comparative method' in anthropology. In the past, the label had marked 'the distinction between anthropology as a generalizing science and ethnography as mere description of one particular society or culture'. The paradigm shift that had occurred in the discipline meant that it was necessary to replace 'comparative method' by 'varying styles of comparison', designed to capture social facts within their frame of reference (Holy, 1987: 2, 5).

Psychologists have gone even further in emphasizing cultural variables, preferring to talk about 'cross-cultural' studies or comparisons (Coolican, 1999: 184; Lyons and Chryssochoou, 2000: 134). Their interest in cross-cultural comparison is explained by its usefulness in determining the extent to which human behaviour is governed by universal laws and processes. In that social psychology, which was recognized as a field of study in the early twentieth century, serves as a bridge between individual and social theories of human behaviour, it also has a bearing on cross-cultural comparisons. An issue that has been of particular concern in cross-cultural studies in Western psychology, as in ethnology, is the danger of ethnocentrism, which in the past took the form of European and American-centredness or colonialism (Coolican, 1999: 184–7). Expressed more positively, Evanthia Lyons and Xenia Chryssochoou (2000: 134) stress the importance of asking whether North American and Western European psychological models can account for the findings from research carried out in non-Western cultures.

The degree to which culture affects psychological structures, and *vice versa*, is seen as a relevant and appropriate subject for a cross-cultural comparative strategy in psychology. The focus on culture and values in cross-cultural comparative studies lends itself to a quasi-experimental approach capable of ensuring methodological rigour in validating theoretical arguments. It can involve various methods of data collection and analysis, often including statistics (Lyons and Chryssochoou, 2000: 146). Experimental psychology, unlike educational research, as noted below, is recognized as homogeneous and relatively free from debates over paradigms (Punch, 2006: 32), although it has been challenged, among others, on ethical grounds, especially in social psychology (Hammersley, 1996: 159). Within psychology, however, it remains that cross-cultural research is not seen as a distinct methodology.

Fragmentation in comparative education

Like many, if not most, of the disciplinary fields examined in this subsection, comparative education was founded on the need to ensure that its parent discipline would become a positive science. Comparative education has its origins in the nineteenth century, when the aim was to reform national educational systems, in what would today be seen as benchmarking. When comparative education was 'rediscovered' in the twentieth century (Hans, 1949: 1), statistical techniques were used to map educational systems and to analyse the relationship between system variables such as *per capita* cost and outcomes, applied for example to the level of illiteracy or incidence of crime or poverty. Drawing on history, philosophy, economics, politics, sociology and psychology, early attempts were also made to compare the quality of education as interest shifted to the causes of educational problems and solutions to them, involving an understanding of the cultural or social forces underlying educational systems (Hans, 1949: 4-5).

The scope of comparative education became ever wider in the early twenty-first century, as illustrated by the journal *Compare: A Journal of Comparative Education*. The editors invited contributions that would 'illuminate the effects of globalisation and post-structural thinking on learning for professional and personal lives', based on analysis of educational discourse, policy and practice across disciplines, the review of processes of comparative and international inquiry, and reports on empirical studies (see www.tandf.co.uk/journals/).

However, by the late 1990s, Val D. Rust and colleagues (1999: 109) noted that, over time, the field was losing its methodological unity and that the leading comparative journals (*Comparative Education Review*, *Comparative Education* and the *International Journal of Educational Development*) were devoting minimal space to research methodology. Those that did focus on methodology paid very little attention to strategies for data collection and analysis, concentrating almost exclusively on conceptual issues. The field had become 'methodologically fragmented and pluralistic' to the extent that every research strategy found in the social sciences would seem to be represented in comparative education, with the notable exception of experimental studies (Rust et al., 1999: 107).

Assessing Disciplinary Approaches to Comparison

This chapter has pursued the longstanding debate over the distinctness or otherwise of the comparative method, both at the level of social sciences and humanities research in general and within and across disciplines. Although it has been possible to identify dominant epistemologies at particular times and to associate them with specific disciplines, the overall picture is more confused. What has emerged, however, is that comparative methods and approaches have been most fully developed and institutionalized at times and in countries where researchers have been seeking to justify their scientific credentials and establish their disciplines as autonomous and legitimate fields of scientific inquiry. The point is illustrated by the case of the founding fathers of sociology and social sciences more generally in the late nineteenth century in Europe, and in the postwar period in Europe and the United States. The closer researchers have been able to come to applying rigorous experimental methods in making comparisons, the more strongly they have been able to argue the case that their strategies allow them to establish general laws and explanations for social and human phenomena, thereby contributing to the advancement of knowledge, irrespective of the disciplinary base.

Although the origins of comparative methods were not tightly bound to disciplines, the emphasis placed on particular methodological approaches as being more 'scientific' than others favoured the development of the large-scale data collection and statistical analysis that came to be associated with much of the research undertaken by comparativists in sociology, political science and economics, aimed at identifying universal phenomena and causal explanations. At the same time, particularly in sociology, researchers drew on smaller-scale studies by anthropologists, who were primarily interested in analysing and understanding cultural phenomena.

During the second half of the twentieth century, two main strands could be identified in both the small- and large-scale studies classified as 'comparative'. On the one hand are studies that set out to describe social and human behaviour, and identify trends and patterns. In the 1960s and

1970s, the aim was often to establish a 'one best way' from a Western perspective, without reflecting on methods; comparisons served as a strategy or a technical device. On the other hand, mainly in sociology and political science, work was undertaken to develop and apply rigorous scientifically sound methodologies based on ever more sophisticated techniques. By the late 1980s, when it seemed that not much remained to be said about comparative methodology, the emphasis was shifting away from technical issues to some of the more practical questions involved in international cooperation. The revival of interest in comparative studies at the turn of the twenty-first century, particularly in the European context with support from the European Commission's Framework Programmes for Research and Development, reopened the methodological debate. By this time, disciplinary boundaries were becoming more blurred as multinational teams of researchers increasingly brought to bear multidisciplinary perspectives in the study of socioeconomic and political phenomena (see Chapter 5).

While illustrating the epistemological divisions within disciplines and the preferences of some disciplines for particular methodological approaches, either in the long term or at certain stages in their development, the examples given in this chapter, especially in the later sections, confirm that disciplinary boundaries are in a constant state of flux, making it difficult, if not impossible, to substantiate claims that international comparative approaches are discipline specific or discipline bound. Just as the originators and leading proponents of scientific and comparative method(s) all subscribed to a mix of disciplinary traditions and epistemologies, only rarely have individual social science and humanities disciplines sought to close their boundaries to alternative comparative approaches. This does not mean that individual disciplines have not strongly advocated certain approaches to comparative research and sought to promote them through their scholarly activities.

Methodological borrowing from other disciplines and the combination of disciplinary approaches in comparative studies are all reminders that, like the founding fathers of their disciplines, researchers have an interest in working together and pooling resources if the social and human sciences are to deserve recognition as scientific disciplines. As a result, the multiple strategies adopted by international comparative researchers in an effort to meet the many challenges they face may bring in their wake the added benefit of contributing to the reconciliation of competing paradigms.

3

Project Design in International Comparative Research

Social science and humanities researchers usually embark on international comparative projects with a view to gaining a deeper understanding of observable phenomena, advancing knowledge, developing new insights, and generating and testing theory. To achieve these challenging objectives, they undertake systematic comparisons across two or more countries, cultures or societies. Despite the long history of comparative studies, reviewed in the two previous chapters, the conduct of comparative projects continues to require a heavy investment in intellectual, technical and physical resources if the innumerable obstacles to successful international cooperation are to be overcome. The likely outcome of any comparative study is largely determined at a very early stage in the research process. Many closely interrelated factors contribute to the research process and outcomes: the selection of the objects of inquiry; the formulation of research questions; the choice of comparators and levels of analysis; the research cultures and disciplinary mix of team members; the theoretical and methodological approaches adopted; and the analysis and interpretation of findings. All these factors, therefore, need to be taken fully into account in project design.

Not all disciplines in the social sciences and humanities have devoted equal attention to exploring comparative research strategies or developing appropriate methodologies (see Chapters 1 and 2 in this volume). Consequently, the degree of reflexivity regarding the research process varies from one discipline to another and over time (Dupré et al., 2003: 15). Sociologists and political scientists have a long tradition, which was particularly dynamic between the 1960s and 1980s, of analysing and debating comparative methodological issues, as testified by the abundant literature from that period cited in this book. Nonetheless, in the early 1970s, Arend Lijphart (1971: 682) could complain about the low level of methodological awareness among politics students. A survey of 947 articles published between 1955 and 1994 in the *Comparative Education Review*, one of the leading journals in the field, recorded only 38 articles dealing primarily with comparative research methodology, and almost none reporting on issues of data collection and interpretation (Rust et al., 1999: 90, 109). Since the 1990s, as noted in Chapter 2, the attention devoted to comparative methods in purportedly 'comparative' research journals has also declined in other disciplines.

Chapter 1 sought to unravel the 'what' and 'why' questions. In this chapter, the emphasis is on the 'how' question. Relatively few research reports on international comparative studies in the social sciences and humanities describe in any detail, or seek to justify, key decisions taken in the early stages of the research process. Even fewer comment on the impact that such decisions may have had on outcomes. The aim in the present chapter is to explore the many components of research design and to show how choices made at the outset can influence the research process and findings. Issues associated with the composition and coordination of research teams are addressed in the final chapter as major components in the management of international research projects.

The first section of this chapter looks at the possible rationales underlying the construction of the object of inquiry, the formulation of the research question and the choice of units and levels of analysis. The second section examines the main research strategies adopted by comparativists. As noted in Chapter 2, certain methodological approaches have come to be associated with specific disciplines, while team projects draw increasingly on a mix of disciplines and a combination of methods, a development that is examined in greater detail in Chapter 5. The second section of the present chapter focuses on the issues raised by data collection, analysis and interpretation, many of which are well documented in methods books. The section reviews the acknowledged advantages and drawbacks of different approaches and the solutions that experienced comparative researchers have proposed in answer to the problems they encounter. The concluding section returns to a theme that recurs throughout the book: how decisions taken in the course of the research can impact on findings.

Rationales for Project Design

The rationales underlying project design are rarely made fully explicit in funding applications, project reports and, even less, in the publications produced by members of research teams involved in large-scale comparative international projects. Yet, the exercise of identifying an appropriate object of inquiry, formulating a tractable research question and choosing the best fit in terms of the unit and level of analysis is a critical initial stage in the research process, as argued throughout this volume.

SELECTING THE OBJECT OF INQUIRY

A trend noted in the literature over the past century is the shift in the substantive focus of comparative research, as illustrated below by the examples of political science, sociology and education. The requirements of funders, as expressed in calls for proposals, have come to play an increasingly important role in prescribing the object of inquiry and the ensuing choices that researchers need to make in designing international comparative projects (see Chapters 6 and 7).

Todd Landman (2000: 213) has tracked the evolution of the focus of comparative politics from the public law phase in the interwar period, through the behavioural revolution between the 1940s and 1960s, to the institutional revival of the 1970s and 1980s, and the new eclecticism of the 1990s, with its emphasis on individual, institutional and cultural foundations of politics. The interest of political scientists has moved on from formal comparisons of political systems, institutions and parties to public policy, electoral behaviour and the political economy. Progressively, the priority themes of the past – decolonization, the foundations of democracy, revolutions or social movements – have been replaced or complemented by topics concerned with the causes and consequences of globalization, the weakening of the nation state, the advent of national or regional forms of modern capitalism, and the convergence of national political systems associated with the acceleration of the cultural, institutional and political diffusion of ideas and practices (Giraud, 2003: 87–8; Jessop, 2004: 11). While remaining 'positivist at heart' and continuing to emphasize 'the predictable and deterministic nature of objective material relationships between variables', Jonathan Hopkin (2002: 266–7) argues that comparative politics has demonstrated its ability to move beyond narrow positivism to analysis of cultural difference, the role of ideas and the social construction of political experience.

A similar shift has occurred in sociology under the influence of globalization and regionalization, and the diffusion of new patterns of social behaviour and value systems (Inglehart, 1990; Berthoud and Iacovou, 2002). International organizations and the all-pervasive media have played an important role in the diffusion process, reflected in the interest shown by governments in policy evaluation and transfer, and evidence-based policy (see Chapter 6). The trend is especially noticeable at European level, with the development of a European social model and the growing concern among governments about demographic issues (Sykes et al., 2001; Vaughan-Whitehead, 2003; Adnett and Hardy, 2005; Hantrais, 2007b). This does not mean that the statistics on income, education, occupation, labour force participation, migration, religion, rural–urban distinctions, marriage, family structure, desertion, divorce or crime, listed by Joseph Elder (1976: 219) as topics for comparative analysis using statistical data in the 1970s, are no longer on the agenda. Indeed, trend data on almost all these subjects are routinely collected at national level and confronted in international league tables. Comparative scientific analysis has developed an additional interest in exploring how concepts are evolving, and in assessing the impact of exogenous explanatory factors on change, as well as the implications of these phenomena for policy making within wider international settings.

Similar trends are also found in comparative education, which has never been characterized by a single research methodology and is often treated as a subset of social science research. By the 1990s, comparative education had progressively expanded its already broad frame of reference from the developed world to global activities, covering human development and policy relevance (Rust et al., 1999: 89).

FORMULATING RESEARCH QUESTIONS

Logically, the research question to be addressed in comparative studies might be expected to be derived from the theoretical presuppositions of the researchers, and serve as the main parameter determining the methods adopted, and how the research is organized and managed. However, other issues generally intervene, including the available time and resources, research culture and methodological preferences of the investigators (see Chapter 7). The international comparative methods literature devotes relatively little attention to the formulation of research questions, presumably on the grounds that this part of the process does not give rise to issues that are any different from those raised by within-country studies. The fact that the researcher decides to undertake international comparisons with a view to gaining a better understanding of observable phenomena, questioning received wisdom, and generating, clarifying or testing theories implies, however, that the comparative dimension should be a central component in the research question. The selection of comparators and research methods need to be determined and justified accordingly.

In essence, researchers are interested in three types of questions: what, why and how (Punch, 2006: 29). Description may be the initial phase in a project seeking to answer the 'what' question in comparative law; it is recognized as an essential first stage (Zweigert and Kötz, 1998: 43). Research that aims simply to describe and juxtapose different systems and practices is not, however, inherently or necessarily comparative, as illustrated by many of the large-scale multinational surveys funded by the European Centre for the Coordination of Research and Documenta- tion in the Social Sciences (Vienna Centre) in the 1960s and 1970s (see Chapter 1). Carefully analysed statistical evidence may suffice when the question to be answered is factual, for example: 'Is the gap between poor and rich countries increasing?' (Dogan, 2004: 335). If concern is with classification and the creation of typologies, whether it be of electoral systems, voting patterns, welfare regimes, value systems or family structures, the research question is likely to be implicitly comparative, insofar as the researcher sets out to identify shared characteristics or deviant cases. Explicit comparison, while not essential, can help in understanding how systems and processes operate.

Systematic international comparisons are most valuable and most explicit in research that is seeking to discover empirical relationships among variables, test hypotheses and draw substantive inferences about the possible causes and explanations for observed phenomena in answer to the 'why' question. The aim in this case is to determine whether an explanation developed in one or more cases has wider applicability. Here, deviant cases can be useful in forcing the re-evaluation of key variables, in generating, testing and refining theory, concepts and measures (see Chapter 4). In this type of research, description and classification are necessary stages in the research design, but the research question focuses on competing or alternative explanations, and on establishing the conditions for their wider application and replication.

CHOOSING COMPARATORS AND UNITS OF ANALYSIS

Comparators, or cases, refer to the countries, societies or cultures that feature in the comparative analysis. Units of analysis are the objects about which researchers collect data or observations, which may, in some instances, be synonymous with the comparator. In international comparative research, depending on the disciplines involved, the units of analysis may be whole countries or regions (political science), societies (sociology) or cultures (anthropology), or they may be subdivisions within larger entities, including subgroupings of individuals sharing specific characteristics or structures such as legal systems.

For political scientists, comparative politics generally means the comparison of countries or nation states. For some authors (for example Mackie and Marsh, 1995: 177; Landman, 2000: 22, 33), comparison may involve the systematic study of only one country, treated as a case study but set within a comparative framework, on the grounds that such studies share the same logic of inference. While single-country case studies may not prove or disprove a theory, they can confirm or contest its wider applicability. Anthropologists have long had recourse to cross-national data to test the validity of theories developed from ideographic accounts limited to particular cases or events, and based on only one country (Elder, 1976: 215; Smelser, 1976: 204).

The scientific rationale for choosing a particular mix and number of comparators is critical in determining not only inputs in terms of methods and materials but also outputs in terms of findings and dissemination. By classifying units, researchers seek to limit and control sources of variation for the phenomena under study. In identifying the unit of analysis, they are making the claim that '*the units so defined do not, for purposes of subsequent analysis, vary with respect to the characteristic defining the class*' (Smelser, 1976: 168, original emphasis).

In international comparative projects, research teams may select cases that will enable them to maximize experimental variance by isolating a particular variable. Alternatively, the aim may be to minimize error variance by choosing representative cases, or to control for extraneous variance by minimizing the effects of other variables (Burnham et al., 2004: 62).

The principles to be applied in any good research design – validity, reliability, replicability and plausibility – are all the more important in international comparative research, but they are also more difficult to achieve. Validity requires the proper choice of cases and relevant indicators so that measurements can be operationalized in relation to theoretical presuppositions, thereby ensuring that they yield consistent results for all the cases under review. Reliability implies that researchers using the same measurement technique or strategy produce the same result (Hammersley, 2008: 43). The cases selected must satisfy the conditions of the research question, allowing for replication. Plausibility implies that the cases are empirically sound and societally relevant (Pennings et al., 1999: 7).

Logically, the selection of comparators and units of analysis should follow on from the research question, but it can often be explained by non-scientific factors, including the researchers' backgrounds or the resources available. The selection of comparators may also be influenced by the requirements of funding agencies in seeking to ensure politically appropriate geographical coverage (see Chapter 7).

Country or nation as the unit of analysis

An important issue frequently raised in the comparative methods literature, particularly in political science, is whether 'country' or 'nation' is the most appropriate unit of analysis, or frame of reference, for international comparative studies, a point already discussed in Chapter 1 (see also Galtung, 1982; Dogan and Pelassy, 1990; Teune, 1990; Dogan and Kazancigil, 1994).

The rationale for selecting countries or nation states is relatively easy to justify in studies where the criterion for inclusion is their membership of an international organization, the most frequently cited being the Council of Europe, European Union, International Labour Organization, Organization for Economic Cooperation and Development, United Nations Educational, Scientific and Cultural Organization or World Health Organization. These organizations collect, process and publish large amounts of data on member countries, thereby potentially providing an important research resource for comparative analysis.

The case for comparing members of international organizations can perhaps be most strongly argued with regard to the European Union, since national governments are directly represented on the Union's supreme decision-making body, the Council of Ministers, and through nationally elected members of the European Parliament. Even in federal states, such as Germany, it is central, rather than regional or local, government that is represented in Brussels.

The advantage for the comparative researcher of examining a particular social phenomenon using nations as the contextual framework when they are members of an international organization is that they explicitly share a common reference point. In addition, nations, or nation states, afford a convenient frame of reference for comparative studies since they possess clearly defined territorial borders, as well as their own characteristic administrative and legal structures. Belonging to the organization confers on them a certain identity of purpose through the common goals to which they subscribe as a condition of membership. At the same time, they exhibit diversity at national and subnational level, due to the specific ways in which their legal, political, economic and sociocultural systems have developed and operate.

Indeed, an objection often raised to studies that take the nation as the unit of observation is that within-nation differences may be obscured. German unification, for example, created a national unit in which internal diversity was greater in some respects (sociodemographic trends for instance) than that observed across the European Union. Mattei Dogan and Dominique Pelassy (1990: 18) refer to 'eight Spains, …four Finlands, …three Belgiums, four Italys, and five or six Frances', and also to the six 'pieces' that made up Yugoslavia and the 15 'independent nation-states' forming the Soviet Union (Dogan, 2004: 325).

Many authors use country and nation interchangeably. For others, nation is a contested, loaded and 'less specifiable' concept than 'country' (Teune, 1990: 39). Richard Rose (1991: 447) argues that comparative analysis in political science excludes 'within-nation' comparison and must focus on concepts that are applicable in more than one 'country'. Another possible alternative is 'cross-polity' (Scarrow, 1969: 6).

A further problem in delimiting nation states is that national borders shift, and it cannot be assumed that they necessarily correspond to cultural, linguistic and ethnic divisions, or to a common sense of identity. Just as national territorial boundaries change, so does member-ship of international organizations. The four waves of enlargement of the European Union between the 1960s and 2007, which brought the total number of member states to 27, altered not only the size of the Union's population and its surface area but also its political, economic and socio-cultural structure. The entry of new member states from Central and Eastern Europe in the early years of the twenty-first century brought momentous changes in the shape of Europe, calling into question many long-held assumptions about the characteristics of Western European societies. In addition, the Union has progressively developed a multi-level system of governance, which means that individual member states contribute to the formation of policy due to their membership of international institutions while, at the same time, being obliged to ensure compliance at national level through their own institutions and their legislation (Marks et al., 1996).

Yet another complication in taking the nation as the context for com-parative policy analysis arises from the way the policy formation process operates both at national and supranational level. Non-governmental organizations, issue networks, policy communities and interest groups play an increasingly important role as policy actors cooperating across national boundaries, again providing material for comparative analysis. Indeed, internal diversity, competing institutions and shifting bounda-ries do not necessarily have to be construed as problems impeding effective research, for they can themselves serve as appropriate objects of inquiry and as relevant units of analysis (Berthoud and Iacovou, 2002).

Societies and cultures as units of analysis

The territorial and administrative boundaries of countries and nations can be determined with some degree of accuracy. The same claim can be made for sub- and supranational territorial and administrative entities, such as regions within or across countries, local municipalities and federal states. Societies and cultures are more fluid, and they do not always readily lend themselves to precise definition or delimitation.

In comparative sociology, reference is rarely made to whole societies as comparators. When used as a unit of analysis, 'society' implies a certain degree of commonality in terms of socioeconomic, political and cultural criteria, making it difficult to distinguish between a 'society' and a 'country' or to adopt a whole society as a discrete unit of analysis. Émile Durkheim (1938, 1990), one of the founding fathers of sociology, made systematic comparisons both of societal units and between societal subsets delimited by age, sex or family type. Talcott Parsons (1966: 1) argued that many social systems (local communities, schools, business firms and kinship units) are not societies but 'sub-systems of a society', adding that many social systems may be parts of more than one society.

The interest of researchers often lies in examining social, as opposed to political, economic or cultural phenomena within subsets or subtypes of societies, or by grouping relatively (historically and geographically) homogeneous societies by region, as in area studies. Comparativists are then able to look for generic categories based on structural criteria, for example stages in socioeconomic development or subsets corresponding to the distribution of wealth. Alternatively, they may take institutions and organizations as the units of analysis. Comparisons can be used to identify social uniqueness, diversity and cross-national contrasts resulting from the specific ways in which legal, political, economic and sociocultural systems have developed and operate.

For the purposes of comparison in public policy, the advice given by Richard Titmuss (1967: 57) in the 1960s still holds, namely that national social policies should be treated 'not by discussing the details for this or that country, but with the aid of concepts and models, principles and goals, and in terms of categories of benefits, contributions and users'. The most meaningful units of analysis, he suggests, should be 'classes of benefit, kinds of entitlement, patterns of utilisation, and differences in goals and objectives'.

Culture is an even more slippery concept than society, described as 'far too broad and complex to serve as an acceptable explanatory variable' (Johnson, 1998: 28). The definitions used in cross-cultural psychology are depicted as 'all-encompassing', both representing 'shared practices and meanings' within particular groups, and constituting an independent variable 'producing differences among groups' (Lyons and Chryssochoou, 2000: 136–7). As a unit of analysis, culture is often closely associated with a linguistic entity studied by linguists and ethnologists.

Anthropologists have tried to resolve the problem of delimiting cultures by developing classifications based on culturally similar ethnographic regions and subregions, or by organizing ethnographic data according to 'interrelated sets of cultural characteristics' (Elder, 1976: 214). The criteria used by anthropologists to define societies include distribution of particular traits, territorial contiguity, political organization, language, ecological adjustment and local community structure. This led Raoul Naroll (1968: 248, original emphasis) to describe the appropriate social unit of analysis in cultural anthropology as a 'cultunit', defined as *'people who are domestic speakers of a common distinct language and who belong either to the same state or the same contact group'*.

In political science, culture has been defined in terms of both 'a system of meaning' and 'the basis of social and political identity that affects how people line up and how they act on a wide range of matters' (Ross, 1997: 42). Accordingly, culture serves as a framework for organizing, analysing and interpreting actions, motives, attitudes and values; to be useful, the term should not, therefore, be defined too broadly.

The definitional task is further complicated due to the fact that the effects of culture on collective action and political life are usually indirect and interact with interests and institutions. In studies involving fine-grain analysis, the ability to understand the way in which units are socially and culturally constructed and expressed through language is critical in gaining a proper understanding of their defining characteristics. The analysis of subunits within societies, or of cultunits, requires a different research design from that adopted when aggregated units are being examined, and this is reflected in the level at which the study is conducted and in the focus of the analysis.

SELECTING THE APPROPRIATE LEVEL OF ANALYSIS AND THE RIGHT DISTANCE

Disciplines vary in their preferences for different levels of analysis and in their perspectives on the object of study, which are, in turn, closely associated with methodological approaches. This section shows how the number of cases examined and the number and mix of units of analysis determine the most appropriate level of analysis and the perspectives adopted by researchers. It also indicates how any changes in the mix or number of cases for analysis may mean adapting the research design, again with implications for interpreting and reporting the results.

Finding the appropriate level of analysis

Comparative researchers are generally interested in one of two main levels of analysis: macro or micro. Macrolevel studies concentrate on groups of individuals, systems, structures and processes, whereas microlevel analysis focuses on individual activities or behaviour. This dichotomy has come to be associated with different methodological approaches and perspectives. In political science, for example, micro-analysts claim that 'the world of politics is shaped by the actions of "structureless agents"', whereas macroanalysts subscribe to the view that 'the world is shaped by the unstoppable processes of "agentless-structures"' (Landman, 2000: 17). These epistemological positions are reflected in preferences for quantitative or qualitative approaches.

As noted in Chapter 2, from the 1980s industrial sociologists were recognizing and exploiting a third level of analysis in international comparisons. Proponents of the societal approach combined macro-, meso- and microlevel analysis in their efforts to identify societal coherence within units of analysis, the assumption being that each unit of observation has a systemic coherence, rooted in national specificity, thereby lending itself to comparative analysis (Maurice, 1989). They stressed the importance of analysing the relationship between the macro and the micro, implying the interaction between a plurality of causal factors, on the basis that actors cannot be separated from structures and *vice versa*, since they are all socially constructed.

By the turn of the twenty-first century, the tendency was increasingly for researchers engaging in international comparisons to draw on inferences from data collected at macro- and microlevel. Multilevel and multidisciplinary analyses lend themselves to a combination of methodological approaches that enable researchers to gain access to an abundance of data on which to base observation, explanation and evaluation (see Chapter 5).

An issue that was identified and documented in the 1950s and 1960s by an American sociologist (Robinson, 1950: 357), and has since been widely discussed in the comparative methods literature, concerns the fallacy of inference. 'Ecological' or 'group' fallacy occurs when observations made at one level are applied at another (wrong) level to draw ill-founded inferences about causality (Smelser, 1976: 227; Peters, 1998: 44). Since the problem is not limited to situations where group analysis is inappropriately applied to individuals, some observers prefer the broader term 'aggregate fallacies' (Riley, 1963: 704–6). A straightforward solution to the problem is to use only individual data to answer questions at individual level and aggregated data to analyse aggregate-level behaviour (Landman, 2000: 51). Michel Lallement (2003: 303) argues, however, that the actual level of analysis selected is less important than the researcher's ability to make sense of the findings by unravelling the interactive relationship between different levels, more especially in multidisciplinary studies.

Finding the right distance

According to the principle of 'variable distance' ('verschiedene Distanz'),
developed by Georg Simmel (1917: 10), the distance from the object
under observation affects the way it is observed. The long-distance
perspective can be exemplified by the large-scale multinational quantitative studies such as those in political science coordinated from the
United States in the postwar period, or the socioeconomic projects
organized by the Vienna Centre and the European Foundation for the
Improvement of Living and Working Conditions in Dublin. Other
examples of the long-distance view are provided by the innumerable
reports published by the European Union, based on data collated by the
Commission's statistical agency (Eurostat), or the statistics collated and
analysed by the many international organizations cited above. Of
necessity, these reports are often confined to description, since their main
purpose is to provide snapshots of situations based on aggregated
statistics in a large number of countries at a given point in time, or for a
more limited number of variables over time.

By contrast, a 'close-up' comparison of a social phenomenon within a
country, society or culture, described as 'narrow-gauge' by Rose (1991:
456), may reveal differences attributable to region, class, age, sex or
ethnicity that may not be apparent when aggregated national-level data
are being compared from a distance. The close-up view allows identification of variations, for example with regard to population ageing, family
structures, levels of poverty or access to social entitlements, that may
result in greater disparities being found within countries, societies or
cultures than between them (Dogan, 2004: 325). This perspective is
particularly useful in the policy field. Most social policies are framed at
national or supranational level, but they are more often than not
implemented at local level, thereby offering scope for identifying
regional and local disparities in delivery.

The implications of changing the mix or number of countries and the
level of analysis may be to add less similar units of observation,
requiring a different research design, which will affect the findings and
their interpretation. Within the European Union, for example, enlargement has altered the European 'mean'. It has changed territorial
boundaries and the cultural and linguistic mix, giving the lie to much
received wisdom. Before the transition of the 1990s, Central and East
European countries tended to be considered as a bloc because of their
shared experience of the Soviet regime. The close scrutiny to which they
have been subjected since they applied for membership of the European
Union reveals, however, that their socioeconomic development during
the Soviet era, and subsequently, is varied. For instance, in the 1990s,

Estonia, which forcefully opposed Soviet rule, moved rapidly towards the Nordic social model, as typified by Finland (Manning and Shaw, 1999). By contrast, Poland's strong religious base and intellectual traditions caused it to align its social policy more closely with the Mediterranean countries and Ireland (Hantrais, 2004a: 205).

When the focus changes from the close-up to the long-distance perspective, what emerge as significant differences within and between countries and within groupings may pale into insignificance. For example, if Western countries are compared to the less developed world, the research design needs to be adjusted to ensure both an appropriate level of analysis and the right distance (see also Chapter 4).

Methods and Methodological Issues

The methodology of international comparative research, understood as a set of principles and theories guiding the choice of a distinctive approach to the study of social phenomena, is largely, but not necessarily, determined by the aims and epistemological positions of research team members (see also Chapter 5). Methods are the means whereby evidence is collected and analysed, with a view to achieving research objectives.

Whole volumes as well as chapters in methods books have been devoted to presenting and analysing 'comparative' methods, especially with reference to survey design (see Chapter 1). The intention in this section is to provide an overview of the most salient features of the main methods used by comparativists, firstly by presenting the interactive relationship between theory and methods. The second subsection provides a succinct summary of John Stuart Mill's 'comparative method' and the critiques made by analysts seeking to apply it in the social sciences and humanities. The third section is devoted to an account of some of the issues associated with different methods of data collection and analysis in international comparative research projects, and to commentary on the attempts made to resolve them.

BETWEEN THEORY AND METHODS

From an epistemological perspective, two extreme positions or research paradigms are usually identified across disciplines, each associated with its own preferred research methods: at the one end of a continuum is the positivist, universalist, experimental or empirical tradition; at the other, is the constructivist, interpretive, culturalist or naturalistic tradition, although even the extremes may overlap (Rust et al., 1999: 104). These positions have been described in terms of nomothetic (lawlike theoretical claims) in contrast to ideographic approaches (Naroll, 1968: 236–9; Smelser, 1976: 204–5; Sartori, 1994: 22, 24) (see also Chapter 5).

Positivists or universalists base their methodology on the ontological conviction that reality is objective and singular, and that all social and human facts are knowable and can be tested through a process of deduction. This process is dependent on indisputable assumptions about human nature that make scientific generalizations and predictions possible (Landman, 2000: 16; Hopkin, 2002: 249–50). Deductive theorists, notably from a rational choice perspective, reach conclusions by applying reason to a given set of premises, thereby making it possible to deduce outcomes. Broadly speaking, positivists prefer quantitative and statistical approaches, encapsulated in what has come to be known as the quasi-experimental method, because they afford greater control over the parameters of the research.

By contrast, exponents of constructivist, interpretist or culturalist theory contend that all knowledge is culturally bound and relative. On the grounds that knowledge is not value free, culturalists exploit qualitative methods and rely on observation of phenomena, located in relation to their social and cultural contexts, to reach conclusions inductively. The qualitative methods that they adopt generally involve in-depth analysis of a small number of cases, from which to build theory and extrapolate. Their interest lies in examining the relationship between the constituent parts of a unit, but usually without claiming to be able to test for causality. For qualitative researchers, reality is seen as subjective and multifarious. The research process involves continual interaction with research subjects, while remaining mindful of their own value biases (Rust et al., 1999: 104).

Comparative case studies, where a single unit is analysed in more than one setting, narrow the focus and enable intensive in-depth study. On its own, a case study can provide neither the basis for valid generalization nor the grounds for disproving established generalization. Case studies can, however, contribute to the formulation of general propositions and to theory building. Lijphart (1971: 691–3) identifies and expounds on six ideal types of case study: atheoretical (descriptive), interpretative (designed to elucidate the case in point), hypothesis generating, theory confirming, theory infirming and deviant. The last four are all useful for theory building. Hypothesis-generating case studies produce new hypotheses, whereas deviant case studies make it possible to refine and sharpen existing hypotheses. Theory-confirming and infirming case studies are implicitly comparative, while deviant cases can serve as an experimental or statistical control group.

Although reference is again made primarily to political science, in his comparative methods book, Landman (2000) makes a further distinction that broadly applies to other disciplines and to quantitative and qualitative approaches. He differentiates between two basic types of theory: normative and empirical. On the one hand, '[n]ormative theory specifies how things in society *ought to be*, given a desired set of outcomes and philosophical position'. On the other, '[e]mpirical theory seeks to establish causal relationships between two or more concepts in an effort to explain the occurrence of observed…phenomena' (Landman, 2000: 15, original emphasis). For both types of theory, comparisons allow the researcher to confirm or contest generalizations.

From his analysis of nomothetic and ideographic approaches, Neil J. Smelser (1976) concludes that these two approaches may involve different research techniques, modes of explanation and organization of variables, but that they 'do *not* necessarily differ substantively with respect to the nature of the causal forces invoked', and 'do not call for different theoretical grounding-points' (Smelser, 1976: 205, original emphasis). This observation would still seem to be valid in the twenty-first century, the more so in a situation where the dividing line between different epistemologies has become less clearly defined (see Chapter 5).

THE COMPARATIVE METHOD ACCORDING TO J.S. MILL

The most widely cited and documented 'comparative method' is that formulated by John Stuart Mill (1843) in the nineteenth century, and subsequently adopted by researchers seeking a quasi-experimental method that could be applied in the social sciences. Although the research designs developed by Mill have been subjected to numerous critiques and are not generally rigidly observed, over the years they have continued to provide a valuable framework for comparative researchers in the social sciences and humanities (see, for example, commentaries by Lijphart, 1971: 688; Smelser, 1976: 205; Ragin, 1987: 36–42; Dogan and Pelassy, 1990: 16; Hopkin, 2002: 252–5; De Vaus, 2008: 252–6).

Mill's methods of agreement, difference and concomitant variation

Of the four methods of experimental inquiry formulated by Mill (1973: book III, 388–406), the three most commonly cited by comparativists are agreement, difference and concomitant variations, outlined in Figure 3.1 and described below. Mill (1973: book III, 388) denotes 'antecedents' – agents or causes – by capital letter, and 'consequents' – effects – by lower

Figure 3.1   Mill's methods of experimental inquiry

	Antecedents/Consequents	Outcomes
Method of agreement	A is similar over a number of cases	
	1. A B C / a b c	X
	2. A D E / a d e	X
	3. A F G / a f g	X
	b c, d e, f g vary	X may be caused by A

If two or more instances of the phenomenon under investigation have only one circumstance in common, the circumstance in which alone all the instances agree, is the cause (or effect) of the given phenomenon.

Method of difference	A is absent from one or more cases	
	1. A B C / a b c	X
	2. B C / b c	not X
	b and c are the same	X may be caused by A

If an instance in which the phenomenon under investigation occurs, and an instance in which it does not occur, have every circumstance in common save one, that one occurring only in the former; the circumstance in which alone the two instances differ, is the effect, of the cause, or an indispensable part of the cause, of the phenomenon.

Method of concomitant variations	The magnitude of A varies over a number of cases	The magnitude of X varies with the magnitude of A
		A may be cause of X

Whatever phenomenon varies in any manner whenever another phenomenon varies in some particular manner, is either a cause or an effect of that phenomenon, or is connected with it through some fact of causation.

Sources: Compiled from Mill, 1973: book III, 388–91, 398–403 (original emphasis and punctuation); and from Jary and Jary, 1991: 104.

case, the aim being to ascertain the effects of a given cause in producing a particular outcome.

Although Mill does not use the term, comparative analysts generally refer to three categories of variables in research designs: dependent, independent, and spurious or intervening variables. Dependent or endogenous variables refer to the phenomenon under investigation that the researcher is seeking to explain, represented by X in the figure. Independent, causal, explanatory or exogenous variables (Mill's A B and a b), together with 'spurious' (seemingly influential) or 'intervening' (in reality influential) variables, are the factors that may serve to explain the dependent variable (Burnham et al., 2004: 62). The distinction between dependent and independent variables is derived from the research question being investigated, the researcher's theoretical position and the selection of cases and units of analysis.

Sociologists and political scientists have tended to choose between the first two research designs proposed by Mill: the method of agreement and the method of difference, which are both methods of elimination. Those who opt for the method of agreement, or what is described as the most different research design, select for comparison cases that are as similar as possible for the dependent variable(s) but as different as possible for other characteristics (independent variables) that are believed to influence the dependent variable or to have a bearing on the relationship between dependent and independent variables. If the cases being compared are found to have only one independent variable in common, that variable can be said to be the cause of the phenomenon. Differing circumstances can thus be discounted as explanations. In other words, the causal relationship is assumed to remain identical notwith-standing systemic differences. The most different research design thus forces analysts to distil out common elements with explanatory power. As Mill (1973: book III, 389–90) points out, it may also be possible to reverse the process and trace the cause of a given effect back to the antecedent. However, he admits that it is hardly ever possible to ascertain all the antecedents, unless the phenomenon can be produced experimentally, which is rarely the case for the method of agreement.

According to the method of difference or most similar research de-sign, which does lend itself more readily to artificial experimentation, cases are selected that are as different as possible for the dependent variable and as similar as possible for the independent variable(s). Cases resemble each other in every respect except for the presence or absence of the phenomenon under investigation. The causal relationship is established by collecting data for all cases assumed to be similar in terms of contextual features, so that variables can be located and investigated as causal or explanatory. Using Mill's (1973: book III, 391) terminology: 'If the effect of A B C is a b c, and the effect of B C, b c, it is evident that the effect of A is a'. As in the controlled experiments of the natural sciences, if all the cases share the same characteristic, a potential explanatory variable can be regarded as controlled. Applying Mill's framework, comparative projects can thus be designed with the aim of explaining empirically the relationship between the core subject and social reality as well as the societal developments that it affects.

The method of concomitant variation has been particularly influential among statisticians in the social sciences (Dogan, 2004: 324). It is relevant to their concerns because it takes account of variables, what Mill calls 'permanent causes', that can neither be excluded nor isolated experimentally, although it may be possible to modify them in some way and to observe corresponding effects (Mill, 1973: book III, 398). Following this method, the research is designed to establish the empirical relationship or correlation between variables, where the magnitude of the first variable affects the magnitude of the second variable. Recognizing the limits of the method, Mill concedes, however, that it cannot be assumed when two phenomena vary in a particular manner that one is the cause and the other the effect, or that some other causal agent has not escaped observation. He therefore recommends using the method of concomitant variations in conjunction with the method of difference, suggesting that it is most reliable in examining variations of quantity. Even then, he warns against assuming that the same numerical relationship exists between variables (Mill, 1973: book III, 398–406).

Critiques of Mill's methods

Not without justification, Mill's method has been criticized on a number of counts. Firstly, it is considered to present an oversimplification of reality, mainly on the basis that, in the real world, it is impossible to take account of all the potential variables that might come into play, an issue of which Mill was himself aware. He believed that experimentation is impossible in the social sciences. It follows that the method of difference, which he describes as 'the most perfect of the methods of experimental inquiry', could not be applied in the social sciences because of the difficulty of finding two cases that are similar in every respect except that which is the subject of inquiry (Mill, 1973: book VI, 881). He therefore suggests applying the 'Indirect Method of Difference…which compares two *classes* of instances respectively agreeing in nothing but the presence of a given circumstance on the one side and its absence on the other', but still the result is likely to be 'a specious semblance of conclusiveness' (Mill, 1973: book VI, 882–3, original emphasis). It remains that the method of agreement does not offer a solution in cases of a plurality of causes, which is characteristic of the social sciences, and the method of concomitant variations may also be inconclusive for similar reasons. At most, it may be possible to conclude that an effect is sometimes produced without a specific circumstance but not that the circumstance, when present, does not contribute to a given outcome.

When, in the late 1960s and early 1970s, the dominant research design for the collection of comparable data was the large-scale survey, it was argued that Mill's method of difference was inapplicable in the social sciences since it required too many variables to be held constant, a problem frequently expressed in terms of 'many variables, small number of cases' (Lijphart, 1971: 685). Mill's method of agreement was, therefore, to be preferred on the grounds that, by seeking out similarities and replicating the relationship between variables, any causal linkages identified would be more likely to be replicated.

From the early 1970s, researchers in the United States engaged in a lively debate over the relative merits of small *versus* large Ns, epitomized in the 1990s in a series of articles by Stanley Lieberson (1991, 1994) and Jukka Savolainen (1994) published in *Social Forces*. In essence, Lieberson (1991) argued that attempts to infer causality by using Mill's methods of agreement and difference on the basis of a small number of cases rested on making several untenable assumptions. These claims were countered by Savolainen, who maintained that Lieberson was confusing the uses of Mill's methods, adopting a narrow conception of causality and failing to appreciate the aim of case-oriented explanations, 'which is not to provide generalizations beyond the scope of the study' (Savolainen, 1994: 1220, 1223). For Savolainen, a small number of cases did not constitute an obstacle to the application of Mill's methods. In his riposte, Lieberson (1994: 1230–3) dismissed Savolainen's criticisms as ill founded and unproven, and went so far as to argue that the methods of agreement and difference were 'outdated and inappropriate' procedures for comparative or historical analysis based on a small number of cases, since they are unable to deal with a probabilistic perspective and data errors, use multivariate analyses, or take account of interaction effects, all of which are central to an understanding of social processes. Lieberson (1994: 1236) concludes by noting that Mill's methods were conceived at a time when researchers were less aware of probabilistic thinking and when techniques were not available for measuring interaction effects and for carrying out multivariate modelling.

Another problem often cited in the literature is the bias introduced by the non-random selection of the units of analysis in comparative research due not only to personal preferences for certain types of cases but also to the deliberate choice of units where the same outcome is present. As recognized by Mill, not only is it never possible to select cases that are identical in all respects except one, but it is also highly unlikely that a single cause can explain the same or a similar outcome, or that the same combination of factors interacts in the same way in cases of multiple or plural causation (Ragin, 1987: 37–41). In addition, factors that might explain the variation in the outcome variable can easily be missed. 'Spurious explanation' refers to the omission of key variables that might account for the outcome and for the other explanatory variables, thereby mistakenly attributing the outcome to an identified factor (Landman, 2000: 38, 47–9).

A related issue first raised by anthropologists in the late nineteenth century is also widely cited by analysts as particularly problematic in comparative research designs such as that proposed by Mill (for example Naroll, 1968: 241, 258–9; Elder, 1976: 217–18; Smelser, 1976: 212–13). The problem was named after Francis Galton. In 1889, Galton challenged a study of the laws of marriage and descent by the early anthropologist Edward B. Tylor (1832–1917), based on correlations between cultural characteristics. Galton argued that correlations between items might be the product of borrowing and diffusion of institutions or traits and could not, therefore, be assumed to reveal causal and functional relations between them. In other words, he contended that societies A and B might be variants of a common overarching society C, or simply illustrations of the same case, and that it was the process of diffusion that constituted the set of operative variables accounting for the association between the correlated variables. The independent variables might, he argued, be interrelated, resulting in the inflation of correlations. In effect, the observed correlations may do no more than 'reflect artifacts of culture-trait borrowing from a common source' (Naroll, 1968: 241). Researchers aware of Galton's problem sought to resolve it by minimizing the variable of diffusion and ensuring greater parametric control, for example by comparing subsets of societies that are similar in size and structural complexity. They also tried to ensure that the units being compared were drawn from different subsets, thereby making it possible for researchers to draw out universal cross-national generalizations.

Many attempts have been made to refine and apply Mill's proposals. The solutions proposed to the small *versus* large N problem in comparative methods include increasing the number of observations over time, comparing subunits within cases to achieve greater overall variation, making comparisons focused on differences, according to Mill's method of difference, or concentrating on key explanatory variables and developing strong theoretical specifications using Mill's method of agreement (Landman, 2000: 40–1). In support of comparative research designs that cover a large number of cases ('large N') from a variety of settings, quantitative researchers argue that they are aiming to establish 'robust and parsimonious generalisations...focusing on communalities (concomitant variation) rather than differences between cases' (Hopkin, 2002: 255).

Many of the problems associated with Mill's methods are relevant to all forms of data collection. They arise not only in large-scale statistical and econometric studies but also in fine-grain qualitative work, thereby confirming the need for research designs capable of taking account of a sufficient number of contextual variables to guarantee that aspects of the wider picture with potentially explanatory value are not overlooked.

DATA COLLECTION AND ANALYSIS

Data collection and analysis have long challenged the resourcefulness of comparative researchers, and they are likely to continue to do so. Writing in the 1970s, Smelser (1976: 151, original emphasis) commented that 'the methodological *issues* facing contemporary comparative analysts have changed much less than their data, methods and theories'. With reference to anthropology, political science, sociology and, to a lesser extent, economics, history and psychology, he stressed the advances made due to the 'revolutionary increase' in the quantity and quality of data, the development of research techniques and the proliferation of new interpretative modes. By the late 1980s, however, in comparative anthropology, the problem was no longer how data should be analysed and interpreted but how suitable data should be gathered in the first place, to the extent that the word 'comparison' had completely disappeared from the vocabulary of methodological discourse. The accumulation of more and more detailed ethnographic data was making general comparison much less feasible (Holy, 1987: 6, 8).

In the mid-1990s, Mattei Dogan (1994: 37–8) claimed that, in political science, the advances in statistical methodology had not been matched in comparative inquiry by 'equivalent progress in data collection and retrieval', compounded by the problem of uncritical use. Writing in the late 1990s, Timothy Johnson (1998: 1) argued that 'the available protocols for conducting cross-cultural and cross-national survey research...would appear to be seriously underdeveloped in comparison to the methodologies available for the conduct of monocultural surveys'. Similar claims were being made in the early twenty-first century, for example to justify the work of the Economic and Social Research Council's National Centre for Research Methods in the United Kingdom. A new initiative on methods and resources for cross-national comparative social science research was thought necessary, designed to build collective capacity, consolidate expertise and foster international cooperation in refining research methods, data enhancement and development (see Chapter 1).

When reviewing data collection and analysis, methods books in most disciplines tend to make a clear distinction between quantitative and qualitative strategies. Although, for a growing number of researchers, the quantitative–qualitative 'divide' is no longer valid, for others it continues to serve as a framework in determining preferences for comparative research strategies (see Chapter 5).

Quantitative data are most often collected using survey instruments, censuses and administrative registers with a view to answering the 'how many' question. Quantification may, it is argued (Dogan, 2004: 336), be unnecessary if contrasts are obvious: some observable phenomena cannot be quantified, for example political corruption, and some theories cannot be tested statistically, for example dependency theory.

Qualitative data are gathered with a view to identifying and understanding the characteristics of the object of inquiry. Ideographic or configurative techniques are available, including documentary searches, historical and content analysis, panel data derived from diaries, biographies, interviews and participant observation, capable of providing discursive accounts of phenomena (for example Rust et al., 1999: 107; Mangen, 2007: 25–9; Nilsen, 2008). The technique of interpretation, as applied in 'thick description', aims to draw 'large conclusions from small, but very densely textured facts' (Geertz, 1973: 28).

Whether the main approach adopted by researchers is quantitative or qualitative, the list of enduring problems associated with data collection and analysis has barely changed over the years. Some of the data issues raised by international comparisons have already been dealt with in this chapter (selection and value bias, small *versus* large N, number of variables and countries, spurious explanation, and ecological and individual fallacy). Others concerning conceptual and linguistic equivalence, vagueness and stretching are examined in Chapter 4. In this section, it remains to review briefly issues of data availability and access, quality and reliability, analysis and interpretation, all of which continue to tax the minds of researchers engaged in comparative research projects.

Issues of data availability, access, quality and reliability

Efforts were made during the 1990s and early 2000s by national research councils (for example the Economic and Social Research Council in the United Kingdom) and international funding agencies (for example the European Science Foundation) to promote more effective large-scale data collection methods, using technological advances to improve data handling and processing techniques. Such activities can be credited with having substantially increased the amount of available data and having made access much easier. Researchers engaging in large-scale quantitative studies now have direct access to many of the aggregate-level international databases and are able to obtain disaggregated datasets.

Data measurement, adequacy and comparability, nonetheless, continue to give rise to problems that may affect the integrity of comparative research projects, to the extent that ease of access to comparable data rather than more scientific factors can drive case selection and shape research design (Hopkin, 2002: 258). In support of his view that Mill's methods could not be applied to small N studies, Lieberson (1994: 1232) argues strongly that measurement errors are 'massive and pervasive in social research' and are not simply a question of quantitative *versus* qualitative research, although they are easier to deal with in large N studies, because they can be absorbed using a probabilistic approach. His list of measurement problems extends to coding and processing, dealing with contradictory evidence, intentional and unintentional distortions by individuals and organizations. Outstanding problems that are commonly identified include lack of national data or missing data, lack of comparable national time series data, changes over time and space in the indicators and categories available for statistical purposes.

Missing data are an insoluble problem, which may result in the relevant cases being omitted from the comparison if new data cannot be collected or simulated. Time series data, like those collated by Eurostat for the European Commission or by the Council of Europe, have to be revised and updated every time new member states join the Union or Council. International organizations issue guidelines for data collection at national level and attempt to harmonize the data supplied, but they cannot require the delivery of non-existent time series data. The United Nations Economic Commission for Europe (2006) regularly supplies detailed recommendations for the collection of census data, but considerable discrepancies continue to be found in the questions asked at national level and in their formulation. Despite the best efforts of international statistical agencies, time series data on sociodemographic topics such as unemployment, part-time working, the informal economy, migration or family structure, remain especially unreliable for international comparisons. These data are problematic not only for practical reasons due to the use of different sources and criteria, but also for political and ethical reasons (for example Kinnear, 1987: 9–11; Brown, 1986: 48–50; Dogan, 2004: 334–5; Hantrais, 2004a: 50–67, 2006b: 146–56, 2007b: 217–19, 230–2; Singleton, 2007: 61–4) (see also Chapter 7).

Researchers selecting indicators for use in international benchmarking exercises may have to rely on the dubious assumption that such indicators retain the same meaning, represent the same variables and are comparable across dissimilar social units over time and space (Smelser, 1976: 242). The case of *per capita* gross domestic product or gross national product is frequently cited as a deceptively precise measure of economic development (for example Hopkin, 2002: 259; Dogan, 2004: 328–9). The compilation of reliable indicators that can be confidently applied across a wide range of situations is a task that exercises the intellectual powers and analytical skills of comparative researchers, as exemplified by the work carried out on poverty indicators (Marlier et al., 2007) or on migration (Poulain et al., 2006) (see also Chapter 4).

Unresolved issues of comparability cannot be ignored. Reliability tests can be performed, raw national data can be scrutinized, and survey questions checked, but the conclusion may be that a large-scale dataset gives no more than an indication of facts, and any findings need to be read and interpreted in conjunction with data yielded by other methods (see Chapter 5). In all events, the effects of differences in data collection and handling need to be known and recorded to show whether they compromise the integrity of the research and the validity of the findings. When new datasets are being compiled, careful annotation is needed to explain how the data have been collected, why they are or are not comparable, and what inferences can and cannot be drawn.

The European Social Survey, developed from the mid-1990s by an international team of researchers intent on establishing a methodological benchmark for comparative attitudinal surveys, provides a noteworthy example of the painstaking preparatory work required to ensure the quality, reliability, validity and, above all, comparability of social survey data (Jowell et al., 2007b). The aim of the coordinating team is to ensure consistent standards not only of design but also of implementation, with a view to producing surveys capable of accurately tracking the speed and direction of change in attitudes and values within European societies. The project, which involved almost a decade of intensive work to identify cross-cutting issues and concepts, to design and translate rigorously tested and optimally comparable questionnaires, and to implement consistent strategies for fieldwork and coding, affords a model for comparative researchers (Bryson and Jowell, 2001).

Issues of data analysis and interpretation

Researchers can now exploit increasingly sophisticated techniques to analyse and interpret ever more complex datasets. Advances in computer software and new analytical techniques mean that the large amounts of data collected using both quantitative (surveys, registers and censuses) and qualitative approaches (official documents, grey literature, in-depth interviewing, participant observation, vignettes and focus groups) can be analysed electronically to enable researchers to make connections, and develop robust typologies and classification schemes.

At the very least, researchers carrying out secondary analysis of existing datasets are generally still obliged to deal with 'statistical noise', to 'clean up' the available data, which may not have been collected according to the same criteria, and to exercise care in interpretation (Dex, 1996: 13, 15). When conducting secondary analysis of datasets, the advice is to examine carefully the national criteria that have been used to compile the statistics and to check for changes over time in national definitions. If data have been harmonized, it may be necessary to go back to the original national datasets and the lowest level of aggregation to locate data that may not have been included in global figures.

Much of the literature on computer software packages for the analysis of data collected in qualitative studies does not specifically address the issues arising in international comparisons and, more especially, the analysis of multilingual data. An exception is Steen Mangen (2004: 320, note 3, 2007: 31), who advocates the use of NUD*IST and Nvivo for this purpose. These packages have proved capable of handling large amounts of multilingual texts, including non-European scripts, in various formats. They offer rapid and easy coding procedures, and are particularly valuable for grounded theorizing in qualitative research.

On the basis that qualitative research often involves complex 'combinatorial' explanations for phenomena that cannot be tested statistically, Charles C. Ragin (1987: 14–15, 85–9) developed a 'configurational' analytic approach based on Boolean algebra, designed to explain phenomena by identifying the combination of causal conditions present in cases containing the phenomenon under study. The approach he suggests uses strict logic rather than frequency, firstly to identify conditions – necessary conditions – present in every available case using dichotomous variables. It then looks for any single factor – a sufficient condition – that produces the phenomenon by itself. By systematically comparing infrequently occurring phenomena, the Boolean approach avoids the descriptive particularism of many small N studies and offers a useful framework for analysing complex data.

Assessing the Impact of Research Design on Findings

This chapter set out to demonstrate the importance of remaining alert to the ways in which the decisions taken at each step in the research design in international comparative projects influence subsequent stages and, ultimately, the findings. The underlying assumption was that it may be possible to develop a theoretically perfect research design, but the materials analysed here suggest that it is never possible to find a design that can be operationalized and implemented in all respects in all the units of comparison. Whether it be in the selection of the object of inquiry, the research question, the number and mix of units and levels of analysis, or the methods adopted for data collection and analysis, trade-offs and compromise are inevitable, both at the research design stage and as the project unfolds. They may be needed to allow refinement of hypotheses, correction of fruitless paths of inquiry, and as a solution to irreconcilable epistemological differences between researchers. The example of grounded theory is instructive in this respect. Because it depends on the systematic discovery of theory from social and human science data, investigators do not foreclose options at an early stage but maintain an open mind throughout the research process (Glaser and Strauss, 1967: 3).

Decisions taken in designing the research are never neutral or immutable. Like objects of inquiry, they are socially, and not infrequently politically, constructed, for research designs are drawn up and implemented by human beings with their own personalities, cultures, ideologies and agendas. From the perspective of the historian and with reference to immigration studies, Nancy Green (1994: 6) argues that 'no comparison…is completely neutral'. Decisions taken about the level of generalization, the variables, and the method of agreement or difference place the accent on diversity or unity, leading her to conclude that '[t]he way in which the question is asked implies part of the response'.

This chapter shows how the choice of units and levels of analysis, and variables in international comparisons are often constrained, if not imposed, by external factors. It also suggests that the constraints are not solely external. The researcher's own cultural and linguistic knowledge, disciplinary affiliations and financial and logistic resources serve as important determinants in the selection of the object of inquiry, the country mix, the variables and strategies adopted. While comparison remains possible and worthwhile, and scientific rigour continues to be a legitimate aim in international comparative projects, the value bias of research team members can result in disagreements over research design and strategies, leading to problems such as skewed case selection, wrong level fallacy and discrepancies in data collection methods and analytical techniques. Issues of research management are examined in detail in Chapter 7, but it is relevant here to signal the importance of the selection and coordination of research teams at every stage in the research process. In multinational research projects, approaches to analysis and interpretation of data need to be discussed, thoroughly critiqued, and supported by the regular exchange of materials, either face to face or by Internet.

Whatever the aims of the research and the composition of the research team, the research strategy agreed in the early stages of a project should make provision for keeping the research design constantly under review, taking account of any unforeseen problems, and seeking collective solutions. Often, one team member will synthesize the country data and carry out the comparative analysis in consultation with partners. When the data are collected, and reports are written in different languages, as is frequently the case in projects conducted under the auspices of

European framework programmes, adequate time needs to scheduled, especially when using qualitative methods, for comparing notes, validating data, developing common analytical frameworks and techniques, translating key documents and scrutinizing possible interpretations of findings. Such planning is essential in international comparative research, the more so in projects that cross disciplinary and epistemological boundaries (see Chapters 4 and 7).

In an assessment of future needs in data collection and analysis, Landman (2000: 215) advocates the development of more systematic ways of collecting, documenting and disseminating data, with researchers paying greater attention to explaining the problems they encounter and to sharing their experience across a networked comparative research community. As suggested in this chapter, if problems cannot be overcome at the design stage, then at the very least researchers need to reflect, individually and severally, on the implications of the decisions they make regarding design and implementation, explaining and justifying any changes in orientation and, at the same time, limiting adverse 'method effects' if it does not prove feasible to apply identical techniques and methods in different cultures (Armer, 1973: 68).

As argued in Chapter 1, comparisons designed to cross national, cultural, linguistic or societal boundaries require additional research skills and strategies that need to be brought into play throughout the research process. International comparisons are, therefore, likely to be more complicated and more demanding in terms of time, effort and resources than comparisons within countries, societies or cultures. Self-conscious observation and critique of the research process are always very cost-effective and informative pursuits, helping to guard against drawing inferences and making generalizations that cannot be validated by the data. Additionally, reflexivity makes it possible for researchers to implement any tactical modifications that may become necessary as the research evolves, with the aim of maximizing the validity, reliability, replicability and plausibility of the findings.

4

Defining and Analysing Concepts and Contexts

The definition and understanding of concepts and the relationship between concepts and contexts are of critical concern in comparative research that crosses national, societal, cultural and linguistic boundaries. International comparisons may be rendered ineffectual by the lack of a common understanding of central concepts and the societal contexts within which phenomena are located. The assertion made in the 1970s by Donald P. Warwick and Samuel Osherson (1973: 14) that variability of concepts presented formidable problems of measurement and interpretation still holds true many decades later, and 'the danger of culturally-bound misinterpretations or misunderstandings' continues to be a largely unresolved issue for researchers from whatever discipline who are engaging in comparative studies (Grootings, 1986: 275).

Reaching a common understanding among international team members about the meaning and measurement of concepts presents major challenges in comparative research. Richard Rose (1991: 451) heralded as a great achievement of comparative politics in the United States in the 1960s a proposal to adopt generic concepts, claiming that a common conceptual vocabulary and common theoretical interests were capable of holding together studies of disparate countries. Expressed in slightly different terms, the aim of comparativists in political science is to create 'a concept capable of homogenizing a heterogeneous series of countries' (Dogan and Kazancigil, 1994: 4).

The underlying assumption in this book, justifying devoting a whole chapter to conceptualization and contextualization in international comparative research, is that concepts cannot be separated from contexts, not only in terms of national, societal or cultural embedding, but also with reference to research cultures and language communities.

The purpose of the chapter is to explore how key concepts in social sciences and humanities disciplines are understood and interpreted in different national settings, and to look at issues of equivalence of concepts, measurement and analysis. It builds on Chapter 3 and offers signposts to Chapter 5, which examines how methodological approaches can be combined to achieve the objectives of comparative research. Interest here lies in providing researchers involved in international comparisons with a rationale and practical guidance for analysing socioeconomic and political phenomena in relation to their institutional and sociocultural settings. The chapter tracks the shift, already identified in this volume, away from universalistic culture-free to culture-bound approaches, which places the theory and practice of contextualization of concepts at the nexus of international comparative studies. It examines the issues surrounding the (non-)transportability of concepts and the selection of appropriate contextual frames of reference, and concludes by commenting on the implications for international comparative research of applying the principle of context-boundedness of concepts.

Defining and Measuring Concepts

In research that crosses cultural and linguistic boundaries, analysis of the social construction, and 'reconstruction' (Sartori, 1984: 50), of concepts is an essential component in the characterization of national, societal and cultural structures and systems. Interest in developing a method for the systematic analysis of concepts was formally recognized in 1970 with the establishment of a Committee on Conceptual and Terminological Analysis under the auspices of the International Political Science Association. Significantly, the committee was subsequently renamed 'Concepts and Methods' (RC01, see www.concepts-methods.org). Fourteen years after its creation, the work of the original committee resulted in the publication of an edited volume on social science concepts. In the introductory chapter, the editor, Giovanni Sartori (1984), constructed a carefully argued set of 'Guidelines for concept analysis', incorporating a series of 'rules' that are of enduring relevance for comparative researchers from most disciplines.

Drawing, among other sources, on Sartori's proposals, the aim in this section is to review some of the numerous attempts to define concepts and the issues that they raise in international comparisons, such as conceptual vagueness and stretching. The section goes on to examine the tools that have been developed to achieve conceptual, linguistic and measurement equivalence.

DEFINING CONCEPTS

In all research, concepts, understood as the ideas or meanings conveyed by a term, serve as the pegs or reference points for identifying and classifying phenomena. Sociologists, political scientists, anthropologists and psychologists, in particular, have therefore devoted considerable attention to defining the concepts to be applied in international comparisons. For Mattei Dogan and Dominique Pelassy (1990: 24), 'there can be no comparisons without concepts', and Rose (1991: 448–9) makes the point that, in political science, concepts come before theories; they provide categories for collecting and sorting information. He argues that it is the operationalization of concepts that enables theories to be tested by empirical observations to produce conclusions that are generalizable because they are capable of being stated in conceptual terms. Sartori (1984: 9) is less assertive about the direction of the relationship between theory and concepts, while acknowledging that, whether concepts are 'theory-formed' or 'theory-forming', they are the basic units with which social scientists operate.

Some social scientists are more reluctant to talk about concepts, preferring instead to use the term 'notions'. The Italian sociologist Vincenzo Ferrari (1990: 67), in a chapter entitled 'Socio-legal concepts and their comparison', observes, for example, how 'notoriously hard' it is to agree on 'the very notion of "law"'. The French sociologist Michel Lallement (2003: 303) comments on the misunderstandings and ambiguities that can result when researchers from different disciplines (economists, sociologists, historians) refer to 'notions' such as 'actor', 'institution', 'forum', 'configuration' or 'time'. In his search for operational concepts, Jean-Claude Barbier (2005a: 47–8) opts to describe the term 'précarité de l'emploi' as a 'notion'. He demonstrates not only how 'précarité', which is sometimes rendered as 'precariousness' in English, is very difficult to define, measure and translate into other languages, but also how the meaning has changed over time in France, with the result that it is far from commanding consensus either within or across societies.

The issues involved in reaching agreement in international comparisons about how to conceptualize universally recognized terms such as 'nation', 'society' and 'culture' due to variations over time and space were raised in Chapters 1 and 3. Sociologists have been unable to find a universally acceptable concept of 'society' to apply in international comparisons. As boundaries have become more difficult to define, and greater importance has been attached to intersocietal connections in a globalized world, the concept of unitary societies has been increasingly contested. In his attempt to codify cross-societal analysis in the 1960s, Robert M. Marsh (1967: 12) defined a society as 'a plurality of interacting individuals', sharing four characteristics: a definite territory; recruitment in large part by sexual reproduction; a comprehensible culture, meaning cultural patterns that are 'sufficiently diversified to enable the members of the society to fulfill all the requirements of social life'; and political independence, when not meaning 'a subsystem' of another 'subsystem'.

In psychology, it is equally if not more difficult to define and opera-tionalize the all-encompassing key concept of culture (Lyons and Chryssochoou, 2000: 138–9). At the one extreme, according to some definitions, 'culture' may be conceptualized interchangeably with 'society' and 'nation', implying that 'national cultures are unitary and homogeneous systems'. At the other extreme, culture can only be useful as an explanatory variable if it is unpacked to reveal the relationship between the different aspects of culture as a complex system, on the one hand, and as psychological structures, processes and social behaviour, on the other (see also Chapter 3).

The very variability of concepts is sometimes presented as a defining characteristic to the extent that variables may be defined in terms of concepts. Hence, '[v]ariables are those concepts whose values change over a given set of units, such as income, political party identification, propensity to join a protest movement' (Landman, 2000: 16). By setting the boundaries of variability ('bounded variability', Rose, 1991: 447), the researcher can hope to gain parametric control over the unit of analysis. However, this is no easy task, and many instances are cited in the literature of 'careless conceptualization' and 'conceptual stretching' that may invalidate empirical generalizations. Careless conceptualization may result from 'conceptual vagueness and inconsistency', for example in the debates over economic development and democracy (Hopkin, 2002: 259–60). The difficulty of finding indicators that accurately measure the properties of concepts such as 'democracy' can lead to 'conceptual stretching', a term used by Sartori (1994: 21) to refer to concepts that are so sloppily defined ('definitional sloppiness') that they fail to discriminate. If a concept is stretched too far, it loses its meaning and its heuristic validity, as illustrated with reference to concepts such as 'pluralism', 'mobilization' and 'ideology'. Conceptual stretching may, however, be avoided if researchers possess a sufficiently in-depth knowledge of all the cases under study (Landman, 2000: 52).

These issues are thoroughly explored by Sartori (1984: 28–44) in constructing a series of rules that he suggests comparativists should follow in systematically defining and operationalizing concepts. He identifies three problems that need to be resolved if a concept is to be accurately defined: concepts may be unsatisfactory, muddled or inadequate if they are based on disorganized or trivial characteristics, undenotativeness, or vagueness and terminological ambiguity. The solutions that Sartori proposes are to establish the connotative definition (properties of the concept) and its referents, or denotative definition (the objects, entities or processes identified by terms), and ensure that the term used is universally understood, unambiguous and consistent. To determine what the properties of a concept are, the advice is that the concept should be reconstructed from a review of the existing literature by collecting a representative set of definitions, extracting their common characteristics and constructing matrices that enable them to be organized meaningfully (Sartori, 1984: 41, rule 4, 50). If concepts are not to suffer from boundary indefiniteness, the number of characteristics needs to be sufficient to identify its referents with respect to all their boundaries, to discriminate *vis-à-vis* membership, for example in the case of elites, and to establish cut-off points for inclusion or exclusion in marginal cases (Sartori, 1984: 42–4, rules 5–6). The ultimate purpose of reconstruction is to provide a firm basis for the formation of concepts.

Sartori (1984) also offers several recipes to ensure that concepts can be meaningfully applied. His much cited 'ladder of abstraction' links universal and particularistic approaches, where universalism represents the highest level of abstraction and particularism the lowest (Sartori, 1984: 44–6, rule 7). The method he describes involves organizing categories according to a basic rule of transformation, whereby the connotations and denotations of concepts are inversely related: to make concepts more general, the number of characteristics must be reduced; to make them more specific, the number must be increased.

The choice of the term to be used to designate a concept is also critical if ambiguity and loss of meaning are to be avoided due to associations with other terms in the same semantic field. This problem can be illustrated with reference to neighbouring words in the semantic field of 'elites', for example 'ruling class', 'power class', or the associated words in the semantic field of 'power', including 'influence', 'authority' or 'force' (Sartori, 1984: 51–4). In the final analysis, it is incumbent on researchers to ensure that definitions of concepts are both adequate and parsimonious. Definitions should be adequate in that they contain enough properties to identify the referents and their boundaries, and parsimonious in that they exclude neighbouring properties that are not necessary as defining characteristics (Sartori, 1984: 56, rule 10).

ESTABLISHING EQUIVALENCE OF CONCEPTS

Establishing equivalence for the theoretical concepts used and the operational indicators applied in multiple contexts is an ongoing challenge for comparative researchers, which is unlikely to be resolved solely by technical means. In an investigation of the types of equivalence that have been discussed or mentioned by researchers from many disciplines in the wide-ranging available literature spanning more than 35 years, Timothy Johnson (1998: 3–6) identifies 50 overlapping varieties of equivalence, to which he adds cross-cultural and cultural equivalence used in a generic sense. He classifies certain forms of equivalence as interpretive and procedural. Interpretive equivalence, which is primarily concerned with subjective cross-cultural comparability of meaning includes conceptual, functional, semantic, linguistic, contextual, idiomatic, experiential, theoretical and substantive equivalence. Procedural equivalence, which is predominant during the data collection phase of a study, is concerned with objective measures and procedures for making cross-cultural comparisons, with emphasis on the application of mechanically identical procedures (Johnson, 1998: 6–10). This section focuses on the issues raised by different forms of equivalence.

Conceptual, functional and semantic equivalence

Comparability of concepts is often defined, particularly by researchers using survey instruments, in terms of functional or semantic equivalence. Functional equivalence of concepts and indicators came into fashion in the 1950s and 1960s. By the 1970s, among the basic problems arising in comparative analysis, 'the most basic theoretical question [was held to be] whether the concepts under study have meaning or equivalent meanings in the social units considered' (Warwick and Osherson, 1973: 11). Functional equivalence does not imply that concepts should be identical or similar, but that they should have the same function, allowing units of analysis with seemingly dissimilar characteristics to be grouped into meaningful categories (Landman, 2000: 43–4). As noted in Chapter 2, 'functionality' is considered to be the basic methodological principle of all comparative law (Zweigert and Kötz, 1998: 34, 44), implying that the concepts selected are broad enough to encompass heterogeneous legal institutions that are functionally comparable. However, just as different structures may perform the same function, the same structure may perform a number of different functions over time and space. In addition, some functions may not be performed everywhere (Dogan and Pelassy, 1990: 37, 41–2). By the turn of the twenty-first century, functional equivalence had become not only one of the most widely used terms qualifying equivalence but also the term commanding the lowest degree of consensus on use (Harkness et al., 2003: 14); conceptual equivalence was generally considered to be a necessary condition for making valid cross-cultural comparisons.

In the postwar period, survey questions were usually developed in the United States and exported to other countries. The uncritical adaptation of techniques that have been developed for monocultural surveys tends, however, to lead to ill-founded assumptions regarding the equivalence of concepts in cross-cultural comparisons (Johnson, 1998: 1). The emphasis placed on producing formally identical items rather than conceptual, functional or semantic equivalence, may make it difficult to know whether any differences reported are due to socio-cultural variations in systems, different interpretations of questions or other extraneous factors.

To illustrate these issues, Sartori (1984: 20–1) discusses the different semantic configurations of 'government' and 'state', in the Anglo-American and European literature, and of 'people' used in the singular and plural. In their chapters, the contributors to his edited volume explore at length the conceptual equivalence in the use of the terms 'consensus', 'development', 'ethnicity', 'integration', 'political culture', 'power' and 'revolution'. Also in political science, Rose (1991: 447) cites the example of the British Prime Minister, the German *Bundeskanzler*, the Italian *Presidente del Consiglio dei Ministri* and the Irish *Taoiseach*, as functionally equivalent units providing a suitable grouping for comparative analysis. Identifying equivalent concepts requires an in-depth analysis of political processes in different countries, as illustrated by the observation that the three different functions of the French President are fulfilled by two officials in the United Kingdom and by three in Italy (Dogan and Pelassy, 1990: 37).

In the field of public policy and more especially welfare, not only the denotations but also the connotations of vocabulary for different benefits vary considerably from one national context to another. These variations can be illustrated by the comparison of 'family allowances' and 'child benefit' in European Union member states (Hantrais, 2007b: 117–19), or 'residualism' and 'universalism' in welfare systems (Mabbett and Bolderson, 1999: 47). In psychology, functional equivalence is said to be achieved 'when two behaviours are related to the solution of the same problem' (Lyons and Chryssochoou, 2000: 142), as illustrated by the example of visits to a priest at his shrine in Ghana and to a psychotherapist in Europe or the United States, or when equivalents for feelings of national pride are identified in different societies: the monarchy in Britain and the Basic Law in Germany.

Authors writing about cross-cultural research methods sometimes make a distinction, taken from anthropology and psychology, between 'etic' and 'emic' conceptual models, which are used to classify concepts, ideas and behaviour in survey questions (Johnson, 1998: 10–11; Coolican, 1999: 188–90; Lyons and Chryssochoou, 2000: 139–40). The differentiation is based on the linguistic distinction between phonetics and phonemics: phonetics are linked to the universal properties of spoken sounds, whereas phonemics are concerned with units of significant sounds in specific languages. According to the 'etic' model, as developed by John W. Berry (1969: 123–4), concepts are universal if they are understood in a consistent way across cultural and national boundaries because they are 'culture-free'. Researchers may assume that a construct taken from their own culture is universal and 'impose' it on new cultures. Ideas and concepts that are 'emic' focus on behaviour that has meaning only for one or a small number of cultural groups, since they are culture or nation specific. Researchers may start by adopting an emic perspective. By becoming immersed in the new culture, they eventually modify 'imposed etics' to produce 'derived etics' (psychological dimensions that are valid cross-culturally), thereby making comparisons possible.

Searching for linguistic equivalence

In international comparative research, language can usefully be analysed at a number of levels: symbolic, as a metalanguage, an object of inquiry and instrumentally. Language acts as a symbol of the cultural identity of the user, whether s/he is a researcher, an interviewer or the respondent. A concern in this case is that researchers and interviewers may not be aware of their own idiosyncrasies and of the effect they can have on respondents. The metalanguage that researchers use to carry out their own studies is an artefact that they need to adapt to the situation in which they are operating. Interest in discourse analysis has become a popular research topic and an important tool for social science and humanities researchers (for example Burnham et al., 2004: 242–8). As an object of inquiry, in sociolinguistics for example, linguistic preferences and codes have long been a topic for comparative analysis (for example Bernstein, 1971). The instrumental use of language, which is the main focus of attention in this subsection, applies when language serves as a stimulus or has an 'incitative' function designed to provoke the same reaction in different linguistic settings in surveys and interviews.

In the 1970s, Warwick and Osherson (1973: 28) observed that '[t]he problems of attaining linguistic equivalence through translation have received more attention from social scientists than any other aspect of cross-cultural research'. They list six dimensions of equivalence that researchers concerned with conceptual–linguistic comparability need to address. These dimensions have retained their relevance for comparative analysis: lexical meaning; grammatical meaning; the differential effects of contextual factors in the construction of questionnaires (question sequence, distribution of response alternatives); the relationship between language and response styles; the salience of culture in the translation of linguistic stimuli; and the equivalence of scale points (Warwick and Osherson, 1973: 28–30). The same authors conclude that linguistic equivalence is inseparable from the theory and concepts guiding comparative studies, and the research design (Warwick and Osherson, 1973: 31). As they note however, in the early 1970s, the pendulum was already swinging away from words to meaning. It was being argued that the primary aim of translation in survey instruments should be to convey equivalence of meaning or conceptual equivalence rather than seeking to attain strict lexical comparability (Deutscher, 1973: 167, 182).

Lexical and syntactic equivalence and comparability are today widely considered to be of less concern than conceptual and semantic equivalence in achieving comparability. In his analysis of the literature reporting on different forms of equivalence in cross-cultural survey research, with the aim of reaching precise similarity of question wording across language groups and cross-cultural consistency of measurement, Johnson (1998: 7–8) accordingly treats exact, lexical, literal, verbal, vocabulary, indicator, stimulus and text equivalence separately from linguistic and semantic equivalence as forms of procedural equivalence.

Translation of survey and interview questions is still by no means a straightforward exercise. Most translations are based on the 'ask-the-same-question' model, on the assumption that the questions are suitable for the different cultures covered in the survey. However, researchers can never assume that questions developed in one society can be straightforwardly translated and exported to another society (Harkness, 2003). Translation concerns the referential meaning and purpose of the original question rather than of the words and sentences, which may also need to be changed, to the extent that the units of translation may not necessarily be the same as the units of expression in the original language. In recognition of the seriousness of the problem, in the European Social Survey, Roger Jowell et al. (2007a: 6–9) go to great lengths to ensure equivalence of survey questions.

The aim in translating survey instruments is to express questions in such a way that the stimulus has an equivalent meaning and purpose, and provokes an equivalent reaction in different societies. Good practice in translation therefore requires attention to be paid to conceptual equivalence rather than lexical comparability based on close scrutiny of the context within which language is used and develops. Several techniques have been introduced to overcome the problems of comparability of questions. For some researchers, the only way of dealing with cultural specificity in surveys may be to use different indicators to tap the same concept (Warwick and Osherson, 1973: 17). In psychology, for example, guidelines for the wording of an original survey instrument include advice on how to achieve clarity and precision and avoid ambiguity (Lyons and Chryssochoou, 2000: 143).

Religiosity and religious practice are good examples of conceptual (mis)understanding and sensitivity of questions where the solution may be to ask different questions to measure the same construct and the equivalence of the reaction. In Western countries, church attendance may offer a suitable indirect measurement in some cultures, whereas in others the frequency of prayer would be more appropriate (Harkness, 2007: 38).

The most common, but not necessarily the most effective, solution is to translate a source questionnaire into the different languages of the countries involved, using back translation to check for equivalence of meaning and purpose. Back translation is a procedure first introduced in cross-cultural psychology in the 1970s. However, it should not be seen as a panacea. Writing after many years of experience of the International Social Survey Programme, based in Mannheim, Janet Harkness (2007: 45) argues that, in terms of results, effort, costs, reliability and viability, back translation is one of 'the less recommendable procedures'.

When carried out with due regard for the many pitfalls associated with it, the process of questionnaire translation and assessment requires not only translators but also reviewers and adjudicators, all of whom need to be familiar with the research subject, survey design and languages involved (Harkness, 2003: 36–7). Back translation can be made more reliable if one bilingual person translates the questionnaire into another language, a second bilingual person translates it back again, and a reviewer then checks the versions obtained, but even this arrangement cannot be guaranteed to eliminate problems of non-equivalence of concepts. It may, in fact, instil a false sense of security by demonstrating a 'spurious lexical equivalence', on the grounds that language is not only a cultural but also a social artefact (Deutscher, 1973: 167).

TOWARDS MEASUREMENT EQUIVALENCE

In addition to formulating theoretical problems, developing conceptual schemes and selecting samples, an important methodological task for comparative researchers is to devise 'measurement and analysis strategies that are comparable or equivalent across the societies involved in a particular study' (Armer, 1973: 51). Analysts of survey instruments have long identified a number of overlapping problems concerning equivalence of measurement, covering differential researchability, and comparability of stimuli, context, response, reliability and validity (for example Warwick and Osherson, 1973: 14–28). Moving from concepts that are theoretically meaningful to manifestations that are empirically observable requires the development of indicators to measure constructs representing underlying concepts (Harkness et al., 2003: 11). Indicators need to be recognized not only as equivalent from one society to another, but also as appropriate, which are two requirements that may conflict with one another (Armer 1973: 53). For example, the measurement of poverty and social exclusion, which is an ongoing topic of international concern, required many decades to develop equivalent and appropriate indicators that could be widely applied (Marlier et al., 2007: 46–53).

The issue of measurement equivalence continues to be of critical concern in comparative survey research. In his analysis of the literature dealing with procedural equivalence in cross-cultural comparisons, Johnson (1998: 7–10) groups together forms of equivalence requiring mechanically identical procedures across groups, including formal, instrument, item, measurement and psychometric procedures, extending to metric, measurement unit, scalar, calibration, structural, factor, factorial, direct or relative equivalence. A further subset is more concerned with validation of survey items and scales, covering construct operationalization, criterion, content, psychological and response equivalence. Other forms refer to situational, motivational, operational, complete and credible equivalence (see also Johnson, 2003: 347–57).

In psychology, attention is most often paid to structural, measurement unit and scalar equivalence (Lyons and Chryssochoou, 2000: 145). Statistical techniques, such as factor analysis, multidimensional scaling and structural equation modelling, are used to determine whether datasets from different cultures have the same structure (share the same psychometric properties) and whether the response options have the same intervals and origins. Measurement unit equivalence is needed to ensure that the scale units for a common construct are identical in different datasets. Scalar equivalence requires that the scales used have the same origin. To improve the equivalence of response scales and to avoid the problem of finding a universally understood set of categories with precise and similar meanings, numerical scales are recommended, as well as dichotomous response options or symmetrical bipolar scales with a clear midpoint (Johnson, 1998: 16–17, 2003: 354–5).

DEALING WITH BIAS IN MEASURING EQUIVALENCE

The examples cited above confirm that researchers cannot assume that the use of similar instruments under similar conditions ensures that respondents from different cultures interpret questions in the same way and that their responses have similar meanings. Nor can it be assumed that techniques widely adopted in one or more cultures are necessarily appropriate elsewhere, or that research instruments cannot be applied in new cultures once they have been adapted to fit a different environment (Harkness et al., 2003: 8–10). The quality of cross-cultural measurement depends on the effectiveness of the instrument design, sampling frame, mode of data collection and analysis, and documentation. Each of these aspects is associated with different sources of error resulting in bias. Concept bias in survey questions refers to non-identity of theoretical concepts across groups. Method bias includes sample incomparability and coverage, instrument differences, interviewer effects and the mode of administration. Another form of bias concerns anomalies at the level of items (Harkness et al., 2003: 13; Johnson, 2003: 349–55).

Concept bias ensues when concepts are not meaningful within the units of analysis. Innumerable instances are cited of stimuli in cross-cultural surveys of opinion or attitudes that may be unintelligible, irrelevant or meaningless in some of the units of analysis (Harkness, 2007). Certain questions may fall outside the experience of some societies; the concept of unemployment was, for example, irrelevant in the Soviet Union; the term was also politically and ideologically charged (Kutsar and Tiit, 2000: 29). In the Central and East European countries that became members of the European Union in 2004 and 2007, the experience of transition called into question the reliability and interpretation of earlier data and showed how important it is to take account of within-country changes over time and revisit data to eliminate bias.

Several of the problems of method bias are associated with the reactions and attitudes of respondents (Johnson and Van de Vijver, 2003: 195–204). Response measurement scales may be unfamiliar, or respondents may not comprehend the task they are being asked to perform. In some countries, respondents may be reluctant or unwilling to discuss sensitive issues, such as politics, sexual behaviour, income or religion, or they may not give honest responses (Grimshaw, 1973: 26; Harkness, 2007: 39). Cultural differences can also be identified in the topics people are able and willing to talk about. Certain topics may not be considered worthy of discussion, because they are taken for granted, for example the responsibility of the state for childcare provision in the Nordic countries in Europe. Nor can it be assumed that, even within societies and cultures, people are speaking the same language and communicating effectively (Deutscher, 1973: 184). Another well-documented source of bias is respondent acquiescence or compliance, when interviewees give positive replies or the answer they think the interviewer wants or expects to hear (Kinnear, 1987: 11). Respondents produce social desirability or courtesy bias if they select the answers that they think will create the most favourable impression (Armer, 1973: 64; Elder, 1976: 224).

The issue of the context-boundedness of researchers is also relevant to an understanding of the reactions of respondents (Lyons and Chryssochoou, 2000: 143–5). The equivalence of measurement of concepts depends to a considerable degree on the comparability of the 'spatio-temporal, political, and perceptual context' of the units of analysis, including the respondents' perceptions of the interviewer (age, sex, ethnicity, education, social class) and the place where the interview is being conducted (Warwick and Osherson, 1973: 23). Respondents may be less reluctant to discuss personal issues with complete outsiders, particularly if they are proficient in the respondent's language. In cross-cultural surveys, the anonymity of electronically administered questionnaires may offer greater protection of privacy for respondents than a questionnaire administered face to face. However, like telephone and Internet interviews, they can result in biased sampling due to differential ownership of telephones or computers in particular regions or socio-economic groups. Even seasonal and weather patterns may affect response rates on topics such as unemployment or emotional well-being (Harkness, 2007: 39). A solution to some of these problems is to obtain data on actual behaviour and match it with attitudinal data, using a combination of methods to check for consistency (see Chapter 5).

Another serious, although not insuperable, problem for procedural equivalence is the lack of 'a calibrated methodology for cross-cultural survey research' (Harkness, 2007: 45). The amount of information provided by research publications and documentation is considered to be well below what is required to ensure that international standards of best practice are being met in the conduct of cross-cultural surveys (Harkness, 2007: 40).

Researchers disagree over the extent to which the many forms of non-equivalence affect comparability. If any of the national studies in a project are flawed because of these different types of bias, however, the similarities or differences identified may be simply methodological artefacts (Braun, 2003: 137). Since the question of the equivalence of indicators in comparisons of large-scale datasets, particularly those concerning attitudes and value systems (Eurobarometer, European Social Survey, World Values Survey), is so difficult to resolve, it has been suggested, pessimistically, that an act of 'faith' may be needed to ensure the same question has been asked, that respondents have a similar understanding of what they are being asked and possess the conceptual and linguistic tools with which to respond (Harkness, 2007: 36).

Whatever the type of equivalence involved, the challenge for social science researchers is to achieve maximum reliability and validity in the measurement of concepts by eliminating bias (see also Chapter 3). Reliability can be enhanced by maximizing measurement consistency and its generalizability to other measures of the same concept or variable obtained using different methods. Validity depends on the extent to which measurement instruments and sets of observations accurately gauge what they are meant to measure, enabling generalizability to other measures of the same phenomenon. Reliability and validity in large-scale surveys can be checked using statistical tests. In small-scale studies, researchers need to rely on their own cultural knowledge and under- standing of the units of analysis, and their judgement, to assess the fit between theoretical predictions and data, and the validity of indicators (Warwick and Osherson, 1973: 28; Hammersley, 2008: 51).

Contextualization of Concepts

In reviewing the definition and measurement of concepts, reference has constantly been made in this chapter to the settings within which concepts are applied. In research that crosses cultural and linguistic boundaries, the social construction of concepts is an essential component in the characterization of different systems. Contextualization may offer a helpful answer to the question that is frequently raised about how to achieve something approaching equivalence of conceptual understand- ing. A useful way of resolving complexity in comparative research is to contextualize by locating concepts in relation to broader socioeconomic and political contexts. By analysing the wider system and including change as one of the parameters, it becomes possible to build up a dynamic picture of processes over time and space.

This section explores in more detail the interconnectedness of con- cepts and contexts. It begins by looking at the progressive shift away from context-free research designs to context-boundedness. It then examines issues surrounding the transportability of concepts from one national, societal or cultural context to another. The concluding section explores some of the solutions adopted in research that takes account of the need to locate concepts within different contexts.

FROM CONCEPTS TO CONTEXTS

International comparisons have long used background information to contextualize data, as exemplified by Karl Marx's analysis of the political economy of nations and the basic mode of production prior to embark- ing on the study of social phenomena (Elder, 1976: 213). In the 1950s and 1960s, attention was devoted primarily to the problem of choosing the right word to convey a particular meaning, rather than locating social phenomena in relation to specific contexts. Much of the comparative research using large-scale surveys in the postwar period was based of the ethnocentric view of the world viewed from the United States (see Chapters 1, 3 and 7), even if the development by Westerners of functional equivalence as a device to understand non-Western countries did help to lessen ethnocentrism (Dogan and Pelassy, 1990: 43).

By the late 1960s, political scientists were advocating recognition of the embeddedness of measures and their contextual grounding in survey-based comparisons (Verba, 1969: 79–80). Following on from the neo-evolutionists (for example Parsons, 1966), a body of theory developed in the United States that took account of the efficiency of different societies in adapting to evolutionary advances. General theories could, it was argued, be formulated if the diversity and mutual interdependence of social structures are recognized, and if phenomena are situated in relation to their spatial and temporal locations. The assumption was that systems are not unique, and social reality may be partly explained by phenomena extrinsic to the system, enabling more general or universal factors to be identified (Przeworski and Teune, 1970: 12–13).

The shift towards conceptual equivalence in the 1970s required an intimate knowledge of context and culture, a point stressed time and again in the literature, to the extent that it was being recommended that investigators should be familiar with the cultural context before constructing research instruments (Deutscher, 1973: 182). From an early stage, the value of the concept of path dependency and 'political learning' was demonstrated in social policy case studies by analysing the constraining or enabling effect of decisions taken in the development of a policy or an institution on the future choices available to policy makers (Heclo, 1974: 284–322).

For anthropologists, the issue in the 1970s was not how to contextualize social phenomena, since culture was, almost by definition, a context, within which they can be 'intelligibly', or 'thickly…described', thereby emphasizing the 'complex specificness', and 'circumstantiality' of findings (Geertz, 1973: 14, 23). By the late 1980s, a general move could be discerned towards a theory of social facts as 'constructions', existing 'only within a frame of reference' and dependent on 'the cultural meanings which people use to account for them and hence to constitute them' (Holy, 1987: 5–6). Although termed 'interpretative anthropology', this approach was shared with other social science disciplines.

Researchers from the British Saxonic tradition (see Chapter 7) applied a contextualized approach in organizational behaviour (Lammers and Hickson, 1979) and industrial relations (Hyman, 1998) to demonstrate the effect of the national context on the object of investigation, heralding a shift away from 'culture free' approaches to analysis of organizations 'in their cultural settings (values and institutions) as cultured organizations' (Grootings, 1986: 282). Their purpose was to determine the extent to which generalizations can be made from the theoretical models and hypotheses that researchers are seeking to test empirically.

By the 1980s, as the practice of working in international teams became more widespread in Europe, researchers were acknowledging that social phenomena 'are related to their context and derive their meaning only within this context' (Grootings, 1986: 284–5). It follows that they can only be understood within specific situations. For some comparativists, 'context-boundedness of social phenomena…is the ultimate rationale for comparative analysis', and attempts made to elucidate the problems raised by context require a distinct methodology (Grootings, 1986: 285).

In comparative projects across countries, societies and cultures, it was accepted that concepts need to be specified in the early stages of the research to ensure agreement about what is to be examined in different national contexts (Rose, 1991: 455). Sartori (1994: 15, original emphasis) maintains that, in definitional terms, research could be considered as implicitly comparative provided that a 'one-country or one-unit study *is* embedded in a comparative context', and the analytical tools used are 'comparable'. Configurative analysis as pursued by some historians, even prior to the French Annales School, relied on a 'context-embedded focus' (Sartori, 1994: 24). By contrast, the lack of attention among political economists in the late 1990s to 'context-specific interests and cross-cultural differences in how interests are conceptualized and articulated' was still seen as a weakness in rational choice theory (Ross, 1997: 74).

The widespread recognition of the importance of contextualizing concepts led some analysts to identify the holistic and contextualized approach as a feature of qualitative comparative research distinguishing it from quantitative comparisons (Ragin, 1987: 3; Bryman, 1988: 64). Whereas quantitative studies abstract phenomena from their contexts, qualitative studies view cases as a whole within their contexts by examining complex combinations of variables (see also Chapter 5). By the turn of the twenty-first century, most disciplines had moved on to develop methods that pay attention to context, thereby helping to bridge the perceived divide between universalist and culturalist approaches and the different methods with which they are associated.

THE CONCEPTUAL LENS OF COMPARATIVE ANALYSIS

The shift towards context-boundedness and the extent to which researchers have been interested in locating concepts in relation to contexts are closely associated with both the level of analysis and the distance of the observer from the object of inquiry (see Chapter 3). Contextualized analysis therefore requires an appropriate conceptual lens. Adopting this metaphor, Dogan and Pelassy (1990: 132, 161) refer to the need to choose between 'a soft-focus or a wide-angle lens', pointing out that similarities and differences are relative and a matter of 'view-point and perspective'. They advocate a regional or area studies approach as a means of controlling the variables that the researchers want to hold constant, allowing them to conduct an in-depth analysis of a 'relatively homogeneous field' and clarify an issue (Dogan and Pelassy, 1990: 133). Most comparative political analysis in the 1990s was pursued using 'diverse conceptual lenses' (Kohli et al., 1996: 2). Kirsten S. Wever and Lowell Turner (1995: 1–7) entitled the introductory chapter to their edited volume on the comparative political economy of industrial relations: 'A wide-angle lens for a global marketplace'. The same metaphor is used to distinguish between qualitative and quantitative approaches. Qualitative researchers can be said to view an unspecified set of concepts through a 'wide lens', whereas quantitative researchers look through a 'narrow lens' at a specified set of variables (Brannen, 1992: 4).

Not only may researchers have a blinkered view of their own society and be convinced that theirs is the one best way, but they may also seek to analyse practices in different cultural settings through inappropriate conceptual lenses. Todd Landman (2000: 43) suggests that the 'explana-tory power of concepts can be enhanced if they are applied in contexts with which the comparativist is most familiar', and that 'local' knowl-edge can enable researchers to 'identify gaps between theoretical concepts and their application'. The languages spoken by researchers, and their knowledge and understanding of other cultures are also critical factors in establishing the conceptual lens that they bring to a study. Their cultural baggage shapes not only their formulation of the research question and the theoretical assumptions underlying it, but also the choice of data with which they will be working and their interpretation of findings (see Chapter 7). Although not without its problems, as noted in the previous section, the researcher's cultural environment is usually considered to be less of an issue in large-scale projects dealing with description and quantitative data, where language is primarily seen as an instrument for obtaining facts. In multilingual qualitative projects involving in-depth interviewing and participant observation, it cannot be assumed that the facts recorded necessarily represent the same reality.

Non-native speakers of English often warn against the practice of accepting ready-made conventions of language and complain that English as an international working language gives rise to unwarranted simplification and misunderstandings (Lallement, 2003: 306). The adoption of English as a world language in international social science and humanities research may create as many problems as it resolves (Barbier, 2005b: 52–61). British researchers do, as Jean Tennom (1995: 278) acknowledges, have the immense advantage over other national research communities of possessing a *lingua franca*, which facilitates their participation in the international arena and explains their frequent leadership role in European research networks and projects. Monolingual speakers of English may, however, be at a disadvantage in international comparative research projects in the social sciences and humanities, because researchers whose native language is English tend, as in the natural sciences, to believe that the concepts transmitted through their language are universally understood. The difficulty many social scientists encounter in studies across linguistic boundaries, as argued by Edmond Lisle in the 1980s, is that:

> language is not simply a medium to carry concepts. It is itself the very matter of scientific observation and discourse. When we study a particular country, we are examining it with the only instruments available, namely a conceptual system and set of ideas produced within and by the society we are investigating, reflecting its history, its institutions, its values, its ideology, all of which are expressed in that country's language. By definition, that overall system and those concepts have no exact equivalents in other societies. When we engage in cross-national comparative studies, therefore, we have to find the nearest approximation. (Lisle, 1985: 24)

It follows that research in different societies confined to the usage of a *lingua franca* results in loss of information and inaccuracy, since it cannot accurately express all the concepts and ideas generated in other cultures and conveyed in other languages. Approximation may, Lisle (1985: 25) suggests, result in misinterpretation. The thought processes and mindsets underlying different modes of expression (French is, for example, more abstract and Cartesian than English) imply that different approaches and interpretations are being called into play.

The advantages of having native informants as team members in gaining access to interviewees may, in addition, be offset by the problems associated with insider involvement and bias. Conducting qualitative research into the attitudes and behaviour of elites in closely knit small countries can, for example, be particularly problematic due to the proximity of the researcher (Randma, 2001).

Richard Hyman (2005: 204–5) concludes a review of a catalogue of untranslatable terms from industrial relations by rejecting simplistic translations that give the illusion of similarity, on the grounds that 'all institutional and analytical categories, applied cross-nationally, [are] provisional'. Rather, he recommends focusing on the elements of reality that are lost in translation with a view to transcending their limitations in pursuit of what he describes as 'a larger totality'. Although he does not refer explicitly to contextualization, in seeking to move from 'particularistic universalisms to universalistic particularisms', his perception of 'reality' would seem to require the contextual embedding of concepts.

TRANSPORTABILITY OF CONCEPTS ACROSS CONTEXTS

Proponents of positivistic, universalist, rationalist, functionalist and structuralist approaches to comparative research argue that theoretical concepts and their indicators must be able to travel if they are to have explanatory power; they must be 'sufficiently abstract to travel across national boundaries' (Rose, 1991: 447). Transportable concepts are needed in studies covering a large number of countries and, therefore, requiring a high level of conceptual abstraction. By contrast, relativists claim that all meaning is determined locally, a position shared by interpretivists, ethnographers and anthropologists. When the focus is on a small number of units of analysis, it is feasible to use less abstract concepts more grounded in specific contexts. A third position advocates modifying concepts so that they are more sensitive to cultural specificity, and combining or reconstituting them to fit the cases being studied (Landman, 2000: 42).

Some concepts may be observationally and linguistically identifiable in most cultures at a very general level, and applicable to all cultures and societies: for example 'mother', socialization', 'illness' (Warwick and Osherson, 1973: 11). However, many concepts do not travel well across national, social or cultural boundaries. The literature abounds with examples from a great variety of disciplines, a number of which have already been mentioned in this chapter, of concepts that are not directly or easily transposable from one context to another. Some, for example 'federal bureaucracy', have meaning in several but not all cultures. Others that are considered theoretically interesting may not be reflected fully or directly in local languages and cultures, and may have to be inferred from behaviour; 'mental deficiency' is a case in point. Yet others, for example 'arctic hysteria', are culture specific and of limited valued in comparisons across cultures (Warwick and Osherson, 1973: 11, 14).

Demographic concepts that do not have readily transferable equivalents in other languages include the French *cadre*, *corps d'ingénieurs* or *grandes écoles* and the German *Angestellte* and *Beamte* (Desrosières, 1996: 25). In industrial relations, even central concepts such as 'trade union', vary in their functions and significance across nations (*Gewerkschaft, syndicat, sindicato*), justifying interest in the analysis of issues presenting equivalent challenges to union identities in different national contexts (Hyman; 1998: 51–2). In psychology, studies of differences in the conceptualization of attitudes towards time are found to affect perceptions of behaviour that may be considered tactless, dishonest or impolite in one culture but are accepted practice in another (Levine, 1987).

Ways have been sought of increasing the 'travelling capability' of concepts across different contexts (Sartori, 1994: 26). If concepts are to be transferred or translated from one context to another, Lallement (2003: 306) argues from a sociological perspective that it is not sufficient to contextualize. Rather, the researcher's task (following Sartori, 1984: 41, 50) is to deconstruct and reconstruct. Surface equivalence, seemingly homogeneous statistics, questionnaires designed for universal application and internationally applied nomenclatures must first be deconstructed if the researcher is to understand how concepts and categories have evolved over time and space and be in a position to proceed to reconstruction.

SELECTING RELEVANT CONTEXTS

Few, if any, comparative studies set out to compare whole societies or to be comprehensive in their coverage of social systems. If an international comparative study is to remain both tractable and credible, a major task for researchers engaged in studies that cross national, societal or cultural boundaries is, therefore, how to select the most appropriate contextual factors for analysis. A distinction can be made here between the selection of the units of analysis (discussed in Chapter 3) and the contextual and systemic environments, or meso variables, determining how microlevel phenomena are socially or culturally constructed. The contextual factors to be examined are likely to be determined, in the first instance, by the object of inquiry, the disciplinary perspective inherent in the research design and the financial, temporal and human resources available.

Figure 4.1 provides a transdisciplinary checklist, indicating some of the most frequently examined contexts in international comparative studies over time and space. These contexts, in turn, enable researchers to select the most appropriate systems, structures, units of observation and analysis, properties of concepts and parametric indicators.

Reading down the table, the first column covers the multiple levels, or frames of reference, at which comparative research is conducted, ranging from global to individual level. The second column lists the main systems or structures that are likely to serve as the object of inquiry at

Figure 4.1   Contextual frames of reference for analysing concepts

Macrolevel	Mesolevel	Microlevel
global	international organizations	political economy
	geophysical environment	ecology, pollution, climate
	technology and industry	information technology, transportation, communications
national	political institutions and systems	ideology, political parties, representation and power, pressure and interest groups, policy networks
	administrative structures	machinery of central, regional, local government, taxation, social security, labour administration, public/private organizations
	economic systems and financial institutions	economic sectors, firms, labour markets, trade, fiscal and employment policy, trade unions
	legal frameworks	national and supranational legislation, social security and labour law, implementation and good practice
societal	social institutions, systems and structures	family, household, kinship, education and training (qualifications, skills)
	social protection systems	funding and benefit structures (housing, health, unemployment, old age, family, social assistance), social services, provision and delivery of welfare
	sociodemographic structures	gender, ethnicity, age, generation, socioeconomic and occupational groups, migratory movements
cultural	cultural environment	values, beliefs, religion, language, media, leisure, entertainment
individual	psychological climate	individual behaviour, mentality, well-being, stress

Source: Developed from Hantrais, 2007a: 11–12.

the mesolevel of investigation, while the third column breaks these down further to suggest the contexts or data categories that researchers can draw on in formulating their research question and defining concepts and variables (Ragin, 1987: 7). The rows in the table move from the general to the particular, shifting from a wider to a narrower perspective, but it is also possible, and indeed recommended, to take account of interactions between items from different rows and columns.

As argued in this and the previous chapters, the boundaries of macro-level frames of reference are usually difficult to delimit precisely. For example, the socioeconomic tasks identified within the key action 'Improving the Socio-Economic Knowledge Base' under the European Commission's Framework Programme 5, launched in 1999, stressed the multidimensional nature of the socioeconomic issues facing the Union, requiring researchers to take account of the overall European context, including European social and economic development models, monetary union, enlargement and the European situation in the world context.

A suitable starting point for comparative contextual analysis is often to situate the phenomenon under study with reference to its systemic or institutional settings. Without knowledge of the political regime or of legislation in a particular field, it may be difficult to grasp why it is, or is not, appropriate to investigate a particular topic. On grounds that the defining concepts used in comparative law may be 'nationally and culturally conditioned', the search for causal factors in legal studies may extend to 'the distribution of political power, the economic system, religious and ethical values, family structure, the basis of agriculture and degree of industrialization, and the organization of authorities and groups' (Zweigert and Kötz, 1998: 11).

An analysis of industrial relations might involve an understanding of political institutions, social protection and educational and training systems, as well as employment policy (Hyman, 1998). The European Social Survey takes account of variations in social structure, legal systems, language, politics, economics and culture (Jowell et al., 2007a: 5). Families can usefully be defined in terms of national administrative and legal frameworks (Hantrais, 2004a: 106–27), and welfare states may best be understood by reference to the political economy in the countries under observation (Jones Finer, 1999) or the impact of globalization (Esping-Andersen, 1996). Understanding equal opportunities in employment as mediated by labour administration in a heterogeneous group of countries may require detailed knowledge about the political regime, degree of urbanization and economic development, national labour and social security law, benefit system, employment trends, provision of education and training, and levels of literacy (Hantrais and Sineau, 1998).

Context-Bounded Concepts

The chapter has shown how issues of conceptualization and contextualization have long been of critical concern for international comparative researchers. Recognizing the importance of the interdependence of social phenomena and of their occurrence in interactive structures, in the early 1970s, Adam Przeworski and Henry Teune (1970: 13) identified the need to interpret specific observations within the context of specific systems. The central problems of comparative inquiry were then how to incorporate contexts into measurement statements and how 'to introduce systemic factors into general, theoretical statements and to retain the systemic context of measurement statements'. The aim in their book was to offer logical and methodological strategies for solving these problems.

By the late 1980s and 1990s, disciplines as diverse as comparative anthropology (Holy, 1987) and comparative law (Zweigert and Kötz, 1998) claimed not to see the context-boundedness of concepts as an insuperable obstacle to effective and meaningful international comparisons. Meanwhile, industrial sociologists had found ways of establishing systemic coherence that incorporated societal specificity (Maurice, 1989), and historical institutionalists in comparative politics were constructing 'important analytic bridges' by working at the level of midrange theory (between state-centred and society-centred analyses), and by exploring the institutional arrangements that structure the relationship between the two (Thelen and Steinmo, 1992: 10).

In the closing decades of the twentieth century, the pendulum was still swinging between two diametrically opposed views about the value of contextualizing concepts in comparative research in line with the epistemological positions adopted by researchers. Interpretists continued to argue that, because social reality is complex and infinitely diverse, sociocultural phenomena can only be accurately observed and compared in relation to the sociospatial and temporal contexts within which they are constructed; they can never be explained by nomothetic (lawlike) statements (see Chapter 5). Cross-cultural survey methodologists pursued their search for categories of concepts that were applicable in any cultural context, while admitting that the increasingly sophisticated methods that were widely available could only be applied in different contexts with adaptation (Harkness, 2003: 45).

Despite the progress made, no universal and enduring solutions have been found to the methodological issues involved in the relationship between concepts and contexts. Rather, awareness seems to have grown that the research process is itself context bound, creating more challenges for comparativists committed to the pursuit of methodological rigour.

5

Combining Methods in International Comparative Research

The difficulties that arise in reaching consensus between different disciplines and research cultures over epistemological positions in comparative research, the choice of comparators and the variables selected present serious challenges for international teams embarking on comparative studies across national, societal and cultural boundaries. Despite scepticism about the extent to which 'a neat correspondence' can be established between 'epistemological positions...and associated techniques...of social research' (Bryman, 1984: 75), traditionally certain epistemologies have come to be closely associated with specific methodological approaches. Although the dividing line between different research strategies has become increasingly porous and blurred, the links between epistemology, methodology and methods continue to be analysed in terms of the broad distinctions that are often drawn between quantitative and qualitative approaches.

While an important body of literature addresses the question of how to combine methods to greatest effect, relatively little has been written about mixing methods in international comparisons. Where multiple strategies are applied in comparative studies, they tend to complicate further what is already likely to be a complex research design, requiring an even wider range of knowledge, understanding, skills and expertise than projects drawing on a single methodological approach.

This chapter explores the costs and benefits of combining and integrating different research methods both within and across paradigms in international comparative research. The first section reviews the reasons for the supposed incompatibility between different epistemologies and the methodologies that are generally associated with them. While acknowledging the limitations and problems of combining methods, subsequent sections examine the various ways in which methodological pluralism, or 'multi-strategy' research, can be exploited to extend the scope of comparative studies, test and reinforce validity, explore new insights, and offer differing or complementary explanations for observed similarities and differences. The chapter draws on examples of how mixed methods strategies have been exploited in international projects as researchers seek to capture more fully the complexity of the objects under study. The concluding section returns to the arguments suggesting that combined methods do not provide a comprehensive or readily applicable answer to the many issues facing comparative researchers.

Reconciling Epistemologies and Methodologies

Comparativists have long been aware that 'many of the difficulties encountered in comparative research could be greatly reduced by creative *combinations* of methods.' (Warwick and Osherson, 1973: viii, original emphasis). However, progress towards methodological pluralism has been slow due to the entrenched theoretical positions anchored in particular epistemologies, even if they are tempered by pragmatic considerations, such as institutional, financial and political constraints (Brannen, 1992: 4).

This section draws on and extends the analysis carried out in previous chapters of the debate between and within social science disciplines over the relative merits and limitations associated with different methodological approaches in comparative research. The section begins by mapping the arguments made by comparativists in support of the methods they adopt, in an attempt to gain a deeper understanding of the paradigmatic divide that often faces researchers seeking to cross national, societal and cultural boundaries. The section concludes with a review of the arguments presented in the literature for and against combining or integrating methodological approaches and techniques.

MAPPING THE PARADIGMATIC DIVIDE

The debate about the relative merits of quantitative and qualitative research dates back at least to the mid-nineteenth century when the focus was on the scientific status of history and the social sciences in contrast to the natural sciences (see Chapter 1 in this volume). By the 1920s and 1930s, the debate had crystallized around the opposition between proponents of case (qualitative) studies and statistical (quantitative) techniques. The immediate postwar period was characterized by the dominance of quantitative approaches in sociology, psychology and political science, until interest in qualitative approaches revived in the 1960s, and they became more readily accepted as a legitimate method of scientific investigation alongside quantitative techniques. In the 1980s, Charles C. Ragin (1987: 2) commented that the gulf between qualitative and quantitative work was probably wider in comparative social science than in any other 'social science subdiscipline', precisely because, almost by definition, as argued below, the qualitative tradition was dominant in this field of inquiry.

In the early twenty-first century, few social scientists would accept that paradigmatic differences can be reduced simply or closely to the quantitative–qualitative divide (Bryman, 2004: 453, 2008: 17–19). Many other factors need to be taken into account, including the search for scientific laws as opposed to the cultural patterns uncovered by ideographic studies, or the arguments supporting deductive *versus* inductive approaches (Hammersley, 1992: 40–1).

Quantitative versus *qualitative approaches in international comparisons*

During the second half of the twentieth century, the competing approaches adopted by quantitative and qualitative comparativists, as well as the epistemological assumptions underlying them, could be broadly characterized in terms of universalist or positivist traditions, as opposed to what have been described varyingly as culturalism (Kohli et al., 1996: 13, 15), 'anti-foundationalist' (Read and Marsh, 2002: 233), phenomenological, constructivist, interpretive or interpretivist positions (Geertz, 1973: 27; Bryman, 1984: 77, 1988: 51–4, 2004: 438). These contrasting approaches, as implemented at the two ends of the epistemological spectrum, came to be associated with different methods of data collection and analysis, as shown in Figure 5.1, which summarizes the main differences between quantitative and qualitative techniques.

Positivists, especially in social and political science, applied quantitative approaches in social surveys, and used structured interviewing and self-administered questionnaires, with the intention of isolating and defining variables and variable categories that could be linked together to frame hypotheses for subsequent testing. As illustrated in Chapter 2 by the example of the large-scale surveys applied in political science to

Figure 5.1   Dominant features of quantitative and qualitative research

	Quantitative	*Qualitative*
associated epistemology	positivist	constructivist
main techniques	survey	participant observation
relationship between researcher and subject	distant	close
researcher's position in relation to subject	outsider	insider
relationship between theory/concepts and research	theory driven, verification	exploration discovery
research strategy	structured	unstructured, open
scope of findings	nomothetic and generalizable	ideographic, contextualized
image of social reality	static and external to actors	processual and socially constructed by actors
nature of data	hard, precise, reliable	rich, deep

Source: Adapted from Bryman, 1988: 94, with kind permission of the author.

compare electoral systems (Lipset and Rokkan, 1967), positivists were looking for a rigorous, reliable and systematic scientific method, by analogy with the natural sciences. However, social psychologists probably came closest to the natural sciences in adopting experimental designs as their main approach to data collection.

By contrast, culturalists, as exemplified by the work of anthropologists, ethnomethodologists, or historians of the Annales School, began by defining general concepts and used qualitative methods to identify patterns of interrelationships (Brannen, 1992: 4). They preferred an approach whereby the formulation and testing of theories proceeded at the same time as data collection (Glaser and Strauss, 1967: 3; Geertz, 1973: 27; Bryman, 1988: 68). For comparativists espousing qualitative approaches, the focus was on differentiation and diversity between and within countries, societies and cultures, and the complexity of the factors involved, making generalizations more difficult. The most fundamental characteristic of qualitative research has been identified as its commitment to viewing events, actions, norms and values through the eyes of the people being studied, involving 'a capacity to penetrate the frames of meaning with which they operate' (Bryman, 1988: 61). Since, from this perspective, researchers engage heavily in reflexivity, their own cultural assumptions are brought into play, making participant observation the preferred research method (Brannen, 1992: 5).

From a cost-benefit analysis of survey research and participant observation, which were the two most highly developed methods in comparative social science and humanities research in the 1970s, Donald Warwick (1973: 203) could conclude that: 'The strength of the sample survey lies in its greater potential for quantification, replication, and generalization to a broader population.' By contrast, according to the same source, participant observation normally has the edge with regard to 'qualitative depth, flexibility for the observer, and appropriateness for the study of social processes and complex patterns of relationships'.

Of particular relevance to international comparative research is the nature of the debate that was taking place among political scientists in the early 1970s about the characteristics of statistical and comparative approaches (Lijphart, 1971). Extending the discussion about the dichotomy between systematic comparative and statistical techniques to a wider comparative social science perspective, Neil J. Smelser (1973: 53) argued that 'As soon as the number of units becomes large enough to permit the use of statistical techniques, the line between the two is crossed.' In contrast to the radically analytic approach of most quantitative work based on the statistical method, comparative research is portrayed as relying on a case-oriented strategy, thereby bringing it closer to the qualitative end of the spectrum. According to this argument, 'applications of the comparative method produce explanations that account for every instance of a certain phenomenon'. They, therefore, have the advantage of enabling researchers to undertake a holistic and interpretive analysis. Statistical techniques, by contrast, do not require the researcher to conduct 'a direct examination of the differences and similarities among cases considered as configurations of characteristics' and conceived as 'meaningful wholes' (Ragin, 1987: 3, 16–17).

Also of interest for international comparisons is the related distinction made between qualitative, or case-oriented (*qua* comparative), and quantitative, or variable-oriented (*qua* statistical), strategies in the ways in which they handle complexity. Case-oriented studies give precedence to an appreciation of complexity as an aid to historical interpretation and a guide to the identification of important causal factors in unravelling the conditions responsible for producing particular outcomes. By contrast, variable-oriented strategies focus on the search for generality, by testing propositions derived from general theories (Ragin, 1987: 54–5). The comparative 'method' is held to be superior to the statistical 'method' insofar as it is 'combinatorial' and capable of investigating situations as 'wholes', while the statistical method examines each relevant condition in a 'piecemeal manner'. The comparative method is, therefore, 'qualitatively different' from the statistical method and 'uniquely suited to the kinds of questions that many comparativists ask' (Ragin, 1987: 15–16). To paraphrase Giovanni Sartori (1994: 24), whereas qualitative researchers know more about less, quantitative researchers know less about more.

Nomothetic versus *ideographic approaches*

Another distinction commonly made between quantitative and qualitative approaches in social science and humanities research lies in their objectives and the scope of their findings. Historically, it is claimed, theory verification has more often been the objective of quantitative studies and theory generation more often that of qualitative studies (Punch, 2006: 35). As noted above, quantitative researchers, following the model of the natural sciences, are usually seeking to produce trend data with predictive value, leading to causal explanations. Generalizations can then be made about the patterning of variables, ultimately providing a basis for scientific laws and statements to be formulated about convergence or divergence across systems. By contrast, qualitative researchers, as exemplified by historical studies, are more interested in identifying cultural patterns with reference to specific objects, places and times (Bryman, 1988: 100).

The choice between nomothetic and ideographic approaches applies as much within disciplines as between them. In the 1950s and 1960s, cultural anthropologists conducted nomothetic sociological studies 'to discover or verify basic laws of society or culture, basic principles which presumably would hold good at least as tendencies in any society, anywhere, any time'. The aim of ideographic historical studies was 'to reconstruct the specific culture history of certain regions or certain traits' (Naroll (1968: 236). In the early 1970s, Adam Przeworski and Henry Teune (1970: 5) noted that historians were debating whether to aim for nomothetic or ideographic outcomes; anthropologists were discussing whether integrated systems should only be treated holistically; sociologists disagreed about whether all existing structures were functional for systems; economists argued over whether a universal definition of their discipline could be constructed; and political scientists debated the value of institution-specific generalizations.

Within psychology, it is recognized that cross-cultural studies can vary in the extent to which they are driven by theory, and findings are generalizable. Cross-cultural psychologists describe the two extremes of the continuum in terms of the distinction between emic and etic approaches, focusing respectively on culture-specific, in contrast to universal, behaviours (Lyons and Chryssochoou, 2000: 139–40) (see Chapter 4).

These intradisciplinary debates show that the distinction between the two seemingly divergent strategies is far from being straightforward and unidirectional. They suggest that the goals attributed to each approach may be overlapping and even interchangeable.

Between deductive and inductive analysis in international comparisons

The opposition between quantitative and qualitative approaches, whether or not with reference to comparative research, has long been presented in terms of the distinction between deductive and inductive analysis. Positivists see science as deductive 'in that it seeks to extract specific propositions from general accounts of reality'; a scientific theory may be constructed to explain laws and test theories (Bryman, 1988: 15). Deductive approaches relying on explanations derived from observation of the external features of human behaviour are often contrasted with the Weberian notion of *Verstehen*, or understanding, which is sought by induction through direct contact with the subjects under study, using insider information, sometimes described as 'the intellectual precursor of qualitative approaches' (Bryman, 1988: 56–7). Deductive argument means that, if the premises on which an argument is based are valid, any conclusions drawn are certain because they are contained in the evidence collected. By contrast, in an inductive argument, the conclusion is no more than probable. It is exploratory and may require a 'creative leap' before any inferences can be drawn based on the balance of available evidence (Preece, 1994: 54–6). Any further supporting evidence that can be adduced by observation or experiment serves to reinforce the conclusions but without necessarily ensuring their validity.

Statements about the divide between the hypothetico-deductive method of quantitative researchers and the inductive approach said to characterize qualitative researchers can be criticized as an oversimplification. Not all quantitative research involves testing hypotheses; some surveys are confined to description, and some quantitative researchers are seeking to generate theories. Nor do all qualitative researchers reject the hypothetico-deductive method. Rather, a strong case can be made for the claim that all research moves between ideas and data, and involves deduction as well as induction (Hammersley, 1992: 48–9). Alan Bryman (1988: 20) presents the logical and idealized structure of the quantitative research process as moving from theory to hypothesis by deduction, through observations and data collection, processing and analysis to interpretation, with induction as an intervening process in the eventual production of findings.

A further distinction is often drawn between 'analytic' and 'enumerative' induction, the first term being associated with qualitative and the second with quantitative research. Whereas qualitative researchers are interested in concepts and categories, for quantitative researchers, it is their incidence and frequency that matter: 'enumerative induction abstracts by generalizing whereas analytic induction generalizes by abstracting' (Brannen, 1992: 7). In qualitative research, a typical example of the steps involved in analytic induction would be: rough definition and hypothetical explanation of the problem; examination of cases to determine whether they fit with the hypothesis; reformulation and redefinition of the problem as necessary until the hypothesis can be deemed to be confirmed (Bryman, 1988: 82). Quantitative researchers may also use analytic induction to move from data through the formulation of hypotheses to their testing and verification, and some qualitative research may not go far beyond description.

Analytic induction has also been contrasted to grounded theory, which was initially formulated in the 1960s as a means of generating theory embedded in data in such a way that '*the theory should fit the data*' (Glaser and Strauss, 1967: 261, original emphasis). According to this approach, the theory develops from the research, and is refined and tested on the basis of empirical work, which continues until the point of '*theoretical saturation*' is reached, when no new information is being added to the categories under investigation (Glaser and Strauss, 1967: 6, 61, original emphasis). As the process of data collection comes to an end, the theory is progressively elaborated at higher levels of abstraction (Bryman, 1988: 84). Grounded theory can be said to differ from analytic induction in three respects: it allows for the development of more complex theories; it adopts a 'constant comparative method' to compare multiple data segments considered to belong to the same category in an attempt to identify its central features; and it selects cases strategically to maximize differences or similarities (Brannen, 1992: 7). However, it can be argued that both analytic induction and grounded theorizing are dependent on the assumption of laws (Hammersley, 1992: 50).

Although these various approaches were developed primarily with reference to single-country studies, and the term 'comparative' has been used very broadly in grounded theory to refer to any comparison of properties in conceptual categories in 'social units of *any* size' (Glaser and Strauss, 1967: 21, original emphasis), they are also of value in international comparisons, where researchers need to remain especially flexible and alert to the many possible ways of collecting, analysing and interpreting data (Turner, 1990; Chamberlayne and King, 2000).

Blurring of the paradigmatic divide

When Przeworski and Teune (1970) published their path-breaking book on the logic of comparative social inquiry in the early 1970s, they were seeking to counter the compartmentalization existing between philosophy of science books, which seemed to have little understanding of the practical problems of conducting comparative social research, and technical methods books, which lacked an intellectual justification for the procedures and techniques they presented. The two authors therefore strongly argued that 'methodological procedures should rely on explicit epistemology' (Przeworski and Teune, 1970: x). The balance subsequently swung heavily in this direction, with some researchers maintaining that methods cannot be separated from basic ontological and epistemological positions, and that the research question, data collection and interpretation are all determined by the researcher's epistemology.

By the late 1980s, however, the argument was already being made that the divide between epistemological positions had been exaggerated and might not be as clear-cut as is often assumed (Bryman, 1988: 105; Burnham et al., 2004: 277). In the early 1990s, in sociological studies both within and across countries, the dichotomy between approaches was no longer considered either valid or useful (Hammersley, 1992: 51). Although the claim is occasionally still made, in political science for example, that 'there is a real correspondence between social ontology, epistemology and research methodology', those making it are prepared to recognize that the search 'for correspondence between theoretical framework and method is rarely achieved' (Burnham et al., 2004: 276–7).

At the very least, it is seldom possible to apply the relationship between theoretical approaches and methods rigidly. For example, although empiricism, predefined research questions and theory-testing are generally associated with positivism and quantitative techniques, qualitative researchers may also seek to ground theory in data and use quasi-quantification to investigate quite specific research questions and test hypotheses. The methods applied (for example participant observation, unstructured interviewing, focus groups) can hardly ever be described strictly as much more 'naturalistic' than those used in quantitative comparisons (Bryman, 2004: 439, 445). Similarly, quantitative researchers frequently try to address meaning, for instance through attitudinal survey questions designed to probe reasons for respondents' actions, and they may be driven less than is generally supposed by hypothesis-testing strategies (Bryman, 2004: 441, 444). For those who claim that quantitative and qualitative techniques are not inherently and necessarily linked to particular ontological or epistemological positions, many other factors are found to influence the choice of methodological approaches (Read and Marsh, 2002: 234, 242). They may include the nature of the research problem and the data, cost, preferences of funders, and the skills, training and experience of researchers.

In any event, the two epistemological positions should not, it is argued (Bryman, 2004: 438), be considered as deterministic or definitive. The methods associated with different positions may be little more than a convention, based on questionable assumptions, and may have been selected on technical rather than epistemological grounds (Bryman, 1988: 124–5). In comparative research, the division or dichotomy between the cases made by proponents of quantitative and qualitative methods is said to be 'false' and mistaken, insofar as researchers adopting both of the two main approaches are seeking to make inferences from available evidence (Landman, 2000: 19), and the two contrasting approaches are neither homogeneous nor consistent (Hammersley, 1996: 172).

FROM CRITICISM TO ACCEPTANCE OF METHODOLOGICAL PLURALISM IN COMPARATIVE RESEARCH

The debate and, at times, hostility between advocates of the positivist and culturalist positions are longstanding, as demonstrated in the previous section. Geographers in the 1970s were said to be tearing their discipline apart in the heated debate between quantitative and qualitative methods (Preece, 1994: 42). In the mid-1990s, the field of comparative politics was 'again embroiled in theoretical controversy' (Kohli et al., 1996: 1). Even if the divide between conflicting positions has become less polarized in most disciplines, and methodological pluralism has been widely accepted, tensions remain due to differences in mindsets (Vigour, 2005: 212). This section shows how mutual suspicion and criticism have persisted, making dialogue and cooperation difficult both within and across disciplines in comparative projects, and calling into question the progress made towards methodological pluralism.

Mutual criticism among quantitative and qualitative researchers

Quantitative researchers tend to criticize qualitative approaches for being unrepresentative, focused on differentiation and too context specific, claiming that, even if they uncover trends or patterns, a central tenet of positivism – generalization – cannot be applied to the findings of qualitative studies. Explanations based on the behaviour of individuals or subgroups of societies cannot, it is argued, be readily or straightforwardly extended to the wider community or to other cultures. Whereas good quantitative research is expected to be systematic, representative, reliable and replicable, studies carried out using qualitative methods are believed to fall short of these requirements in a number of respects. Their units of analysis are thought to be untypical and unrepresentative. They rely too heavily on subjective and unscientific interpretations that may be influenced by insider and ideological bias, liable to manipulation, and lacking in transparency. Their findings are difficult to replicate, and they often encounter problems of access and reactivity, given that subjects are likely to behave differently when they know they are being observed. In addition, qualitative studies are held to be time-consuming and costly.

The criticisms made by quantitative researchers of qualitative analysts are also levelled against quantitative researchers. Their samples may be open to bias and manipulation. Their ideological bent may influence the nature and formulation of survey questions and interpretations of responses. Reliability, validity and replicability cannot be taken for granted. Fieldwork and data analysis are found to be just as time consuming and costly, if not more so. Qualitative analysts identify shortcomings in large-scale surveys due to oversimplification and the propensity to reduce complex phenomena to the lowest common denominator in an attempt to justify generalizations and causal inferences, using predefined concepts. Quantitative approaches are criticized for being reductionist, for reifying social reality and treating it as if it is no different from the natural order. The measurement process is said to be flawed and to produce an artificial and spurious sense of precision and accuracy (see Chapter 4).

These comments are frequently made with reference to single-country studies (Preece, 1994: 43–4; Harrison, 2001: 78–83; Bryman, 2004: 78–9, 284–5), but the criticisms apply equally, if not to an even greater extent, to research across nations, societies and cultures (Hantrais, 2005b).

Towards methodological pluralism in comparative research

Several developments in the latter part of the twentieth century help to explain the growing acceptance of methodological pluralism, which can be seen as an important stage on the way to combination methods or 'multi-strategy' research (Bryman, 2004: 452–64). At a time when methodological pluralism was still in its infancy in the early 1970s, Warwick and Osherson (1973: 40–1) were arguing that 'surveys...are often mounted when simpler methods of data collection would produce the same or better results', and that comparative research would often be much improved 'if several methods were used simultaneously'. For example, surveys would be much more effective if studies contained extensive qualitative information about the units of analysis.

This advice has been widely heeded since the 1970s, more especially in comparative research carried out by multinational teams using new technologies. The 1980s and 1990s saw a series of methodological breakthroughs, as researchers became more interested in identifying multiple causes for observed phenomena, and sought to explain and interpret them with reference to their wider societal settings, an approach developed by Marc Maurice (1989) and the Aix School in the study of business organizations (see Chapter 2). The various approaches introduced in organization studies in the 1980s had in common that they were dealing with different levels and stages of technological change. When taken together they were shown to 'form a complex multi-level model of technology and work in society' (Grootings, 1986: 283), not very different from the models of multilevel governance applied by political scientists in the European context (Marks et al., 1996).

The evolution of comparative politics in the second half of the twentieth century maps onto developments in methods. For example, in his analysis of issues and methods in comparative politics, Todd Landman (2000: 214) notes a 'certain disillusionment with large-scale comparisons', leading to an increase in the interest shown in studies of a small number of countries, or single countries, committed to providing explanation and understanding of observed phenomena at global level. He argues that the shift in focus militates in favour of 'a more inclusive set of methods', able to transcend traditional boundaries and draw on new analytical software and comparative techniques.

Another explanation for the growing interest in methodological pluralism can be found in technological change. While survey techniques were becoming ever more sophisticated, qualitative researchers developed a whole raft of methods and applied them in comparative studies. In addition to participant observation, semi- and unstructured interviewing, interpretive, constructivist and naturalistic–ethnographic methods, researchers adopted techniques such as focus groups and discourse analysis to examine reflexive human beings (Breakwell et al., 2000; Read and Marsh, 2002: 233; Bryman, 2004: 267–8). These and other innovative techniques that had not hitherto been widely exploited in international comparative research were developed for use in comparisons: biographical and oral history (Bertaux, 1990; Chamberlayne and King, 2000), archival historical research (Whitehead, 2004), qualitative interview data collection and analysis (Mangen, 2004, 2007), focus groups (Smithson,

2008: 365–6), vignettes (Soydan, 1996; Hetherington et al., 2002: 13–23), simulation (Eardley, 1996), cross-border interview observation and interpretation of data by multinational teams (Hantrais, 2004b: 21).

The paradigmatic shift from positivistic to interpretative anthropology that had taken place by the 1980s meant that, from being unitary in terms of its objectives and methods, different styles of comparison could be distinguished aimed at establishing functional correlations, facilitating description and identifying common cultural logics (Holy, 1987: 9–12). In comparative education, where the pervasive tendency is to rely on qualitative analysis, the field has long been recognized as 'methodologically...pluralistic' (Rust et al., 1999: 107). By the 1960s, a stage had been reached where quantitative methods from economics, political science and sociology were being used alongside more qualitative approaches in the search for explanation of social and educational phenomena, but they lacked a systematic, consistent and defensible methodology, concepts were elusive, and data were unreliable (Noah and Eckstein, 1969: 4, 185–9). The research strategies adopted in comparative education range from large-scale surveys, literature reviews, historical studies and project evaluations, to content analyses, participant observation and in-depth interviews. This diversity could be seen as a problem insofar as it may prove difficult for the field to retain a sense of identity and cohesiveness. However, it is also claimed that the heavy reliance on qualitative approaches, characteristic of the discipline, indicates that the field is unified by the ontological, epistemological and axiological assumptions underpinning its research strategies (Rust et al., 1999: 107–9).

Within Western Europe, the growing interest in comparative approaches in social sciences and humanities was further stimulated during the 1990s by the development of the European Research Area and enlargement of the European Union to the East, which created an incentive to extend the knowledge and methodological skills base to a wider Europe. The experience of working in international teams acted as a spur for theoretical and methodological developments in the social sciences, with the result that, whether they are in the habit of working qualitatively or quantitatively, the pressures on social scientists are, increasingly, to work 'qualitatively and quantitatively' (Brannen, 2003).

In a helpful summary table, Landman (2000: 213) shows how the methods used in comparative politics evolved during the twentieth century towards combined strategies. Similar patterns can be identified in other disciplines. In the interwar period single countries and small numbers of countries were studied using formal and configurative analysis. Between the 1940s and 1960s, larger numbers of countries were examined using cross-national indicators and quantitative analysis. Coinciding with the 'institutional revival' of the 1970s and 1980s, qualitative and quantitative techniques were used in few-country comparisons to draw inferences that could be applied to countries outside the scope of the study. In the 1990s, studies were conducted covering many, few and single countries, again using qualitative and quantitative techniques, with a view to making universal generalizations as well as drawing regional and country-specific inferences.

Integrating Methods in International Comparisons

The two contrasting epistemological positions considered in the previous sections have become less firmly entrenched in international comparative social science and humanities research as awareness has grown that account must be taken of a whole range of contextual factors: the cultural backgrounds of researchers; the language communities to which they belong; the socioeconomic and political environments impinging on the phenomena that they are analysing; and the institutional frameworks within which they are operating (see Chapter 7).

Recognition of the value of methodological pluralism, which has accompanied this trend, does not, however, necessarily imply the integration of contrasting methodological approaches. Despite shifts in the boundaries between different paradigms, social science methods books published in the early twenty-first century continue to make a clear distinction between quantitative and qualitative approaches, by devoting separate chapters or sections to each position. Further chapters may be allocated to combined methods or the qualitative/quantitative divide (for example Read and Marsh, 2002; Burnham et al., 2004: 270–8, in political science; Bryman, 2004: 451–65; Alasuutari et al., 2008, in social research), and/or to comparative methods, whether or not they are treated as a distinct methodology (for example Coolican, 1999: 180–95; Lyons and Chryssochoou, 2000, in psychology; Hopkin, 2002; Burnham et al., 2004: 58–79, in political science). Mixed methods handbooks (Tashakkori and Teddlie, 2003) have not explored the potential for systematically combining several methods in international comparisons.

Whereas proponents of a necessary link between epistemologies and methodological approaches would maintain that quantitative and qualitative research cannot be combined because the two traditions represent contrasting and competing views of social reality, and of the ways in which it should be studied, proponents of what Bryman (1988: 126) calls the 'technical version of the debate' can more easily accommodate the two distinct approaches to data collection and analysis, and are prepared to acknowledge their relative strengths and weaknesses. This section begins by analysing the reasons for combining methods and techniques in international comparisons, using a framework based on three types of strategies. It reviews the ways in which quantitative approaches have been deployed to support qualitative studies and *vice versa*, and assesses some of the ensuing trade-offs, costs and benefits.

MULTIPLE METHODS STRATEGIES

Two main reasons are generally found in the literature in support of multiple methods: to enable researchers to address all aspects of a research question; and to increase the validity of research, by using different methods to cross-check findings (Read and Marsh, 2002: 237). Expressed in more detailed terms, combined methods are found to be useful in generating insights capable of providing a more integrated picture of a phenomenon (Brannen, 1992: 14). By bringing to bear different methodological approaches, researchers can gain a deeper understanding of complex social phenomena and produce 'much more complete accounts of social reality' (Bryman, 1988: 126). The expectation is that each additional approach will contribute further evidence to test research hypotheses by shedding more light on the subject being investigated and by drawing attention to the relative importance of different factors making up the wider picture. A mixed methods design has the advantage of being able to combine inductive and deductive approaches. The risks of drawing erroneous conclusions, as reported in Chapters 3 and 4, can be reduced, if not eliminated, by applying a variety of methods in addressing research problems.

Methodological pluralism refers to the combination of quantitative and qualitative approaches; it also implies the application of a mix of methods within quantitative and qualitative paradigms. Although the value of using multiple methods and integrating data has been amply demonstrated in single-nation and single-discipline studies (Devine and Heath, 1999: 4; Fielding and Fielding, 2008), methodological pluralism is all the more valuable in multinational research and, more especially, in international comparisons that are seeking to capture the effects of linguistic and cultural diversity on the phenomena under study (Hines, 1993).

Three different approaches are usually applied in multi-strategy research, and are explored in more detail in this section: triangulation, facilitation and complementarity (Hammersley, 1996: 167–8; Bryman, 2004: 454–64). Methodological triangulation involves the combination of two or more different research strategies to study the same empirical issue and corroborate findings (Denzin, 1970: 308). Facilitation means that one research strategy is employed to support another strategy. Complementarity implies that the two strategies are dovetailed in an investigation of different aspects of the phenomenon under study.

Triangulation as a combination strategy

Methods textbooks have long advocated the combination of methods, or method triangulation, to enable theory construction, cross-checking and quality control of data (Denzin, 1970: 300; Bryman, 1988: 131–4; Fielding and Fielding, 2008: 555–8). Triangulation may be within or between methods. Triangulation within methods involves using the same method for different datasets, at different levels of analysis or on different occasions; and between methods implies using different methods to investigate the same phenomenon (Brannen, 1992: 11–12). For example, qualitative researchers may use a variety of techniques – participant observation, unstructured or small-scale structured interviews, archival research, life history methods and survey questionnaires – to draw inferences from one data source that can be corroborated by another (Bryman, 1988: 47). Quantitative researchers may combine their own postal or telephone surveys with secondary data analysis and structured interviewing; quantitative studies may be used to corroborate the findings from qualitative research or *vice versa* (Hantrais, 2005a: 404–11).

In their analysis of the uses of comparative history in macrosocial inquiry, Theda Skocpol and Margaret Somers (1980) first consider how historical comparativists have used one of three distinct approaches: parallel, contrast-oriented and macroanalytic comparative history (see Chapter 2). They go on to illustrate how 'works of comparative history sometimes *combine* (especially in pairs) the major logics' contained in what they present as a 'triangle of comparative history' (Skocpol and Somers, 1980: 187, original emphasis). The same authors note that pairs of logics often share common characteristics: parallel and contrast-oriented comparative history share an interest in applying theories and themes to each case; in contrast-oriented and macroanalytic comparative history, direct comparisons between or among historical cases are intrinsic to the argumentation; parallel and macroanalytic comparative history are both concerned with developing explanations, whether deductively or inductively, but for contradictory purposes (Skocpol and Somers, 1980: 187–90).

Triangulation is not confined to methods (multiple strategies), data-sets and theories, but can also apply to investigators working across disciplines and countries (Denzin, 1970: 301). Robert Burgess (1984: 158–9) argues that 'multiple investigators' from diverse sociocultural backgrounds can help overcome the bias that is often associated with individual researchers in single-culture and single-discipline studies, while warning of the difficulties that can arise due to conflicts of interest and differences in theoretical positions (see Chapter 7).

Facilitation by combining approaches

In considering multiple methods strategies as a facilitating device in international comparisons, the distinction can also usefully be made between combining different techniques within quantitative or qualitative research, on the one hand, and combining qualitative with quantitative approaches, on the other (Read and Marsh, 2002: 237). In triangulation, quantitative and qualitative approaches are generally used in parallel. When the aim is to facilitate the research process, more often than not, one approach is dominant, and the different techniques selected may be used sequentially rather than simultaneously. For example, Landman (2000: 19, following Sartori, 1970: 1038, 1994: 23) supports the view that 'the qualitative distinction made among categories in comparative classification schemes necessarily precedes the process of quantification'.

Quantitative researchers are increasingly recognizing that qualitative data can help in throwing up hypotheses, framing and formulating survey questions, defining, elaborating and exemplifying complex concepts, and interpreting and contextualizing findings from data collected in surveys. An exploratory qualitative study is often used to inform a quantitative study. It can aid measurement by using in-depth knowledge of social contexts to help formulate survey questions. Qualitative research can facilitate quantitative research by providing hypotheses for subsequent testing using quantitative data. Since qualitative research is more processual, it can be used to gain access to the perspectives of the individuals or groups under study and to explore specific issues and their dynamics in more depth, thereby facilitating the interpretation of the relationship between variables by looking for intervening variables and connections between different levels and stages in the research process (Bryman, 2004: 457–61).

Timothy Johnson (1998: 31) concludes his analysis of approaches to equivalence in cross-cultural and cross-national survey research by advocating multiple methodologies to ensure the cross-cultural equivalence of survey measures. He notes, for example, how ethnographic and other qualitative approaches have been recommended as methods for developing interpretively equivalent measures. His advice to researchers is to exploit as many techniques as possible to ensure equivalence, on the grounds that certain methods may prove to be more appropriate to one form of equivalence than to another (see Chapter 3).

Qualitative comparative analysis may also be seen as a route to generalizations. In political science, Jonathan Hopkin (2002: 261) underlines the value of small N qualitative comparative studies in controlling some variables, while detecting concomitant variation in others. Rational choice theorists generally use quantitative techniques, but they may also resort to case studies, not to identify specificities or to emphasize contingency, but to seek explanation and generalization, as do comparative historical sociologists, with a view to testing more general propositions and causal hypotheses about large-scale change (Hopkin, 2002: 263). Rather than seeking to establish generalizations that can be applied across a large number of cases, historical institutionalists in comparative political economy may use qualitative comparative analysis to emphasize the particularities and specificities of individual cases. They are interested in showing how 'large-scale social, economic and political forces can produce divergent outcomes in different countries as a result of the diversity of their institutional arrangements' (Hopkin, 2002: 263)

An important way in which quantitative research supports qualitative studies is by identifying respondents with the required characteristics for in-depth interviewing, when designed to study the meanings that they attach to actions or behaviour (Bryman, 2004: 457). Due to their greater universality and 'apparent objectivity' (Preece, 1994: 44), quantitative approaches can provide background information for qualitative studies to draw on in identifying broader trends, against which to locate in-depth analysis. Some quantification may help to uncover the generality of phenomena (Bryman, 2004: 460). Among the comparative education studies analysed by Val D. Rust and colleagues (1999: 106), the quantitative studies were mainly based on secondary analysis of existing data, but the pervasive analytical orientation was qualitative.

Complementarity of approaches

Complementarity is distinguished from triangulation and facilitation by the integration of different approaches rather than using them in parallel or subordinating one to the other. The dividing line between facilitation and complementarity is not, however, always easy to establish. For example, researchers may apply one of the two main approaches to help fill gaps in data that are not accessible using the other approach, and to avoid having to trade off precision against breadth of description (Hammersley, 1992: 51, 1996: 168). In seeking to combine deductive and inductive analysis, researchers may proceed by trial and error in their fieldwork, constantly shifting between data collection and theory building, while developing and refining the analysis through a process of discovery and justification of hypotheses (Vigour, 2005: 195–7).

Complementary approaches have been applied effectively in a number of disciplines. In cultural anthropology, Raoul Naroll (1968: 237) describes the progression from an ideographic to a nomothetic approach enabling researchers to seek general patterns of correlation or causation in a small number of cases that might apply to other cases yet to be investigated, thereby changing the character of the study along the way (see Chapter 4). In grounded theory, both quantitative and qualitative forms of data are considered to be necessary 'as supplements, as mutual verification and...as different forms of data on the same subject, which, when compared, will each generate theory' (Glaser and Strauss, 1967: 18). Combined approaches in comparative history are found to be most effective when their individual strengths are used to complement one other. Thus, the advantages of 'holistic, rich descriptions and full, chronological case accounts' can be complemented by the capacity of macroanalytic comparative history 'to validate (and invalidate) causal hypotheses about macro-phenomena of which there are intrinsically only limited numbers of cases' (Skocpol and Somers, 1980: 193).

Examples are cited in social and political science of variable-oriented analyses supplemented with case studies, and of case studies reinforced with quantitative analyses. The Boolean approach (see Chapter 4), advocated by Ragin (1987: 171), allows researchers to move away from 'traditional case-oriented methods by focusing on large numbers of cases but retain[s] some of the logic of the case-oriented approach'. He thereby provides 'a link to historical interpretation', demonstrating that 'qualitative comparative researchers are both holistic and interpretive in their approach to comparative materials' (Ragin, 1987: 17).

In the 1990s, Sartori (1994: 23) described the potential of the comparative and case study methods as 'mutually reinforcing and complementary undertakings', allowing trade-offs to be made between gains and losses. Case studies, he claimed, hinge on comparable concepts; they can be hypothesis generating, and contribute to the conception of generalizations and theory building, whereas they cannot, in his view, be used to confirm or control theory.

APPLYING MULTIPLE METHODS STRATEGIES ACROSS INTERNATIONAL PROJECTS

International comparisons in the social and human sciences lend themselves to multiple methods strategies due to the added complexity of studying phenomena across national, societal and cultural boundaries. It is rare for comparativists to start with a *tabula rasa*. Most researchers embarking on international comparative projects begin by carrying out a review of the literature to establish what is already known about the subject and what new avenues of inquiry remain to be explored. This stage in the research usually involves identifying earlier work on the topic under investigation in the countries, societies or cultures to be compared. The techniques of triangulation, facilitation and complementarity may all be applied not only within a single project, but also across projects when research teams look for areas where a new methodological approach may enable them to confirm or refute earlier findings. They may also decide to use an earlier study to facilitate their own work by introducing different techniques to analyse existing data, or they may design their projects to fill gaps in knowledge and country coverage, and thereby add greater depth of understanding.

In the past, analysts of multiple methods research strategies in the social sciences took most of their examples from single-case and, consequently, single-country studies, because relatively few instances of 'multisite/multimethod' studies were available to illustrate 'methodological integration' (Bryman 1988: 129–30). The European framework programmes and, more especially, the clustering of social science projects and networks around selected topics provide a body of material that lends itself to an analysis of both these approaches.

Under the key action for 'Improving the Socio-economic Knowledge Base' in the Commission's framework programmes, several projects and networks were grouped together in an attempt to implement an integrated approach towards research fields. The aim in creating thematic clusters of projects was, initially, to maximize European added value within a given area and establish critical mass in an effort to find effective solutions to complex multidisciplinary problems (European Commission's 1999 Guide for Proposers, Part I: 10). The Commission was not concerned about methods, except insofar as the research community would be able to demonstrate that it was contributing to methodological advancement and refinement, thereby ensuring greater reliability of data. Project teams were expected to show that they would generate and exploit high-quality reliable and comparable data, while also improving access to datasets that other researchers could use as an empirical basis for theory building and scientific explanations in comparative analysis.

In 2003, the Directorate-General for Research and Development commissioned 20 policy reviewers to identify policy directions in close to 300 socioeconomic projects and networks funded by the framework programmes (see http://ec.europa.eu/research/social-sciences/newsletter/

policy_reviews_en.htm/). Many of the projects and networks in the clusters were contributing to research infrastructures that support the work of research users by developing conceptual and analytical toolkits capable of capturing changing concepts and serving as a resource for analysis of the policy process. The reviewers were required to draw out important policy conclusions or policy lessons, and to advance scientific understanding on matters relevant to policy in the European Union. The reviews afford examples of how the three strategies – triangulation, facilitation and complementarity – can be exploited across projects with the aim of validating findings, taking forward the research process and gaining a fuller understanding of the complex social phenomena being investigated in comparative research (Hantrais, 2005a: 413, 2006a).

The projects and networks in the clusters drew on a variety of quantitative and qualitative approaches. In most cases, a dominant approach could be identified. At the one end of the methodological spectrum were projects aiming to develop large-scale databases. Some carried out new surveys to fill existing gaps in information and to refine variables. Cross-sectional and longitudinal data analysis and mapping exercises of a number of datasets, including household panel studies, were used to study the dynamics of social change, interpret variations between countries, make generalizations and draw out causal explanations. Projects in which qualitative approaches were dominant invariably drew on macrolevel data to provide a backcloth for in-depth interviews and other observational techniques. They devoted a considerable amount of time and effort to developing interview guidelines and analytical frameworks that could be operationalized in very different national settings. Many of the projects used a range of microlevel observational techniques, often in combination, including elite interviews with key policy actors, in-depth interviews, ethnographic case studies, focus groups and vignettes. Most of the projects and networks using qualitative methods were following an approach that emphasizes differentiation between and within countries to take account of the complexity of the factors involved and of subnational diversity. They carried out new fieldwork in an attempt to capture the complexity of intervening factors, which enabled them to complement and extend the analysis resulting from the projects and networks focusing on large-scale datasets.

Although almost all the projects in the cluster subscribed to a dominant methodology, none could be said to represent a pure form of either a quantitative or qualitative research paradigm as traditionally portrayed. Even the projects that came closest to meeting the widely recognized criteria for rigorous quantitative research required very detailed qualitative work to achieve comparability, which led to the admission that methodological compromise may be necessary to achieve functional equivalence in cross-national surveys (Hantrais, 2005a: 417). The projects at the other end of the methodological spectrum were no less rigorous in their efforts to avoid insider bias and interpret findings with reference to a much broader socioeconomic and political context.

These examples lend support to the claim that the combination of methods within and across projects and networks can result in the production of more reliable datasets and a more sensitive appreciation of diversity. It is less certain that the *post hoc* synergy across the projects that the Commission was attempting to stimulate through clustering succeeded in producing an integrated approach towards research fields and projects, capable of offering effective solutions to complex multi-disciplinary problems, since the projects in the various clusters had not been designed at the outset to complement one another (see Chapter 3).

The Limits of Multi-Strategy Research

This chapter has explored not only the advantages of integrating different research methods within and across paradigms in international comparative research but also the issues raised by multiple strategies. Although combining methods, for example by triangulation, may increase internal validity, analysts have found that it does not necessarily produce a 'rounded unity' (Brannen, 1992: 14), and its value may not be as 'straightforward as is sometimes supposed' (Hammersley, 1996: 169). Facilitation implies the subordination of one approach to another, making it difficult to maintain a balance between them. The findings produced by triangulation or complementarity of different methodological approaches may be concordant or mutually reinforcing. They may also be contradictory or discrepant, or they may fail to corroborate findings, indicating that the presumed relationship may not exist or has to be understood differently (Gillham, 2000: 29–30; Bryman, 1988: 133, 2004: 456). Skocpol and Somers (1980: 190) suggest that the result of 'mixed type' work in comparative history, when two or more logics are applied to the same units of analysis, may be an ambiguous message, unless the different logics are kept relatively separate.

These findings offer support for the claim that multi-strategy research combining quantitative and qualitative approaches should not be seen as a panacea. Bryman (2004: 452–3) comments on the two main arguments – embedded methods and paradigm – that are frequently used against multi-strategy research. According to the embedded methods argument, the integration of different approaches is neither feasible nor desirable due to the irreconcilability of the epistemological positions associated with them. According to the paradigm argument, integration can only ever take place at a superficial level and within a single paradigm, since paradigms are, by definition, incommensurable and incompatible. Both these contentions are, as Bryman (2004: 454, 463) points out, based on the much disputed case made by proponents of non-integration about the interconnectedness of methods and epistemologies. This debate can only be resolved by demonstrating that quantitative and qualitative approaches are by no means as distinct as is often supposed, particularly if they are regarded essentially as techniques for data collection and analysis. Moreover, after once again revisiting the arguments, Bryman (2008: 23) concludes his chapter in a handbook on social research methods by admitting that 'even the rise of mixed methods has not brought the paradigm wars to an end, although it may have lessened the mutual hostility'.

While these recurrent debates also apply to international comparative research, they do not necessarily detract from the value of adopting multiple strategies to add breadth and depth in comparative studies. As shown in this chapter, the combination of approaches within and between paradigms is all the more valuable in research that crosses national, societal and cultural boundaries due to the great complexity of the phenomena under study in a variety of sociocultural and political environments.

If multi-method strategies are to help resolve the many epistemological, methodological and technical issues that are inherent in international comparative research, rather than contributing to the problems it raises, careful reflection and scientific justification are needed before multi-method research designs can be confidently adopted as 'an attitude of inquiry, an approach to quality standards' and for the achievement of 'adequate explanations of social phenomena' (Fielding and Fielding, 2008: 566).

6

Research and Policy in International Settings

Many personal and scientific reasons are evoked in this volume to explain why researchers embark on the daunting and complex task of conducting comparisons across nations, societies and cultures. Comparativists are seeking to develop their own awareness and understanding by comparing the familiar with the unknown, advance knowledge by testing theory against practice, search for scientific explanations for observed phenomena, and learn from the exchange of information and experience. Increasingly, funding agencies require social and human science researchers to demonstrate the relevance of their findings for society and, by implication, for policy. Comparisons across time and space are called upon to produce evidence of the effectiveness of policies implemented in different spatiotemporal environments in response to similar socioeconomic trends, and to provide examples of good practice.

Globalization, the more prominent role played by international organizations in addressing policy issues in the latter part of the twentieth century, the launching of the European Research Area and the enlargement of the European Union to the East in the early twenty-first century gave national governments a fresh incentive to take advantage of opportunities for cross-border learning and transfer. The transportation of policies between countries, like that of concepts, demands a discriminating and contextualized comparative analysis of the relationship between macro- and microlevel structures in exporting and importing countries (see Chapter 4 in this volume). Contextualization assumes particular significance in comparative research with a policy focus, entailing fine-grain analysis of policy environments if researchers are to understand how a particular phenomenon has been socially, culturally and politically constructed.

This chapter examines how international comparative research in the social sciences and humanities can assist policy development. It asks how researchers can contribute to the research–policy interface, what policy actors can learn from international comparative research into socioeconomic and political phenomena, and how such research can inform policy. It reviews the many ways in which research is relevant to policy, paying particular attention to evidence-based policy, policy evaluation, learning and transfer in international settings.

Understanding the Research–Policy Relationship

Data gathering has long been carried out to underpin policy decisions. Since the mid-nineteenth century when the first international statistical conference was held in London, common statistical tools and methods of data presentation have been sought to build up an international network of standardized objective observations, covering topics such as population trends and international trade. Initially, international databases were expected to serve as an information resource supporting efforts to reduce tensions between nations. Subsequently, they were used to provide the materials researchers and policy actors needed to undertake meaningful international comparisons to underpin policy development. Universalization of techniques does not necessarily resolve the problems that arise due to national specificities in statistical traditions, which are in turn shaped by political pressures. It took almost a century before international organizations such as the United Nations were able to establish harmonized economic indicators. Social indicators have proved to be even more resistant to universal development and implementation (Desrosières, 1996: 17–19; Marlier et al., 2007: 38–9).

This section explores the relationship between research and policy with reference to theories about the utilization of social science and humanities research by policy makers and practitioners. It goes on to examine the differing nature of research and policy making, the limitations of the social and human sciences, the extent to which research governance can integrate research and policy, and the attempts made to bridge the communications gap.

INCOMPATIBILITY BETWEEN RESEARCH AND POLICY

The pioneers of comparative social policy in the 1960s and 1970s, particularly in the United Kingdom, argued that valuable knowledge and insights could be gained from looking across countries (Rodgers et al., 1968: 11–13; Rodgers et al., 1979: xi). Meanwhile, the United States saw a period of government supported expansion of social science research in the 1950s and 1960s when positivism was in the ascendancy (see Chapter 2). The 1970s were marked by disenchantment about the value of research for policy, leading to significant cuts in government spending in the 1980s (Bogenschneider et al., 2002: 188).

At that time, Harold L. Wilensky and colleagues (1985) made a strong case for developing comparative social science research in support of policy making in the United States. They identified three ways in which they believed basic research could usefully contribute to social policy (Wilensky et al., 1985: 4). Firstly, international comparisons can help policy makers to improve their understanding of constraints on social spending, policy development and political choices. Secondly, international comparisons can heighten awareness of the policy options adopted by different countries confronting similar problems. Thirdly, by drawing attention to the socioeconomic and political consequences of different policy choices, they can enable policy actors to gain a fuller understanding of real opportunities and constraints. The analysis by Wilensky et al. (1985) has since been refined and expressed in different terms, as demonstrated in this chapter, but their assessment is still relevant in the twenty-first century.

Despite what are often shared objectives, the relationship between academic researchers, on the one hand, and policy makers and practitioners, on the other, has never been easy. Several widely applicable theories have been developed to explain the underutilization of social science research findings by policy makers, aptly summarized by Karen Bogenschneider et al. (2002) with reference to a series of state-sponsored Wisconsin Family Impact Seminars, designed to encourage greater use of research in policy making.

The first theory portrays policy making as a 'fast-breaking, self-serving, influence-driven process incompatible with the methods of social science, which are more time-intensive, intellectual, and rational' (Bogenschneider et al., 2002: 189). This incompatibility can be demonstrated by differences in the time horizons and ambitions of politicians concerned about short-term outcomes that may influence the results of the next election and their public image, and those of researchers who are trained to probe ever more deeply into the complexities of social life with a view to producing robust and reliable findings. As argued by a research officer in a British government department, 'policy makers not only want "good evidence" and examples of "good practice", but they want it on a timely basis and have a keen eye for cost-effectiveness' (Williams, 2004: 45). Without convincing evidence and the will to use it, politicians are inclined to base policy pronouncements on atypical examples, quotes and percentage figures taken out of context, with little regard for meaning or causation. The force of the time horizon and ambitions argument may be weakening, however, as researchers become increasingly constrained by limited resources and externally imposed deadlines, and as public confidence and trust in the ability of politicians to deliver election campaign promises are eroded.

Secondly, social scientists, according to Bogenschneider et al. (2002: 189), are reluctant to communicate research findings to policy makers and practitioners, because they are aware of the limitations and incompleteness of their own knowledge. Researchers are trained to be cautious, sceptical and reflective. The limitations argument applies to both quantitative and qualitative international comparative research. In the case of quantitative research, reliable comparable data are often difficult to obtain and analyse (see Chapter 4). In the case of qualitative research, the findings are, of necessity, restricted to a small, often unrepresentative, sample (see Chapter 5).

Thirdly, the underutilization of the findings from social science and humanities research may be 'an artifact of a democratic, free-market system, which lacks institutional structures for integrating knowledge and power' (Bogenschneider et al., 2002: 189). This theory raises questions not only about research capacity building and the strengthening of links between academia and services, but also about how research is funded and managed, how different research methodologies are applied, and how shared standards can be developed for all stakeholders in the research–policy process (see also Chapter 7).

These issues are all the more difficult to resolve in global research markets, since national research cultures and traditions are influential in determining how power relationships are constructed between researchers and policy actors, for example as mediated through research councils. Intermediaries in research councils or government departments, such as policy advisers, can and do play an important role in 'helping researchers to understand the needs of policy makers, and helping policy makers gain a better understanding of how research can be used both to inform and evaluate policy decisions' (Williams, 2004: 45). Careful consideration therefore needs to be given to deciding how delegation should be carried out and how best to manage conflicting interests (Arve-Parès, 2005: 13). The exercise of research governance can also become a negative force working against the integration of research and policy, since 'research findings may disturb power relations in the policy process that support certain financial and societal arrangements' to the extent that 'some policy actors...may resist changes that a given research project might imply or recommend' (Stafford, 2001: 85).

The pessimistic conclusion drawn by Bogenschneider et al. (2002: 191) is that the first three of the four theories they examine to explain why policy makers and practitioners underutilize social science research would be difficult to alter because they are the result of structural factors. Their fourth theory – 'two communities theory' – identifies a communications gap between researchers and policy actors, portrayed as two communities with 'different goals, information needs, values, reward systems, and languages' (Bogenschneider et al., 2002: 189, 192). The authors are more optimistic about building bridges to fill such a gap (a proposition examined in greater detail below). Accordingly, they recommend that researchers should avoid an advocacy orientation designed to promote a particular (ideological) view, and instead adopt an 'alternative education' orientation, whereby a range of policy alternatives are presented objectively without suggesting or expressing personal preferences (Bogenschneider et al., 2002: 192).

BRIDGING THE COMMUNICATIONS GAP BETWEEN RESEARCH AND POLICY

Despite the optimism expressed by Bogenschneider et al. (2002: 192) about reducing the communications gap between academic researchers and non-academic users of social science research, it continues to be recognized as a major obstacle to cooperation between researchers and users of research findings (MacGregor, 2005). The information needs of researchers and policy actors are very different, as already noted: policy actors want to know what works and what findings matter. At the formal level, researchers may not know how to present their findings in language that is jargon free and comprehensible to stakeholders, who do not have time to read academic papers and are looking for conciseness and immediately applicable findings. Researchers are also prone to overemphasize concepts, theories and methods, which are far removed from the everyday work experience of practitioners, making it difficult for them to see how the information could be applied in practice.

The reward systems of the two communities constitute another barrier to effective communication. For politicians, the main reward is to be re-elected and remain in power. The policy-oriented work of social sciences and humanities researchers may be undervalued in a situation where their reputation and career prospects as academics depend on research ratings, which are primarily determined by their ability to publish their findings in internationally peer reviewed journals. In addition, research funding institutions increasingly require applicants to involve stake-holders in the research, evaluation and dissemination processes.

However, reports to sponsors, as exemplified by the situation in the United Kingdom, may carry relatively low weight in assessing the performance of aspiring academics. Contract researchers, for their part, once they have embarked on the process of attracting grants from government departments, foundations, industrial funders, research councils and international funding bodies, have little time to publish findings in academic journals. They thereby jeopardize their chances of pursuing a career in academia in countries where recruitment is based largely on scientific publications (Hantrais, 2006c: 227–32).

The communications gap between researchers and policy makers may be more difficult to bridge in some countries than in others. Wilensky (1997: 1244, 1254) argues that researchers in countries with more 'corporatist' systems, exemplified by Austria, Germany, Japan, Norway, Sweden and, to a lesser extent, Belgium and the Netherlands, are more effective at fostering dialogue between researchers, bureaucrats and politicians than in decentralized, fragmented political economies such as the United States. Countries where different policy actors form coalitions and achieve consensus are also more likely to be successful in integrating knowledge and power (Wilensky, 1997: 1248).

Differences are found in the extent to which researchers are committed to demonstrating the policy relevance of their research (see also Chapter 7). For British researchers funded by research councils and government departments, for example, the policy relevance of the research and the involvement of stakeholders have become basic requirements, forcing researchers to formulate their research questions in terms of policy issues, and to draft their proposals with an eye to wider dissemination strategies and opportunities for further funding. By contrast, social science and humanities researchers in France, even when, paradoxically, they are under the direct tutelage of a government department for social affairs or employment, still cling to the notion that researchers should not compromise their intellectual integrity by embarking on what is often derisorily referred to as 'applied' or 'problem-solving' research. Applied research is widely considered to be in conflict with their true vocation, which is to conduct 'basic' or 'fundamental' research, and contribute to grand theory, free from external influences. As full-time researchers employed by the state, their career development was not, in the past, influenced by their success in fundraising or their policy evaluation activities, and even less by their ability to disseminate their findings outside the research community.

A more positive perspective on the potential for meaningful dialogue between the two communities is illustrated by the symbiotic relationship that can exist between researchers and policy actors in some Central and East European countries (Kutsar, 2005). In Estonia for example, most of the policy advisers at the Ministry for Social Affairs in the late 1990s and early 2000s had undergone university training as researchers in public administration before taking up their positions, making them aware of the interest of studying the experience of other countries and of comparing notes on ways of addressing similar problems. Their experience shows how policy makers can rely on researchers not only to collect, analyse and interpret data, but also to identify examples of good practice and find new ways of tackling persistent problems that prevent policy from being more effective. Researchers are expected to collate information on policy options, drawing on the experience of other countries facing similar issues, and to present it in a form that is readily accessible and understandable for stakeholders.

Findings from social science and humanities research are, however, only one form of information feeding into policy. Politicians are also influenced by the findings from opinion polls, pressure groups, think tanks, journalism and media reporting, the more so when they do not like the message conveyed by social scientists. 'Policy relevant research', it is suggested (Stafford, 2001: 85), 'will contain both "good" and "bad" news for policy makers; and the latter may be politically embarrassing.' Even when communication between the two communities is effective, policy makers may choose to ignore robust research findings due to political resistance or apathy (Alcock, 2004: 26).

POLICY-RELEVANT RESEARCH IN INTERNATIONAL SETTINGS

In the early years of the twenty-first century, at least in the European context, researchers seemed to have become more aware of the need to take account of the policy dimension in their work, and policy makers and practitioners were showing more interest in research findings. Even if the linkages were not always made explicit, the many ways in which research can be relevant to policy had been widely recognized by the two communities. They can usefully be expressed in terms of different models presenting the relationship between research and policy (adapted from Alcock, 2004: 28–9):

- a knowledge-driven model where the assumption is that research leads policy;
- a problem-solving model where the assumption is that research follows policy and that policy issues shape research priorities;
- an enlightenment model that sees research as serving policy in indirect ways, providing a broader framework for understanding and explaining policy;

- an interactive model that portrays research and policy as mutually influential;
- a political/tactical model that sees policy as the outcome of a political process, and where the research agenda is politically driven.

Despite the renewed interest in comparative social policy in the late 1990s and early 2000s, demonstrated by the literature on the subject (for example Clasen, 1999, 2004; Kennett, 2001, 2004; May, 2008), it is less certain that either researchers or policy actors are fully convinced of the value of systematically incorporating an international dimension into their work. International comparative policy research is expensive and time consuming; it requires experienced multidisciplinary researchers, specialized management and people skills, and an intimate knowledge of diverse economic and social systems, and national research cultures (see Chapter 7). For institutions and funders, it is more difficult to control, which further complicates the already complex tasks of designing and conducting international comparative projects on the one hand, and formulating and implementing effective public policies on the other.

Evidence-Based and Policy Evaluation Research

Research that is relevant for policy or has a policy orientation is concerned not only with understanding social issues but also with providing answers and evidence that can contribute to the improvement of policy formation and delivery. Increasingly, governments are calling upon social and human scientists to assess both the potential and actual impacts of policies. The evidence adduced to evaluate policy effects is expected to be independently observed and verified, allowing a broad consensus to be achieved about content, if not interpretation (Davies et al., 2000a: 2). Accordingly, evidence-based policy research can be defined as an approach that contributes to well-informed policy decisions based on reliable objective evidence produced from research (Davies et al., 2006: 175). By informing the various stages in the policy process, evidence-based policy is expected to lead to improvements in practice and more cost-effective interventions. The 'better-informed, pluralistic and pragmatic approaches' of the early 2000s are said, however, to be concerned less with 'evidence-based policy' than with the *'evidence base for policy'* (Alcock, 2004: 51, original emphasis).

This section looks at developments regarding both these approaches from an international comparative perspective. It begins by reviewing how evidence from comparative research can be utilized in policy evaluation before examining the ways in which the evidence base is exploited in policy and the problems of identifying and interpreting policy effects.

DEVELOPING INTERNATIONAL POLICY EVALUATION RESEARCH

Policy evaluation research, like policy-relevant and policy-oriented research, has a long history dating back to the beginning of the twentieth century when experimental designs and statistical techniques were used in the United States in agricultural research to examine the practices most likely to produce the highest crop yields. Already in the 1920s, educational research was developing models that could be used in assessing classroom performance. Survey techniques were applied in the 1950s and 1960s to evaluate the cost-effectiveness of public policies and their success in achieving their objectives in areas covering education, public health and equality of opportunity. The quasi-experimental methods of psychologists and the multivariate analyses being developed by sociologists were combined to establish the techniques needed for experiment-based quantitative approaches to evaluation during the 1960s and 1970s in the United States, while sociologists in Europe were refining qualitative methods (Chelimsky, 2006: 34; Stevenson and Thomas, 2006: 202–3). The 1970s have been described as the 'coming-of-age for evaluation as a discipline', by bringing to bear a variety of intellectual traditions (Stevenson and Thomas, 2006: 210).

The next decade was marked not only by greater awareness of inter-national applications and a more multicultural vision of evaluation in the United States, but also by the surfacing of 'paradigm wars' (Stevenson and Thomas, 2006: 210–11). In line with the dominant positivistic paradigm, scientific methods were widely believed to produce un-equivocal results, although the conviction that social progress could be achieved through policy evaluation was criticized for the prominence it gave to social engineering (Dahler-Larsen, 2006: 143).

The aims of the managerial reforms introduced under the banner of 'new public management' in the 1990s were to produce 'rational, efficient and transparent decision-making with respect to the allocation of resources', highlighting 'value-for-money, cost containment, account-ability and effectiveness' in service provision (Clarke, 2006: 560–1). The resulting demand for systematic monitoring and evaluation of the impacts of policies, programmes and practices, most notably in clinical practice, social work and criminal justice, became an international phenomenon, reinforcing the role attributed to research-based evidence.

Like policy-relevant and policy-oriented research, policy evaluation research fulfils a variety of purposes, albeit with greater emphasis on the direct implications for policy effectiveness (Spencer et al., 2003: 36–8; Chelimsky, 2006: 35; Mark et al., 2006: 12–13). These aims can be succinctly summarized under four main headings:

- generating information that can then be used to improve agency capability and the decision-making process;
- developing the operation and practice of policies;
- advancing and testing knowledge about social problems and their solutions;
- determining accountability and improving the effectiveness of practitioners.

By the early twenty-first century, the United States were considered to be market leaders in policy evaluation, whereas the United Kingdom under the Labour government was at the forefront of evidence-based policy making (Walker and Wiseman, 2006: 362). The major purpose of policy evaluation and evidence-based policy, as applied in both countries at that time, was to promote accountability by informing governments about the impacts and cost-effectiveness of policies, thereby enabling them to reduce waste and engender trust in public management, to the extent that evaluation had become a central feature of evidence-based policy and practice (Chelimsky, 2006: 34; Davies et al., 2006: 165). The two countries were said, however, to be pursuing different objectives in using pilot studies. For example, in the United States, the aim was to establish whether a policy works in a particular setting, and to design policy and implementation simultaneously to ensure a high degree of precision in the assessment of policy impacts. By contrast, in the United Kingdom, pilot studies were used to test policies prior to introducing large-scale implementation (Walker, 2000: 161).

REVIEWING INTERNATIONAL POLICY EVALUATION

Opinion differs about whether the procedures used to evaluate policy proposals, programmes and outcomes meet scientific criteria and can be considered as research (Spencer et al., 2003: 29–30). As with comparative research over time and space (see Chapter 1), the question also arises as to whether policy evaluation is characterized by a distinct method or methodology. Like social policy research more generally, policy evaluation is usually considered to be a multidisciplinary applied social science, drawing on the disciplinary perspectives of sociology, public administration, economics (econometrics), psychology, ethnology and anthropology, extending to cultural studies, management and communication. Taken individually these disciplinary perspectives may be in conflict or competition with one another. For example, whereas economists tend to treat monetary policies as if they are universally applicable, sociologists and political scientists are alert to the importance of context-embeddedness. By applying the methods and methodologies developed in the disciplines on which it draws, policy evaluation research seeks to integrate a variety of approaches aimed at making sense of social phenomena (Mark et al., 2006: 21–4). In combination, they can be complementary and mutually reinforcing (see Chapters 4 and 5). The wide range of methodological approaches available means that they can provide both summative and formative evidence, but the social, relational, political and ethical dimensions of policy evaluation may hamper its objectivity (Mark et al., 2006: 18).

International comparisons in the social and human sciences have been described as 'quasi-experimental' in that they seek to control for the cultural environments in which a given phenomenon occurs, following the model of the 'controlled experiment of the natural sciences' (Lisle, 1985: 16). Social experiments have been widely utilized in the United States, for example, to evaluate welfare-to-work programmes, education and training initiatives, low-income housing assistance and negative income taxes. Experimentation is less frequently applied in Europe for paradigmatic, technical and practical reasons, which are not, however, considered to be insuperable obstacles provided that the evaluation strategy includes other methods to explore why and how questions (Stafford, 2002: 282). Since policy evaluation studies make wide use of matching situations or time series data to provide control groups in an attempt to limit the number of contextual variables, the approach resembles that frequently adopted in international comparative research designs (see Chapter 3). As in comparative studies, spatiotemporal contextualization is essential to an understanding of how the policy process operates. However, while researchers in comparative public policy may be seeking explanations for observed differences and emphasizing contextual details in their findings, governments are more interested in the effectiveness of policy interventions in terms of inputs, outcomes, implementation and delivery.

Evaluation research is also prone to many of the same paradigmatic controversies, especially the quantitative–qualitative debate (see Chapter 5). The two approaches may serve to achieve different ends. Systematic reviews, randomized controlled trials for social intervention evaluation, matched comparisons, community audits, quasi-experimental research designs, attitudinal surveys and econometric modelling are expected to provide evidence about cause and effect, often focusing on performance measures and indicators of efficiency. By contrast, qualitative interpretative approaches, including participative, observational and consultative techniques, in-depth interviews and focus groups, provide evidence about experience and process (Spencer et al., 2003: 31–5; Alcock, 2004: 57; Robson, 2004: 123–4; Davies et al., 2006: 178–80). It has been argued persuasively that evidence-based policy and practice should seek to foster an intellectual environment in which quantitative and qualitative approaches complement one another (Davies, 2000: 308–9). A major challenge for the 2000s is to develop combined methods enabling policy actors and researchers to gain a more comprehensive understanding of the complexity of interventions and practices (Clarke, 2006: 576).

Whatever the methods and techniques adopted, policy evaluation research is subject to the same scientific criteria of transparency, validity, replicability, reliability and plausibility as comparative social policy research. Since evaluators generally draw on the paradigms, concepts, methods and practices of critical thinking characteristic of the social and human sciences, and adhere to the same standards of 'quality of the conceptual approach' and 'rigor of the method', the distinction between evaluation and evaluation research can be said to lie in the 'scale, scope, context, and utility' of the work (Dahler-Larsen, 2006: 151).

As in other types of policy research when carried out in international settings, and as noted above when reviewing the relationship between researchers and users of research findings, policy evaluation is likely to be influenced by the requirements and expectations of stakeholders and evaluators, and by interpersonal relations, which can call into question the status of policy evaluation as research. In addition to the ethical questions raised by direct contact with policy clients, often to a greater extent than researchers working with non-policy related research designs, policy evaluators have to contend with issues regarding their independence *vis-à-vis* their sponsors and the ways in which their work will, subsequently, be applied by practitioners (Chelimsky, 2006: 53).

In that the objective is to assess the quality of a programme, policy or practice, the qualitative techniques used in policy evaluation mean that it is, of necessity, interpretive and judgemental (Spencer et al., 2003: 21). At the same time, evaluation knowledge is, by definition, context bound, and the interpretation of findings is value laden, raising controversy about the extent to which evaluators should and can remain politically neutral, or whether they should 'strive to enhance democratic processes and help achieve democratic ideals' (Mark et al., 2006: 12). Moreover, politicians commissioning evaluations may seek to prioritize timely over robust results in their efforts to rally evidence in support of a political argument. For the same reasons, they are also likely to prefer tried, tested and uncontroversial methods (Walker and Wiseman, 2006: 369–70), thereby potentially undermining the scientific value of the research.

THE EVIDENCE BASE FOR INTERNATIONAL COMPARATIVE POLICY RESEARCH

The postwar period was marked by the creation of a number of international organizations and agencies responsible, among other tasks, for gathering information about sociodemographic and economic trends in the countries under their jurisdiction (see Chapter 1). By the turn of the twenty-first century, Eurostat, the European Union's statistical agency, was constantly working in conjunction with the United Nations, International Labour Organization, World Health Organization, Council of Europe and Organization for Economic Cooperation and Development in collating socioeconomic data. Technological progress has meant that the capacity to handle and process large amounts of data has substantially improved (Dale et al., 2008: 521–4), although the demand in policy-oriented research for fully comparable aggregated and disaggregated datasets is far from being satisfied (see Chapter 3). Like sociodemographic and economic data, regularly updated information on policy measures and implementation is notoriously difficult to collect.

Since the 1970s, the European Commission's agencies, networks and observatories have monitored trends and tracked policies across member states in an effort to build an information base that can be drawn on to compare the situation in different countries and inform policy. The Commission's social situation and demographic reports, for example, present and analyse trend data collated by Eurostat and other national and international statistical agencies. The Mutual Information System on Social Protection produces an annual online publication covering the social protection systems in the member states of the European Union, European Economic Area and Switzerland.

Other noteworthy examples of databases used by researchers engaged on European funded projects and by the European Commission's observatories are the Luxembourg Income Study, the Multi-National Time Use Study, the Cross-National Equivalence File of panel data and the European Community Household Panel survey, which was replaced in 2003 by the European Union Survey of Income and Living Conditions (EU-SILC). The long-running European Values Study and the Eurobarometer survey have been supplemented by the European Social Survey. These data sources are used increasingly for benchmarking with the aim of monitoring and measuring the performance of national governments as they strive to meet international targets (see, for example, the website of the Directorate-General for Employment, Social Affairs and Equal Opportunities at: http://ec.europa.eu/employment_social/emplweb/publications/index_en.cfm).

If policy actors have tended to show more interest in the findings from international comparisons of policy developments since the 1990s, at least in the European context, it may be partly due to the requirement on member states to produce national reports tracking the progress made towards meeting the targets set under the open method of coordination. This institutionalized form of monitoring makes extensive use of benchmarking to gauge the performance of member states (for example Trubek and Trubek, 2005; Büchs, 2007).

Reports commissioned by governments may, however, be blunt instruments for checking on policy implementation when national interests are at stake. As demonstrated by the national reports on measures taken to promote employment, they may provide an indication of good intentions rather than effective actions. The gathering of evidence at national level required by the open method of coordination may, nonetheless, put pressure on governments to carry out policy evaluations and result in the introduction of what might be unpopular or politically contentious legislation.

ASSESSING EVIDENCE IN INTERNATIONAL POLICY RESEARCH

Comparative policy evaluation has to overcome many of the same technical obstacles as other types of comparative research, particularly with regard to comparability of the units of observation and data, the need to take into account what may be an inordinate number of intervening variables, and the limited generalizability of findings over time and space (see Chapter 4). In addition, evidence-based policy is required not only to determine whether specific policy measures are achieving their stated objectives but also to explain why they are effective. In international comparative policy research, the quantitative data collected by international organizations, although useful as a mechanism for informing policy, do not usually provide meaningful indicators of the success, or otherwise, of policy measures that can then be used as evidence on which to base policy. Qualitative approaches that take account of context specificity and the motives and meanings of actors provide a valuable, complementary tool for fleshing out the possible effects of social policies (Davies, 2000: 309). They are particularly useful when they examine the totality of the process from policy formulation through to implementation and practice, as translated into the lived experience of the individuals and groups targeted. Such comprehensive studies are, however, rare since they are costly of time and effort. The costs increase exponentially as the number of units of investigation is extended. Policy evaluators need to be able to identify unequivocal policy effects and to explain the outcomes they observe in a manner that can be readily assimilated by policy actors. This section explores some of the problems facing researchers seeking to isolate policy effects and interpret findings about outcomes, drawing on practical examples of how these can be addressed.

Isolating policy effects

The effects of a specific policy measure across countries are particularly difficult to isolate in situations where policies have multiple objectives. Isolating policy effects is further complicated by the fact that the outcomes of policies may not necessarily be what was sought or intended. Measures enacted in one policy area to meet a particular target may achieve unanticipated effects in another policy area. Policies designed to redistribute resources vertically using means testing may, for example, not be of greatest benefit to those most in need, if take-up is limited due to the stigma attached to means-tested benefits. Policies targeted at specific age or socioeconomic categories may encourage a dependency culture or provoke intergenerational tensions, which are both unintended and unwanted outcomes. Just as improved provision cannot be assumed automatically to have the desired effect, the with-drawal of previous support, or the lack of policy, may not be the only cause explaining behaviour. These observations also raise the issue of whether policy measures can be deemed to have worked if they achieve unintended but positive effects (Hantrais, 2004a: chapter 7).

Knowing whether a particular policy measure has achieved its stated objective is sometimes gauged by asking 'customers' whether they are satisfied, but satisfaction ratings, like attitudinal data, are notoriously unreliable and difficult to compare across societies. In addition, the public may not share the perceptions that political and administrative actors have of the success of policies. Where policy actors have raised expectations during an electoral campaign, it may be difficult for them to meet their promises when they are in power. Moreover, recorded satisfaction may have little to do with the actual service received. What is believed to be an acceptable level and quality of provision in one country may be judged differently elsewhere. People who may be considered, objectively, to have benefited from a specific policy may report that their experience was negative, making outcomes difficult to interpret, as argued below (Davies, 2000: 298).

Evidence of the extent to which policies formulated at supranational or national level are effectively implemented at national or local level remains difficult to identify for the same reasons. When, as in the case of the European Union, member states are left to choose their own policy mechanisms, the effectiveness in monitoring, reporting, policing and applying sanctions can vary considerably from one country to another. Although governments may be required to transpose European legislation into national law, the number of rulings by the European Court of Justice on social policy differs markedly from one member state to another (Leibfried, 2005: table 10.4). Legal action may offer no more than an indication of the effectiveness of policing and the provision of access to legal services, while the evidence supplied by member states about the efficacy of policy practice may be unreliable, the more so when governments are left to decide on the form and method of implementation and are responsible for reporting on their success in meeting targets.

Interpreting policy outcomes

Determining why a policy does or does not work is equally, if not more, difficult than determining whether it worked, particularly in view of the absence of direct and unequivocal evidence confirming causal effects. Even when policy evaluation is undertaken regularly, it is often difficult to interpret observed outcomes that appear to mark the success or failure of specific measures. The wider economic and social climate or the state of labour markets may be more discriminating factors in shaping decisions than the policy measure being studied. A whole bundle of measures and their different configurations may need to be taken into account to ensure ecological validity (Davies, 2000: 295–6).

The problems in understanding, interpreting and explaining policy effects can be illustrated by the findings from projects funded by the European Commission, comparing perceptions of public policy provision across member states in the European Union. One mixed methods study found that opinions about the relationship between policy for families and behaviour were ambivalent (Hantrais, 2004a: 149–51, 166). Irrespective of the level of provision, few respondents were satisfied that public policy does enough to support families. In France, where provision is relatively generous, public policy for families tends to be taken for granted, and French respondents complain about the inadequacy of childcare facilities (Hantrais and Ackers, 2005: 199–202). Where standards of living are generally low, and confidence in governments to deliver is limited, the public may be satisfied to 'make do' with provision that is elsewhere considered to be poor, due to low expectations.

The findings from another study funded by the European Commission examining households, work and flexibility in the early 2000s point to a paradox between the objective situation and subjective perceptions. Countries in Northern Europe with a long history of policies to help balance work and family life, and reporting the greatest degree of sharing of domestic labour, were found to be those where the family–work conflict was experienced as most difficult to manage. By contrast, because they had no expectations of equality, respondents in Central and East European countries did not, on the whole, claim to experience family–work conflict, although they were working the longest hours and might have been expected to be most dissatisfied with their working arrangements (Wallace, 2003: 37–8).

Analysis of the fit between policy objectives, public perceptions and practice highlights many of the tensions resulting from competing interests and ideologies among different policy actors, and within and between countries. Conflicting, contradictory, confused or non-explicit objectives make outcomes difficult to interpret, particularly across national, societal and cultural boundaries. The interpretation of outcomes is further complicated by the lack of consensus over objectives and the difficulty of identifying specific policy effects. Different objectives may be in competition or they may unintentionally coincide, whereas similar objectives may produce divergent outcomes.

The problems in explaining the impact of the European Union's open method of coordination on domestic policy making are not very different from those that occur when attempting to assess the impact of findings from comparative social science and humanities research designed to analyse the policy-making process more generally. Policy actors may not be prepared to acknowledge that they are influenced by what happens in other countries, because they want to present a policy initiative as their own. They are likely to choose examples of best practice that suit their own purposes and support developments that were already taking place, thereby demonstrating what has been termed 'invited dutifulness' (Büchs, 2008: 27). The ambiguity in the relationship between policy and outcomes is accentuated by the ever greater interdependence of national policies within international organizations, to the extent that a direct causal relationship can rarely be assumed to exist between specific policy measures and observed patterns of behaviour (Ní Bhrolcháin and Dyson, 2007), lending a new salience to Galton's problem (see Chapter 3).

Although, as in other areas of comparative research, multiple methods strategies and contextualized approaches cannot be considered as a panacea (see Chapter 5), they are particularly valuable in evidence-based and policy evaluation research where an understanding of why a particular policy works in a specific setting is of critical importance.

International Policy Transfer and Learning

Much of the work on policy evaluation reported in the specialized literature is limited to single-case or within-country studies, generally undertaken in response to the need to assess the efficacy of a specific policy measure or programme (Davies et al., 2000b; Shaw et al., 2006; *International Journal of Evaluation*). By contrast, references in the literature on policy transfer and policy learning usually focus on international comparisons. International comparative policy tools and techniques are, therefore, more often applied in analysis of policy transfer and lesson drawing than in policy evaluation research.

Policy transfer and lesson drawing are concerned with the process whereby 'knowledge about policies, administrative arrangements, institutions and ideas in one political system (past or present) is used in the development of policies, administrative arrangements, institutions and ideas in another political system' (Dolowitz and Marsh, 2000: 5). Within this definition, policy transfer can be broadly couched to cover a variety of topics: 'goals, structure and content; policy instruments or administrative techniques; institutions; ideology; ideas, attitudes and concepts' (Dolowitz and Marsh, 1996: 350). Policy learning occurs when governments seeking to improve their policy responses to socioeconomic change and what are perceived as similar problems look to other countries, both for examples of how best to respond to the challenges they are facing and for ways of avoiding the mistakes made elsewhere.

This section considers the many dimensions of policy transfer and learning, including preconditions for successfully importing or exporting policies. It looks at how international institutions are stimulating the development of policy learning in their efforts to promote best practice.

UNDERSTANDING INTERNATIONAL POLICY TRANSFER

Policy transfer can be seen as a development from policy diffusion, which became a topic for scientific inquiry in the 1960s in the United States. Jack L. Walker (1969), for example, sought to explain why some American states adopted innovations more rapidly than others. This led him to investigate the system of social choice in policy making, as manifested in the parameters of policy decisions, including interstate communication networks, where emulation and competition play an important role. According to the diffusion hypothesis, social policy initiatives can be seen primarily as 'the outcomes of processes of imitation, whereby nations copy the efforts of welfare-state pioneers'

(Wilensky et al., 1985: 12). Early policy diffusion studies were more interested in process than in the content of policies. The focus shifted during the 1980s to the analysis of policy transfer, which directed attention towards comparisons of the substance of policies (for example Heidenheimer et al., 1983).

Two contrasting types of policy transfer are relevant to international comparative research: obligated or coercive transfer, often from international to national level; and voluntary multilateral transfer within and between countries, either during periods of socioeconomic transition that create the need for policy reform, or following periods of political change requiring innovative decision-making structures and policy ideas.

In the case of obligated transfer, supranational institutions directly impose policies on the countries in their ambit, for example the International Monetary Fund when it compels countries requesting loans to observe prescribed conditions (Dolowitz and Marsh, 1996: 348). Even though policy actors may not be interested in looking for examples of policy practice in other countries, their status as current or prospective members of an international organization, such as the United Nations, International Labour Organization, Council of Europe or European Union, draws them into policy transfer. Obligated policy transfer operates through treaties, regulations, directives, charters and other forms of hard and soft law, including the open method of coordination, agreed at supranational level and implemented at national level.

European Union social policy provides a widely cited example of obligated policy transfer, illustrating the difficulties policy actors face in reaching consensus across countries with very different socioeconomic and policy environments. Not only does the Union draft legislation that it imposes on member states, but the European Court of Justice also forces compliance and imposes sanctions for failure to comply. Although the open method of coordination offers a softer form of governance and opportunities for comparing practices, it nonetheless involves a degree of coercion through the naming and shaming of countries that do not meet the standards set at European level. Governments in the Central and East European countries came under considerable pressure during the late 1990s and early 2000s to adopt European law and adapt to the European social model as a condition for membership of the European Union; they were required to implement the large body of *acquis communautaires* that they had no hand in shaping. Membership of the European Union forced careful scrutiny of their welfare systems, questioning the traditional assumptions of longstanding member states, and opening up new policy perspectives.

Voluntary bilateral or multilateral transfer has become a topical issue in a context where governments at different stages of socioeconomic change and policy development are looking for lessons to guide them in formulating effective responses to similar challenges. The media regularly compare statistics on national practices with those of other countries, and international meetings of representatives of policy actors, including non-governmental organizations, provide opportunities for the exchange of ideas and experience, which can then feed into the policy process at national level. The benchmarking of national performance can be an important element contributing to policy learning since it involves constant comparison and mutual surveillance, often resulting in the questioning of received wisdom and stimulating greater competition between member states, while at the same time facilitating the exchange of information about best practice.

PRECONDITIONS FOR INTERNATIONAL POLICY TRANSFER AND POLICY LEARNING

Comparisons of the responses of different countries to common problems produce examples of measures that appear to have been successful in achieving their policy objectives. The aim of lesson drawing is to 'adapt and adopt' policies or programmes that have proved to be effective elsewhere (Rose, 2002: 5). Although it may occasionally be possible to implement a policy or programme introduced in another country without adaptation, more often than not some adjustment is necessary. Adaptation is, however, not a simple process. Countries start from different points. They do not have the same resources or policy mechanisms. Their policies are path dependent, which means that they need to be in a position not only to implement the practices that they want to adopt but also to escape from previous commitments. Learning from other countries may allow them to make progress, but will not necessarily enable them to catch up or to converge (Rose, 2002: 7, 21). A key question in lesson learning is, accordingly, about 'contingencies: <u>'Under what circumstances and to what extent will a programme that works there also work here?'</u> (Rose, 2002: 11, original underlining).

The transferability of policies between countries is largely dependent on the match between prevailing circumstances in the lesson-exporting and lesson-importing countries, and the interplay between policy environments and processes. A number of conditions thus need to be met before policies can be transported between countries (Rose, 2001: 7–9). The exporting and importing countries must be ideologically compatible; they need to have common objectives, a shared definition of the issues to be tackled, and governments that subscribe to similar political orientations, resources and values.

Richard Rose (2002: 6) argues that 'psychological proximity', implying political values and ideology, is more important than 'geographical proximity' in determining where a country should look for lessons. The United Kingdom and Ireland are, for example, much more likely to look to the United States or Australia than to Europe. The Nordic countries exceptionally combine psychological and geographical proximity (Rose, 2002: 15). Relatively little policy learning seems to have occurred between countries within the former Soviet bloc during the period of transition (Elster et al., 1998: 245). In areas such as old-age security, the Czech Republic, Hungary and Poland might have been expected to draw on their common legacy prior to and during the Soviet era. While the Czech policy choice can be seen as a return to its precommunist welfare traditions and a move towards Western Bismarckian and Beveridgean paradigms, Hungary and Poland were less restrained by their institutional legacy, and were encouraged by the World Bank to draw lessons from Latin American pension reform models (Müller, 2001: 59). The psychological affinity between the Baltic states would seem to be a major factor encouraging Latvia, Lithuania and, especially, Estonia to look to their Scandinavian neighbours for social policy lessons (Manning and Shaw, 1999). In addition, ideological compatibility may shift according to the government in power, further complicating the issue of where to look for the most suitable policy models.

Secondly, the policy process in provider and receiver countries needs to be both appropriate and compatible in terms of welfare design principles, structure and agency to enable formulation, implementation and delivery in another country. Within the European Union, where member state governments are responsible for determining their own funding arrangements, regulatory mechanisms and methods of delivery, policy learning may involve one or more of these stages, and exemplars may need to be sought in more than one country. Another complicating factor is that policies may be delivered at national or local level through public services in the exporting country, but through partnerships with business and the voluntary sector in the importing country. Differences in the structure of public finances and welfare delivery, and the public–private mix impose constraints on policy transfer. For instance, a policy measure borrowed from Sweden, where funding is from general taxation and provision is universal, might be financed in the importing country by employment-related insurance contributions and confined to contributors in the scheme, as in Italy or Spain.

Thirdly, policy learning and transfer have to be seen as desirable, feasible and practical, implying consideration of national opportunities and constraints, covering legitimacy and public acceptability of state intervention. Even in the case of obligated policy transfer, governments are left to adapt policies to suit national circumstances. It is rare that a policy can be transported without being adjusted in some way, requiring consideration of feasibility and practicality. Account also needs to be taken of the receptiveness or resistance to change at government level and among the public at large. Policies that are readily legitimated in one jurisdiction may not command public acceptance in another context, as demonstrated, for example, by reactions to supranational intervention to regulate working hours and conditions in the European Union. Legislation in the exporting country may impose strict regulatory conditions with high penalties for infringement, whereas, in the importing country, firms may be issued with general guidelines based on the business case, and left to devise their own implementation strategies.

Fourthly, policy transfer must be affordable and accountable in terms of available resources, perceived economic and social benefits, the costs of importation and adaptation, and the ability to demonstrate value for money. Affordability raises questions about the extent to which tax payers (individuals and businesses) are willing to contribute more for social protection, and about the most acceptable balance between public (national, regional or local government) and private (family and private sector) funding and delivery of welfare. Countries with high *per capita* incomes are unlikely to look for models in countries with low *per capita* incomes, although the reverse is sometimes true, for example when the International Monetary Fund recommends the best practices of advanced industrialized nations for developing countries (Rose, 2001: 8).

Although policy transfer may help to shape change, it may also contribute to implementation failure (Dolowitz and Marsh, 2000: 17). Three reasons are offered to help explain failure: if the importing country is insufficiently informed about how the policy or programme operates; if the transfer is incomplete so that some of the elements capable of explaining its success in the exporting country are not transferred; if insufficient attention is paid to the social, economic, political and ideological differences between exporting and importing countries.

When they are not obliged to follow international prescriptions and are not exposed to international scrutiny, or compelled to exchange experience, policy actors, whether they represent government, the economy or civil society, may show little interest in policy innovations in other countries. They may not consciously draw lessons from elsewhere. Nor do they necessarily keep a record of any examples of good practice that they choose to emulate. Governments may believe they do not have much to learn from experience elsewhere, precisely because their socioeconomic systems and policy environments are so different. They may, therefore, prefer to look to their own past and build on their own regional, national or local legacy (Büchs, 2007: 26).

The extent to which shared objectives can be translated into practice using the same or similar policies thus depends not only on their appropriateness for the importing country but also on the compatibility of the socioeconomic, political and cultural environments in the exporting and importing countries, and the willingness of governments to draw lessons from other jurisdictions. The closer countries are in terms of their political and welfare structures, psychological proximity, ideological compatibility, and socioeconomic and cultural characteristics, the more likely they are to be able to pool, and learn from, their policy experience. Countries with similar socioeconomic, political and cultural backgrounds tend to look to each other for examples of policy measures that have been implemented in response to similar problems. This does not mean that countries that are further apart may not also be able to learn from experience elsewhere, but they may need to make greater adaptations to the policies they are importing, or to consider more far-reaching changes to their structures of governance and the instruments they have available for policy formulation and delivery.

Enhancing Synergy between Research and Policy

Despite the seemingly insuperable obstacles to cooperation, the contribution made by the social and human sciences to the relationship between research and policy is considerable. Whether it be in the construction of the evidence base enabling the evaluation of policy effects, or in the analysis of the process of policy diffusion and the preconditions for successful policy transfer and lesson learning, the theoretical underpinnings, methods and techniques developed in international comparative research can be seen to apply in policy-relevant and policy-oriented research. They are particularly useful in enhancing the potential synergy between researchers and policy actors.

Drawing together the various dimensions explored in this chapter, the value of policy-oriented international comparative research in the social sciences and humanities for policy development can be said to lie in the contribution it makes by:

- extending the international knowledge base about socioeconomic change that policy makers draw on when formulating policies, thereby enabling the refinement of the concepts and indicators used by policy actors in determining policy responses;
- raising awareness among policy actors about how policy processes operate at various levels in society in diverse cultural contexts, and

how different policy instruments can be used to deal with similar problems;

- developing international indicators and benchmarks to assess the relative efficacy of policy delivery and evaluate policy outcomes;
- helping policy actors to understand the implications of policy for social practice by examining what works (or does not work) and, if so (or if not), why, with reference to different socioeconomic and political settings;
- assisting policy actors involved in policy transfer between countries by showing how a particular policy may need to be adapted if it is to be introduced in a different national policy setting;
- contributing towards making policy more effective in dealing with common socioeconomic issues by identifying good practice and the conditions required for successful implementation.

Although many of the sources on policy evaluation (for instance Davies et al., 2000b; Spencer et al., 2003; Shaw et al., 2006) referred to in this chapter do not set out specifically to address comparative issues, they provide a wealth of material and guidance that can be applied in international comparative studies. When policy processes and performances are being compared in a number of national, societal or cultural settings, multidisciplinary and multinational networking is a common response in assembling the range of knowledge, skills and competencies required to analyse and interpret observed phenomena, and assess the transferability of policy responses. As in other areas of comparative research, policy-oriented studies across nations, societies or cultures raise challenging issues of such great conceptual and contextual complexity that few researchers are equipped to deal adequately with them until they have been appropriately trained and have acquired considerable experience in the field. Effective management of team projects is therefore critical in ensuring that such studies are valid, reliable, valuable and relevant for policy formation and implementation.

7

Managing International Comparative Research

Managing multinational teams engaged in comparative social sciences and humanities projects that cross national, societal or cultural boundaries is infinitely more complex than organizing single- or two-country studies carried out by lone researchers or small national teams. Whether it concerns the conceptualization of the research topic, the formulation of research questions, the selection of units of comparison, team members and methods, or the interpretation and dissemination of findings, the coordination of international teams is rarely a straightforward process. Just as reports on projects and articles in internationally refereed journals tend to gloss over many of the practical problems encountered, and the findings of projects that fail to meet their objectives may never be publicized, it is all too easy to disregard the challenging and divisive issues that arise when researchers from different cultures, languages and disciplines work together to explore a question of mutual interest from a comparative perspective.

Nor can international research teams escape the habitual pressures exerted by funders and stakeholders compelling them to meet tight deadlines while remaining within limited budgets. Few, if any, externally funded projects are open ended, and most contributors to international team projects are not in a position to devote themselves single-mindedly to the task in hand, ignoring the competing demands made on their time and resources by other academic commitments. A further complicating factor in international comparative research in the social science and humanities is the need to take account of a whole range of contextual factors, not least the cultural backgrounds of researchers, the language communities to which they belong, the socioeconomic and political environments impinging on the phenomena under analysis, the institutional frameworks within which they are operating, the agendas of national and international funding agencies and the innumerable assessment procedures that researchers must undergo.

In revisiting the many issues raised throughout the book from an organizational perspective, this concluding chapter seeks to provide guidance on how to improve the effectiveness of international comparative research management. It first examines how the composition of research teams across disciplines and countries impacts on research design and implementation. In addressing the question of access to external funding for comparative research, the chapter explores the implications of different funding mechanisms for international cooperation, findings and dissemination, taking account of the expectations of sponsors and stakeholders, and the constraints they impose. It considers how the classification of disciplines as social or human sciences can influence funding opportunities and the subsequent conduct of international comparative research. The chapter concludes with a tentative assessment of the contribution that international comparative research is making to scientific inquiry, international understanding and the knowledge base in contemporary societies.

Developing International Research Governance

The chapters in this volume illustrate the great variety of approaches to international comparative research not only between countries but also between and within disciplines. International comparative researchers in the social sciences and humanities, interested in describing, understanding and explaining social phenomena in relation to their socioeconomic, political and cultural settings, call upon a wide range of disciplinary and cultural knowledge and expertise, all of which needs to be harnessed in managing multidisciplinary international research teams, if comparative projects are to fulfil their objectives by extending and deepening the international knowledge base.

This section begins by tracking changing practices in the management of international research projects and presents a set of guidelines derived from a professional and ethical code of practice, which was initially drawn up for socioeconomic research in Europe. The section examines some of the attempts that have been made to classify epistemologies according to national characteristics and in relation to national research cultures and traditions, before considering how they impact on the management of international cooperation in comparative research projects.

CHANGING PRACTICE IN INTERNATIONAL PROJECT MANAGEMENT

Much of the path-breaking literature analysing the comparative research process in the 1960s and 1970s was written from the perspective of single-nation research teams based in the United States. The early postwar years were characterized by the increasing predominance of American sociology, which then moved outside its own national borders, using foreign societies to test the validity of theories developed at home (critiqued, for example, by Armer and Grimshaw, 1973: xii). The emphasis in the literature in this early period was primarily on technical issues of conceptual equivalence, measurement reliability and inter-viewer bias, although awareness was growing in the United States of the need to earn the cooperation of local communities in other countries and to take account of the ethical issues raised by international projects (Portes, 1973: 149–50).

The conduct of large-scale fieldwork in different societal settings gave rise to a whole catalogue of previously uncharted problems. Topics were selected with little regard for the concerns and sensitivities of the countries involved, or political acceptability. Project organization was unsystematic making duplication a continual risk. Local social scientists were assigned a subordinate role, and were not given access to data. Countries (in Latin America for example) were exposed to a never-ending flow of researchers with little in return for local communities (Portes, 1973: 159–60). In addition, state-sponsored international surveys were charged with infringing national autonomy and perpetuating 'scientific colonialism' by treating foreign collaborators as 'hired hands'. They were suspected of facilitating armed intervention in the affairs of other countries by gathering 'intelligence'; and anthropologists using participant observation were accused of 'international imperialism', mainly because their fieldwork depended upon the cooperation of former imperial powers (Warwick, 1973: 202).

Already in the 1970s, a major challenge facing enlightened compara-tivists was to ensure the appropriateness of the methodological tools at their disposal in different research environments (Armer, 1973: 51). In reaction to the colonialism and imperialism of what is referred to as the 'safari' approach to international research (Szalai, 1977: 69), the East–West projects conducted in the 1980s under the auspices of the European Centre for the Coordination of Research and Documentation in the Social Sciences, based in Vienna, depended on consensus being reached among team members in the countries under study, and their active participa-tion in project design and delivery (Grootings, 1986: 275–6, 284). The projects coordinated by the Vienna Centre were, however, rarely strictly speaking comparative, defined in the first chapter of this volume as studies of societies, countries, cultures, systems, institutions, social structures and change over time and space, carried out with the intention of using the same research tools to compare systematically the manifestations of phenomena in more than one temporal or spatial sociocultural setting.

The administrative experience gained from managing international research projects at the Vienna Centre in the 1980s led Peter Grootings (1986: 295) to realize that the larger the number of countries involved and, accordingly, the lower the level of agreement about basic paradigms, the more likely it was that the organizational structure would be bureaucratic and that the output would take the form of a series of parallel national monographs. By contrast, the smaller the number of countries and the more they shared basic paradigms, the more likely it was that cooperation would be intense and substantial throughout the research, and the more rewarding would be the comparative analysis. Despite these observations, Grootings was aware that research design needed to be flexible enough to cope with different organizational structures and objectives (see Chapter 3 in this volume).

In terms of research governance, a major shift in emphasis had occurred by the turn of the twenty-first century. In place of national research teams venturing into unknown territory equipped with Western research tools and perceptions, international networking was being actively promoted as the most viable and productive form of international cooperation. Researchers had to learn how to adapt their research objectives and methods to make them applicable and acceptable in the different societies they were investigating, at the risk of reducing comparisons to the lowest common denominator. A legitimate aim for members of research teams in the twenty-first century is to work together to find the greatest common ground capable of commanding a consensus.

In many respects, the comments and insights of the 1970s, as well as the scepticism expressed in the 1980s about the rigour and reliability of comparative approaches, remain relevant for international comparative researchers in the twenty-first century. International teams involved in large multinational projects are invariably operating across several nations, societies or cultures, with which researchers from any one of the contributing countries may not be familiar. In line with the Vienna Centre's large-scale project model, standard practice is for national teams to work in parallel, each on their own part of a study. In the past, the research coordinator or national coordinating team would design the project alone and then issue instructions for its implementation. Today, it is more customary for international project team members to develop the research design jointly, using matching samples, and agreeing on conceptual equivalence. Occasionally, in accordance with cultural preferences and practices, individual national teams may agree to differ in selecting the techniques to be applied, for example when deciding whether to prioritize quantitative or qualitative approaches, or whether to conduct postal or telephone surveys, or face-to-face interviews. The contractual project specifications are then usually implemented simultaneously at the relevant study sites. In well-managed and integrated projects, the analysis, interpretation and dissemination of findings are often carried out collectively, with national teams taking responsibility for coordinating and reporting on a specific topic or stage in the research.

As with the Vienna Centre projects, however, many of the studies conducted by international teams of researchers may fail to meet systematic comparative criteria due, in no small part, to cultural incompatibilities between team members, making the composition and management of research teams a critical factor in determining the likely outcome of a project.

MEETING INTERNATIONAL STANDARDS IN THE MANAGEMENT OF INTERNATIONAL PROJECTS

Many coordinators of international comparative research projects learn about project management on the job. The inflation in the number of international networks and projects being funded, particularly at European level, has created the need for codes of practice if the work is to comply with internationally recognized professional standards. It has also become incumbent on sponsors to ensure good governance of research by underwriting high ethical and technical standards, requiring a delicate balance to be struck between the control over research by funders and the autonomy of research teams.

The list presented below is an abridged and adapted version of the guidelines drawn up by the RESPECT project (Dench et al., 2004) as the basis for a voluntary code of practice for the conduct of socioeconomic research in Europe. The code is founded on three main principles, which individual researchers, their funders and employers are required to respect: upholding scientific standards; compliance with the law; and avoidance of social and personal harm. The bullet points under these three headings in the checklist below record the items extracted from the code that are most relevant for the effective management of teams and networks engaged in international comparative research projects. The annotations indicate how they would need to be interpreted to take account of the international comparative dimension.

Upholding scientific standards

- declare any conflict of interest that may arise in the research funding or design, or in the scientific evaluation of proposals or peer review of work by other researchers;

In international comparative research, conflicts of interest can arise due to the different requirements of national institutions and the expectations associated with competing schools of thought.

- critically question authorities and assumptions about the research design to avoid predetermining the research outcome and excluding unwanted findings;

In international projects, it is important to bear in mind that funding agencies may be politically motivated and inclined to support teams that share the same ideological assumptions and research traditions.

- ensure the use of appropriate methodologies and the availability of appropriate skills and qualifications in the research team;

In constituting an international team of researchers, coordinators need to strike a balance between team members capable of working together across cultures and those known to possess specific and complementary research skills and qualifications.

- acknowledge fully previous and concurrent research (data, concepts and methodology), including research that challenges findings;

Literature reviews in international comparative projects need to take account of a very wide range of national and disciplinary studies, of which they may not previously have been aware and which may not concord with their hypotheses.

- ensure factual accuracy and avoid fabrication, suppression or misinterpretation of data;

In international comparisons, coordinators need to remain especially alert to issues of linguistic and cultural understanding and interpretation that may result in misuse of data and discrepant or discordant findings.

- ensure that research findings are reported truthfully, accurately, clearly, comprehensively and without distortion;

International comparative research projects are notorious for collecting large amounts of data that not all team members are able to access in the original language. Reports are necessarily selective. Research coordinators need to ensure that all possible means are used to cross-check for accuracy, consistency and optimal comprehensiveness.

- demonstrate an awareness of the limitations of the research, including the ways in which the characteristics or values of the researchers may have influenced the research process and outcomes;

report fully on any methodologies used and any results obtained, including the probability of errors;

Researcher bias is a problem at all stages in international comparative research. Reports should record fully the issues raised by the different methodological approaches involved and their impact on findings.

- honour contractual obligations to funders and employers;

Coordinators need to remain mindful of the reputation acquired by researchers from different national backgrounds for being more or less efficient in meeting deadlines, observing the specifications stipulated by sponsors, delivering agreed outputs and remaining within budget.

- declare the source of funding in any communication about the research.

In international comparative research, information about funding sources should be noted in recognition of the expectations of sponsors regarding the various stages in the research process and the findings.

Compliance with the law

- find out about the laws governing the countries involved in the research;

Different countries have different legal requirements, for example about managing budgets and peer reviewing, which may affect cooperation.

- comply with national and international laws, with particular reference to intellectual property (permissions, attribution of author- ship, acknowledgement of sources) and data protection (collection, processing, security and confidentiality of personal data).

Variations in the substance and strictness of implementation of laws regarding data protection and intellectual property between countries can affect participation of team members at different stages in the research.

Avoidance of social and personal harm

- ensure that the results of the research carried out do not harm society but are of benefit to it by improving knowledge and understanding, and maximizing utility and relevance;

Not all national governments, funding agencies and research institutions attach the same importance to the social impact of research, resulting in different expectations among participants in international projects.

- Avoid social and personal harm, including harassment and discrimi- nation, by ensuring that participation is voluntary and based on informed consent, that the views of relevant stakeholders are taken into account, and that results are accessible to them.

Research coordinators need to remain alert to the varying ways in which ethical codes are laid down and observed in different countries. High ethical standards may not be universally applied.

Most of the items included in the list have been addressed at some point in this volume. Since they are not always self-evident for researchers participating in international teams, and may lead to incompatibilities and disagreements between team members, a number of key points are reiterated and developed further in the remainder of the chapter.

BUILDING INTERNATIONAL RESEARCH TEAMS

Reasons are not difficult to find to explain why international research that sets out to be comparative does not always conform strictly to the criteria contained in the definition of comparative studies or adopt the requirements of the code of practice presented above. The lack of agreement over the very existence of a distinct comparative method or methodology reported in Chapter 1 could alone explain why it may be impossible to reach consensus among researchers about research design. The wide-ranging survey of the development of disciplinary interest in international comparative research in Chapter 2 highlights variations from one discipline to another in the amount of interest shown in comparative studies over time and space, in the approaches and strategies adopted, and in the amount of reflexivity regarding comparative methods. Reference is also made at the beginning of this section to differences in the ways in which international comparative research has developed in particular countries, illustrated by the dominance and ethnocentrism across disciplines in the methods literature emanating from the United States in the immediate postwar period. In the European context, by the early 1980s, comparativists were beginning to recognize the need, when constituting international research teams, to take account of the impact that different national research traditions, 'prevailing theoretical and methodological approaches' and 'the extra-scientific context of investigation' could have on the research process (Nießen, 1984: xv).

Although it might appear logical to form a research team once decisions have been reached about research design, in practice, as noted in Chapter 3, the order of events is frequently reversed. Constituting and managing an international team of researchers, brought together to investigate a predefined and specified topic in response to a call for proposals, is far more demanding than inviting researchers who have already worked collectively on similar topics to cooperate in designing a project on a research question of their own choosing. In small-scale projects, especially in the humanities, the research design is most likely to be decided by an individual researcher's disciplinary background, cultural and linguistic knowledge and expertise, and material resources. Large international teams are, of necessity, frequently built around existing networks or a core of researchers who share similar research cultures and linguistic affinity, expectations and working practices. Whatever the order of events, size of projects and teams, the disciplinary mix and national backgrounds of team members are of primary importance if international cooperation is to be successful. An essential task for project coordinators is to seek to avoid counterproductive clashes of cultures and conflicts of interest, resulting from differences in intellectual styles and national research traditions.

Exploring intellectual styles

At the time in the early 1980s when the Vienna Centre was considering ways of developing alternatives to large-scale international surveys, Johan Galtung (1982: 25–8) devoted part of his contribution at a seminar on the problems of theory, methodology and organization in cross-national comparative research to the question of intellectual styles. He identified differences at the epistemological level between three dominant 'intellectual styles' in the Western world: Saxonic, Teutonic and Gallic, corresponding to ideal types in the Weberian sense. These Western styles were contrasted with the Nipponic (oriental) style.

The distinction between the four styles is based on the way that intellectuals in each country perform certain tasks: those involving the exploration of paradigms (what kinds of phenomena exist); empirical tasks associated with description; explanatory or theoretical tasks; and the commentary produced on the performance of other intellectuals. The relative emphasis placed on these four tasks, illustrated in Figure 7.1, makes it possible to characterize the intellectual styles of the four research communities.

The Saxonic and Nipponic styles are shown to be strong on data collection and facts, but weaker on the philosophical basis and theory formation. Within the Saxonic style, Galtung distinguishes between the American tendency to favour extensive data collection (large number of cases but limited information on each in the search for universal laws) and the British preference for intensive data collection through case studies, ideographic history and social anthropology. Richard Rose

Figure 7.1   Characterizing intellectual styles

	Saxonic	*Teutonic*	*Gallic*	*Nipponic*
paradigm (exploration)	weak	strong	strong	weak
description (empirical, data)	very strong	weak	weak	strong
explanation (theoretical)	weak	very strong	very strong	weak
commentary	strong	strong	strong	very strong

Source: Galtung, 1982: 26, with kind permission of the author.

(1991: 450) makes a similar distinction when he claims that American political scientists are often universalistic in interpreting American evidence, whereas British writers lean towards 'excessive particularization'. In epistemological terms, the two Saxonic-style countries could be said to 'share the conviction that knowledge rests on documentation', although their perception of what is a fact differs (Galtung, 1982: 26). In addition to a strong emphasis on descriptive data, the Nipponic style is, by contrast, most strongly characterized by its attachment to the commentary task.

The Teutonic and Gallic intellectual styles are depicted as more cerebral, with data being used for illustration rather than confirmation. Again differences are noted between the Teutonic style, with its 'search for the axiomatic pyramid that facilitates the much honoured pursuits of *Zurückführung* and *Ableitung*', and the more complex Gallic style, with its 'pyramidal exercises couched in highly embroidered, artistic forms of expression where *elegance* plays a key role as a carrier of conviction power' (Galtung, 1982: 26, original emphasis).

Galtung (1982: 27) bases his search for variables to explain the differences in emphasis on two related assumptions. Firstly, he suggests that data unite and facilitate dialogue, whereas theories divide. Secondly, the Saxonic and Nipponic styles are founded on consensus and harmony, whereas the Teutonic/Gallic styles thrive on dissent and disharmony. These are shown to be important factors determining the extent to which researchers associated with different styles are likely to be able to cooperate constructively in international comparative research projects.

Historians of statistics have identified similar characteristics in the sociopolitical traditions of Britain, France and Germany. For example, Alain Desrosières (1996: 21–4) shows how differences in political styles influence national statistical systems. While Britain is recognized for its empiricism and a much less codified system, described as 'political arithmetic', the term 'statistics' is used in Germany, with its tradition of legalism, to refer to all aspects of the formal description of states. French centralism and Cartesianism resulted in a high level of legitimacy being attributed to statistical institutions. Desrosières (1996) examines how these differences in intellectual traditions result in disparities in the categories used to collect and analyse data and, consequently, in their comparability (see also Chapters 4 and 6).

Contrasting national research cultures

The contrasts in cultural backgrounds between French (Gallic) and British (Saxonic) researchers have been examined in greater detail by Jean Tennom (1995). He uses the Franco-British comparison to illustrate why, despite the geographical proximity of the two countries, Franco-British cooperation can often be difficult. While French researchers tend to operate in a closed self-contained world of discourse and debate, as depicted by Galtung (1982), British researchers, like their American counterparts, with their undoubted advantage of possessing an international language as their mother tongue, are more likely to hold an Anglocentric view of the world and to expect other research communities to adopt their *modus operandi* in international networks. Tennom (1995: 271–4) argues that the very different research traditions and contexts of British and French researchers inform their approaches to international cooperation. The status of civil servants conferred on the researchers employed by the Centre national de la recherche scientifique (CNRS) in France affords them protection from external interference, enabling them to concentrate on fundamental research, theoretical and conceptual work, and the production of new knowledge.

At the time when Tennom was writing in the mid-1990s, CNRS researchers were relatively well cushioned from the major economic, political and social concerns of the day. They were not obliged to attract external funding to enable them to engage in research on topics of their own choosing. In a situation where evaluation did not directly determine funding, they lacked the incentive to disseminate their findings widely through internationally reviewed publications.

By contrast, Tennom (1995: 275) portrays British researchers at that time as driven by the market demands of productivity, 'maximum output for minimum input', forcing them to become entrepreneurs. He argues that they are more likely than their French opposite numbers to concentrate on applied, policy-relevant research and the 'user interface' (see Chapter 6), implying that they will seek to avoid 'theoretical excursions and intellectual adventurousness'. Operating within a context of transparency and public accountability, the onus is on British researchers to demonstrate value for money. They know that their performance is being constantly monitored, assessed and called into question, which may help to explain why they adopt an instrumental approach to their work, maximizing opportunities to cooperate with industry and other potential funders and engaging with stakeholders in the policy arena.

By the early 2000s, these differences were becoming less marked. Social science and humanities researchers in France were being increasingly exposed to market forces. They were under pressure to become more accountable like their British counterparts, in principle thereby easing some of the barriers to effective Franco-British cooperation.

Implications of different intellectual styles and research cultures

Differences in intellectual styles and research cultures help to explain many of the obstacles to international cooperation and understanding between national research communities. The preference in international studies carried out by British researchers for cross-Atlantic or for Antipodean rather than cross-Channel partners can, for example, be largely attributed to their common intellectual and linguistic roots. Researchers in the United States and the United Kingdom have more difficulty in cooperating with Britain's European neighbours, illustrated in the examples cited above by the Gallic and Teutonic intellectual styles.

The problems resulting from differences in research traditions and cultures are not confined to the countries mentioned in this section. Galtung's (1982) description of the Nipponic style and the many reports emanating from researchers associated with the Vienna Centre commenting on East–West cooperative projects (for example Berting, 1987; Deacon, 1987; Kinnear, 1987; Lesage, 1987) provide some indication of the extent to which cultural diversity can affect the coherence and integrity of international comparative research across a much wider range of countries and paradigms. Researchers in Western Europe faced a steep learning curve when research cooperation among the existing member states in the European Union was extended to Central and Eastern Europe through the European Commission's framework programmes in the 1990s, in preparation for new waves of enlargement. Cooperation with countries in the Middle East, South East Asia, Latin America and Africa is, in relative terms, still in its infancy and raises many more cultural issues.

The cultural and 'touristic bias' associated with the preferences of researchers for working in particular environments has long been a concern for team coordinators in international collaborative research (Warwick and Osherson, 1973: 34). The value bias of researchers, due to their sociocultural, ideological and epistemological predispositions cannot be ignored in data collection, analysis and interpretation, since it may result, among other problems, in skewed case selection and flawed interpretation of data, ultimately affecting the outcome of the research (see Chapter 4). Operating within international teams provides a powerful test of objectivity if the potential value bias created by national research cultures and epistemological traditions is to be overcome.

As demonstrated by Galtung's (1982) examples, the preferences for certain epistemological approaches related to different intellectual styles and research cultures may reinforce barriers to effective international cooperation. It is, for instance, difficult to generate productive discussion and exchange of ideas and experience between research team members that consider themselves to be strongly wedded to either quantitative or qualitative methods (Hantrais, 2005a: 412). Within the two opposing paradigms, the issues that have to be addressed by national teams conducting comparative research may be more obvious for proponents of qualitative than of quantitative approaches, precisely because qualitative analysis is so closely concerned with the cultural embedding of phenomena (see Chapters 4 and 5). Whereas the most challenging problems identified by researchers using quantitative approaches largely involve the availability, reliability and comparability of data, many of the difficulties encountered in projects and networks adopting qualitative approaches relate to potential subjective bias and differences in understandings of concepts and cultural contexts within research teams. While these issues are by no means absent in quantitative project design and implementation, they tend to be magnified in qualitative studies due to the importance attributed to in-depth analysis and variations in conceptual understanding.

In addition, and irrespective of the methodological approach adopted, the key concepts involved in international research are frequently politically and ideologically charged. Interpretations of events by participants – insider knowledge can easily become insider bias – is therefore likely to be influenced by national politics and the ideologically driven preferences of sponsors, as well as by national and disciplinary research cultures. One of the potentially useful scientific by-products of differences in intellectual styles, research traditions, ideologies and cultures is that researchers, as well as the environments within which they are trained and work, can become objects of comparative study in their own right, as illustrated in this chapter.

Confronting cultural and linguistic barriers to effective cooperation

In constituting research teams, all cooperative ventures have to face practical issues, such as constraints on the time that individual researchers can devote to the research, their engagement with a particular topic, commitment to the work, and the compatibility of personalities. In international comparative research, project teams have to contend with additional barriers. Issues concerning familiarity with other cultures and languages, and ideological preferences for working in certain contexts or on certain topics can prove to be greater obstacles than anticipated, even among seasoned international researchers. This may help to explain why project reports and publications may take the form of a series of parallel country studies and lack an integrated comparative analysis.

The development of a European Research Area within the European Union and the extension of its boundaries to Central and Eastern Europe undoubtedly created a new openness to the rich variety of cultures and languages that it contains. In recognition of the centrality of research in a knowledge-based society, the aim of the European Research Area is to increase the global impact of European research and, thereby, prevent Europe from falling behind the United States. However, in the social sciences and humanities, the very diversity of the cultures being investigated presents major challenges to a common research endeavour. At the same time, the enlargement of the Union has reinforced the dominance of English as the working language for trans-European networks and teams, and hence of British researchers as project coordinators. They bring with them their intellectual styles and working practices, potentially creating a new form of imperialism, but without dispelling the widely held impression that British researchers are insular and not fully committed to the European concept.

Even if project members are fluent in two or three languages and use English as their working language, it is unusual for researchers involved in multinational projects to have an equal command of all the languages concerned, the more so when few European projects or networks in the social sciences and humanities are limited to only three or four language communities. It is axiomatic that researchers who cannot operate in several languages will have to rely on intermediaries to provide what is inevitably filtered and selective access to other cultures, thereby reinforcing concern about latent bias.

An initial response to the problem is to insist when selecting team members that all the contributors to contextually embedded comparative projects have prior experience of working across languages and cultures, making them aware of the issues involved. Problems of access to data and inconsistencies in the available data can often be resolved by using local informants and expertise (see Chapter 4). To avoid insider bias and misinterpretation of national situations, opportunities can usefully be created for bilateral cross-border fieldwork, collective analysis and interpretation of data, and the participation of team members in the drafting of interim reports using the Internet (Hantrais, 2004b: 21).

Regular project workshops throughout the duration of the research are an occasion for team members, and especially research assistants, to reflect collectively on central concepts and the most appropriate ways of conducting fieldwork, processing and interpreting findings, while remaining alert to the need to record any differences in procedures that may impinge on findings. Intensive discussion of concepts, scrutiny of interpretations among team members, research subjects and stake-holders, and the confrontation of findings obtained by combining a variety of methodological approaches are valuable devices in helping research teams to avoid bias, prevent paradigm wars, and guard against drawing ill-founded conclusions (see Chapter 5).

Just as the mix of intellectual styles can create barriers to effective team working, management styles are also likely to be contested by team members from different research cultures. The success of the European Social Survey in standardizing data collection and maximizing compara-bility, seen as a major problem in large-scale surveys, is attributable to its tight '"top-down" organizational structure', which is combined with 'a bottom-up process' (Bryson and Jowell, 2001: 14; Jowell et al., 2007a: 26). However, some team members may resist top-down management, and subgroups may form among researchers who share similar perspectives and research cultures. Negotiating and diplomatic skills are, therefore, key competencies that coordinators of international comparative projects need to possess, again underlining the importance of the ability to select sufficiently compatible team members and to ensure that, in the short time available, they work together productively despite, or even because of, epistemological and cultural differences.

Funding International Comparative Research

Much of the funding for international social science and humanities research in the postwar period was provided by national agencies (research councils and academies) or international organizations interested in collecting economic data, tracking sociodemographic trends, and mapping political systems and behaviour across large numbers of regions and countries (see Chapter 1). The concept of national and international team working was progressively extended from the natural to the social and human sciences. A decade after the establishment of the Vienna Centre, national research councils and academies in the wider Europe came together to fund international initiatives conducted by multinational teams under the auspices of the European Science Foundation, which was set up in 1974 to represent all scientific disciplines. Within the context of the European Union, the launch of a Targeted Socio-Economic Research strand in the European Commission's fourth framework programme for research and development in 1996 provided a fresh incentive for the development of international networks of researchers in the social sciences and humanities, independently from national funding agencies. An important objective of the European Research Area, when it was created in 2000, was to reinforce the coherence of research activities and policies conducted within Europe, including 'socio-economic intelligence at national and European levels' (Commission of the European Communities, 2000: 28).

This section examines not only how the requirements of national and international funding agencies can affect the conduct of comparative projects, but also how the opportunities for obtaining financial support and sponsorship can be influenced by national and international practices with regard to the classification of research within the social sciences and humanities. It concludes by commenting on the ways in which the requirements of funders impact on outputs and dissemination strategies in international comparative research.

IMPLICATIONS OF FUNDING ARRANGEMENTS FOR COMPARATIVE RESEARCH

The requirements of funders, as expressed in calls for proposals, particularly in policy-relevant research (see Chapter 6), have come to play an increasingly important role in prescribing the object of inquiry and research methods in the social sciences and humanities. They also influence the ensuing choices that researchers need to make in designing international comparative projects. This trend is especially apparent in a situation where funding agencies seeking to promote large-scale programmes, notably the European Commission's framework programmes, have reduced the number of opportunities for responsive (bottom-up) mode funding.

Few, if any, large-scale multinational research projects are accomplished without financial support from external sponsors. In most research projects, the object of inquiry, comparators and methods are predetermined by funding agencies when they draw up programme specifications, generally following a process of consultation within the research and policy communities, with the purpose of identifying future research needs. The large-scale multinational networks and team projects in the social sciences and humanities, funded by the European Commission are, for example, designed to answer the needs of the policy directorates-general, who, in parallel, fund their own desk studies on topics relevant to their policy concerns.

The European Science Foundation, like many national research councils, academies and foundations, offers relatively few opportunities for completely responsive-mode project funding for international projects (see Chapter 1). Although researchers usually have some flexibility in programme mode to determine the parameters of specific projects, they must nonetheless be able to demonstrate how their work will contribute to the overall objectives of the programme.

Priority setting inevitably entails political bias, but political imperatives also affect the conduct of research in less overt ways. The selection of project and network partners and coordinators may be driven less by scientific criteria than by the need to include countries representing different regions, for example in the European Research Area, and to avoid overrepresentation of certain member states or disciplines within a programme. In Framework Programme 5, for instance, the Commission required proposers to involve at least two different member states or one member and one associated state. It also sought to ensure that less frequently chosen member states would be adequately represented, and that candidate countries would be integrated into the European Research Area. The politics of the selection of participating countries raises further methodological issues concerning the impact of sampling criteria on the findings: the question of how representative the countries selected are of the phenomena under study; the extent to which partners acting as native informants are influenced by insider bias; and the conditions under which policy-relevant findings can be extrapolated to different socioeconomic environments (see Chapters 3, 4 and 6).

Funding agencies, for example some national research councils, supporting both thematic programmes and responsive-mode grant schemes are often faced with a dilemma when deciding whether to prioritize political or scientific objectives. They have to maintain a delicate balance between support for research that meets the highest quality criteria and research that corresponds to programmatic needs, which brings other factors into play. When projects and networks within a programme are selected primarily on grounds of scientific quality, several projects may address the same topic, while other important parts of a call may not be covered. To fill gaps in thematic coverage, subsequent calls may need to be reshaped to exclude certain areas and stimulate interest in undersubscribed or emerging topics, but duplication of effort is more difficult to avoid in cases where several high quality proposals address the same topic, and may be using similar approaches (see Chapter 6).

Given that most funding agencies, of necessity, concentrate their resources on topics that are likely to be of current interest and to have policy relevance, it is not easy for researchers to open up new fields of inquiry, unless they are able to influence the research agenda of major funders by becoming closely involved in consultation and lobbying activities. In 2007, the European Union's newly created European Research Council adopted an approach more open to innovation when it began funding individual scientists from any discipline to conduct world-class research on topics and at locations of their own choosing, thereby directing the available funds towards individual research excellence rather than international networks and predetermined topics.

CLASSIFYING SOCIAL AND HUMAN SCIENCE DISCIPLINES

Over the years, clusters of disciplines have come to be connoted together in different combinations to the extent that the distinction often made between the social and human sciences may vary from one country to another. The lack of consistency between countries in the ways in which disciplines are classified as belonging to the social sciences or humanities can present problems in comparative studies carried out by international teams when they are applying for funding. The distinction that is generally drawn between social science and humanities disciplines is thus another aspect of the linkages between epistemologies and national characteristics that is relevant to an understanding of the theory, methodology and practice of international comparative research.

This subsection examines further the impact that the value bias associated with the national and disciplinary composition of international research teams can have on cooperation in comparative research projects. It explores the implications of this bias, which can be seen not only in research careers, assessment and access to funding and technical resources, but also in the design of international comparative projects, since disciplinary classifications also determine the likelihood that researchers in particular disciplines and countries will be able to cooperate successfully within international teams.

Disciplinary groupings within social sciences and humanities

When the social and human sciences are contrasted with the natural sciences, they are frequently considered as a composite grouping. More than a century after the founding fathers of sociology and the social sciences set out to demonstrate that the research methods used in 'non-natural' science disciplines can be scientific, many natural scientists remain unconvinced, and some social and human scientists are also doubtful, as to whether certain disciplines and subdisciplines should bear the scientific label. Subdisciplines or specific areas within disciplines – economics (macroeconomics), linguistics (phonology), psychology (experimental psychology) and archaeology (carbon dating) – are generally considered to come closer to the natural (and life) sciences due to their ability to quantify and replicate observations, and this is reflected in the approaches they adopt in comparative studies (see Chapter 2).

When they are in competition with natural sciences for funding, these subdisciplines are able to argue the case on 'scientific grounds' for large-scale equipment to be used by research teams. They are generally in a stronger position to attract substantial funding than disciplines that are thought to rely essentially on archival and documentary materials being used by lone researchers. Hence, comparative studies in social sciences and humanities that are dependent on techniques for large-scale data collection and analysis are often able to attract the resources needed to invest in expensive hardware, whereas the disciplines unable to make a convincing 'large science' case tend to remain underfunded.

This pattern is reflected in the ways in which the social sciences and humanities are forced to 'sell' themselves to the public and to government (Commission on the Social Sciences, 2003; British Academy, 2004; European Science Foundation, 2007), and, consequently, in the numbers of researchers they employ. It is also found in provision for training in research methods, where substantial resources are more readily invested in quantitative methods, prompted by fears that the coming generations of researchers will be ill equipped to handle the data needs of national governments and international organizations. When, for example, in the late 1990s, the British Economic and Social Research Council launched a major programme specifically targeting research methods, effort was heavily concentrated on quantitative skills. Between 2003 and 2007, the European Science Foundation supported a programme of integrated workshops and seminars to train social scientists in the quantitative skills needed for the analysis of complex social scientific data, such as pan-European datasets, with the aim of advancing comparative quantitative social science. This followed on from the significant contribution made to the advancement of comparative methods in the late 1990s and early 2000s by a multinational team of researchers, supported first by the Foundation and then by the European Commission's framework programmes, in a collaborative project that was aimed at achieving 'uncompromisingly high standards' in social surveys (Mohler, 2007: 166).

Attributing disciplinary labels

The epistemological traditions associated with different disciplines come into play when groupings for the social sciences are distinguished from those for the humanities. The components of these groupings and the positioning of particular disciplines vary within and between countries and at supranational level. The first column of Figure 7.2 illustrates the composition of the core disciplines in the European Science Foundation's two Social Science Standing Committees: one for social sciences and the other for humanities. The remaining columns in the two sections show how disciplines are distributed between the social sciences and humanities in France (CNRS and university assessment panels) and the United Kingdom (two research councils and university assessment panels). In the British case, assessment panels are not classified as belonging explicitly to the social science or humanities. Rather, the panels are organized according to generic groupings. This means that the relevant panels would, for example, be assigned all research in education, history, linguistics or psychology irrespective of methods and subject matter.

In some cases, disciplinary distribution is consistent across all five columns: business and management studies, demography, economics, environmental studies, geography, law, political science, social anthropology and sociology belong to the social sciences; and archaeology, arts, history, linguistics, languages and literature, philosophy and religion come under the humanities, suggesting that researchers in these disciplines work within similar parameters. In the United Kingdom, ESRC also classifies economic and social history, and linguistics as social sciences, and AHRC includes law as humanities, indicating how they straddle the disciplines. Education and psychology are assigned to British social sciences, whereas they are classified as humanities in France. They appear in both groupings for ESF, as do anthropology for ESF and geography for French universities. Media and communications appear under social sciences for ESF and as humanities elsewhere, while sports-related subjects are social sciences in British universities and humanities subjects in French universities.

Some disciplinary labels are peculiar to one of the two countries considered or to one institution: area and development studies, science and technology, social policy/social work belong to British social science, as does librarianship (also RAE humanities); comparative literature is specific to French university research in the humanities; women's studies is under ESF social sciences, and Oriental and African studies under ESF humanities. ESF and British research share a social science interest in international studies, statistics and computing, and ESF and French university humanities have a common interest in history of science.

Figure 7.2   Distribution of social science and humanities disciplines, early 2000s

ESF Social Sciences	UK ESRC	FR CNRS Social Sciences	UK Research Assessment Exercise	FR University Research Assessment
business & administrative sciences	management & business studies	management	business & management studies	management
demography	demography	demography	demography	demography
economics	economics	economics	economics/econometrics	economics
environmental sciences	environmental planning	environment	architecture & built environment, planning	environment, urbanism
geography	human geography	geography	geography, development & environmental studies	space, territory & society
law	sociolegal studies & criminology	law	law	history of law & institutions
political sciences	political science	political science	politics	political science
social anthropology	social anthropology	anthropology & ethnology	anthropology	ethnology & anthropology
sociology	sociology	sociology	sociology	sociology
	economic & social history			
	linguistics			
communication sciences			sports-related subjects	
pedagogy & education	education		education	
psychology & cognitive science	psychology		psychology	

ESF Social Sciences	UK ESRC	FR CNRS Social Sciences	UK Research Assessment Exercise	FR University Research Assessment
women's studies	area studies & development studies; science, technology & innovation; social policy, social work		library & information management; social work, social policy & administration	
international relations; social statistics & informatics	international studies; statistics, methods & computing		international studies	

ESF Humanities	UK AHRC	FR CNRS Human sciences	UK Research Assessment Exercise	FR University Research Assessment
archaeology	archaeology	archaeology	archaeology	history, civilization, art & archaeology
art & art history; music & musicology	visual & performing arts, music	arts	art & design, art history, music, performing arts	arts, history of art & music
history	ancient history, medieval & modern history	pre-history, ancient & medieval history, modern & contemporary history	history	pre-history
linguistics; literature, classical studies	linguistics; language & literature, classics	language(s) & discourse; language & literature	linguistics; language & literature	linguistics; language & literature, regional languages & cultures

ESF Social Sciences	UK ESRC	FR CNRS Social Sciences	UK Research Assessment Exercise	FR University Research Assessment
philosophy	philosophy	philosophy	philosophy	philosophy
religion & theology	religious studies	religion	theology, religious studies	theology
anthropology, ethnology & folklore	law			physical, human, socioeconomic geography
psychology, cognitive science		psychology		clinical & social psychology
pedagogical & educational research		science of education		science of education
	media	communication	communication, cultural & media studies	information science & communication
				communication
				sports-related subjects
Oriental & African studies	librarianship, information & museum studies			comparative literature
history & philosophy of science				epistemology & history of science

Sources: www.esf.org/research-areas/social-sciences.html; www.esf.org/research-areas/humanities/about.html; www.cnrs.fr; www.rae.ac.uk; www.cpu.fr

Key: ESF – European Science Foundation; ESRC – Economic and Social Research Council; AHRC – Arts and Humanities Research Council; CNRS – Centre national de la recherche scientifique.

Implications of disciplinary labelling for research funding

The ways in which disciplinary boundaries and traditions have been constructed within and across countries are likely to affect the ability of researchers from different disciplines to obtain funding and to work together in international teams. For example, although ESRC and AHRC in the United Kingdom liaise closely to decide how best to support researchers who straddle disciplinary boundaries, ESRC commands a much larger budget than AHRC, on grounds that the needs of the humanities are more modest. Consequently, British researchers in disciplines that are considered to belong to the social and human sciences may have an interest in presenting their proposals for funding as social scientists, whereas the reverse might apply in France where the humanities cover many more disciplines than the social sciences.

Researchers employed by CNRS are funded to work full time on their research, whereas university researchers in France and most other countries are usually expected to devote a large proportion of their time to teaching and related activities. A particular complication for French researchers in some disciplines, as indicated in the figure, is that their area of study is not supported by CNRS. Some disciplines are overrepresented in the university sector and un(der)represented in CNRS, most notably psychology, education, and sports science, language and communication, languages and literature, philosophy and arts; the situation is reversed for ethnology and anthropology. All the social science disciplines are underrepresented in CNRS (Hantrais, 2006c: table 17). The implication is that researchers in un(der)represented disciplines in CNRS will have difficulty in pursuing a research career in France, due to the small number of research positions available in their respective disciplines.

This ambivalence can give rise to anomalous situations when applications are made for international funding such as that provided by the ESF. Proposals from researchers in disciplines classified as social sciences in one country and as humanities in another need to apply to different standing committees, and funding for awards has to be approved by national research councils and disciplinary panels that may not be using the same scientific criteria (Hantrais, 2005b: 281–2).

Such is the extent of the bureaucratic complications that arise in preparing funding proposals and managing budgets for international projects, not least in the social and human sciences, that institutions encouraging researchers to seek external funding often put in place specialized offices or employ dedicated agencies to handle applications, process claims and oversee budgets, thereby enabling the coordinators of projects to concentrate their efforts on the research process.

OUTPUTS AND DISSEMINATION OF INTERNATIONAL COMPARATIVE RESEARCH FINDINGS

Sponsors of research are required to ensure that the projects they fund provide value for money. Research councils and international agencies usually stipulate that their support should be acknowledged, and that findings should be widely disseminated. Occasionally, for example in policy evaluation studies or evidence-based policy research involving government sponsors, an embargo may be placed on findings for political or strategic reasons (see Chapter 6).

A distinguishing characteristic of Anglo-Saxon research cultures, which is being widely adopted by the Nordic states and the Netherlands, as well as by countries like Portugal, is the requirement to publish in internationally refereed scientific journals. Here too, English native speakers have an advantage over other countries because of their language and training. Publication ratings are calculated from databases originally established by the Institute for Scientific Information in the United States for bibliographic searching, and are generally acknowledged to have a strong bias towards Anglo-American literature. The impact factor of individual articles reflects the extent to which different research communities have sought to internationalize their output by publishing in English-language journals, thereby increasing the chances that their findings will be widely read and cited. In the social and human sciences, the work of Dutch, Finnish and Swedish researchers, who routinely publish in English, is, for example, much more widely read beyond national borders than work in French, German or Spanish. In conjunction with financial and academic pressures, these advantages may help to explain the relatively high ranking of British social and human science researchers in relation to their continental neighbours, who are less accustomed to publishing in English-language outlets, as measured by international performance indicators derived from citations indices (Oksanen et al., 2003: table 5.10).

These national differences in publication strategies are reflected in practices within the various social sciences and humanities disciplines: whereas economists rarely publish monographs, historians are, for example, more likely to publish book-length monographs than articles in specialized journals. Comparative researchers working in large international teams are more likely to contribute chapters to edited books than to author monographs. While multi-authored or edited collections of papers by research teams are common forms of publication in the natural sciences, and are interpreted as an indicator of international recognition, it is more difficult to estimate the share of the work carried out by an individual contributor in the social and human sciences. The team spirit and tight cooperation required of large-scale international comparative research projects run counter to the criteria that were traditionally the hallmarks of the vast majority of social and human science researchers.

These comments are also relevant to the assessment of applications for international funding and project reports. Assessors bring with them their own epistemological, ontological and cultural preferences and expectations. As with interdisciplinary research, the shortcomings and difficulties embodied in the peer review process combine to make the assessment of international comparative research proposals and outputs a delicate operation, requiring careful monitoring and an in-depth understanding of the issues involved in international cooperation, networking and project management.

Assessing International Comparative Research

This concluding section draws on the analysis carried out in preceding chapters in an attempt to assess the theoretical, methodological and practical contribution made by international comparative research in the social sciences and humanities to international cooperation and understanding, and to the socioeconomic knowledge base. The intention is not to confine discussion to the European context, although the impetus provided since the mid-1990s by the European Union's framework programmes and the European Research Area has, arguably, provoked an unprecedented concentration of comparative research effort in the social sciences and humanities on international cooperation within Europe. In its attempt to implement a coherent international engagement strategy in research and development designed to strengthen the socioeconomic knowledge base, the European Commission reinforced emphasis on practice and outcomes, particularly when they are relevant for policy, rather than focusing on theory and methods, where most of the major developments were taking place in previous decades.

The early chapters in this volume suggest that international comparative research made an important contribution to the recognition of the social and human sciences as legitimate scientific disciplines, capable of meeting international scientific standards. Although comparative approaches may come close to the experimental method, often validity, reliability, replicability and plausibility cannot be straightforwardly demonstrated. The subject matter, theoretical underpinnings, variety of methodological approaches and great complexity of the international comparisons conducted by social and human scientists also mean that their scientific credentials cannot be adequately assessed according to the indicators widely applied in the natural sciences. In addition, unlike the natural sciences, social and human scientists are required to show that their findings 'benefit society' (Dench et al., 2004: 17).

The heyday of methodological advances in comparative studies can, however, be located in the late 1960s and early 1970s. Since then, the focus has shifted primarily to the improvement of methodological rigour, and refinement of data collection and analysis techniques, rather than innovation, with the continued aim of consolidating the scientific credentials of comparative studies. Recognition of the need to accept methodological trade-offs, compromise and flexibility has encouraged the development of multidisciplinary and multi-strategy approaches as useful devices to achieve greater validity and reliability, while encouraging the extension of the geographical and cultural reach of comparative studies and building up the body of comparative knowledge.

Systematic international comparative research, as conducted at varying stages in the United States and the wider Europe during the second half of the twentieth century can also be credited with having developed the linkages between general sociological theory and method. Comparative research has extended the empirical basis for theory. Researchers have learnt how to draw on comparative studies to generate hypotheses, interrogate and test the generalizability and robustness of theories. They routinely use the tools and techniques offered by international comparisons to control the variables making up theoretical relationships, verify or falsify relationships between variables, identify necessary and sufficient conditions under which relationships occur in reality, and establish scientific explanation. Systematic comparative case studies serve as instruments in the search for constant factors or general laws capable of explaining phenomena, while existing theory is utilized to illuminate, confirm or validate cases, and identify deviance.

Comparative researchers at the turn of the twenty-first century will most probably be remembered for their input to practice and policy. The contribution made, directly and indirectly, by the social and human sciences during this period to the relationship between research and policy is noteworthy, not only in the construction of the international knowledge base, and the development of more meaningful and reliable tools for the qualitative evaluation of policy effects and policy diffusion (Spencer et al., 2003), but also in creating the preconditions for successful policy transfer and lesson learning (see Chapter 6). The research skills and specialist contextual knowledge needed by social and human scientists, and their ability to work cross-, trans- and internationally, and inform policy have been more widely recognized and called upon.

The sheer volume and intensity of international comparative research activity do not mean that the communications gap between social and human scientists and their many stakeholders has been wholly bridged, or that researchers no longer need to devote time and effort to overcoming national, cultural, logistic and linguistic barriers to international cooperation. Nor have the internal divisions within and between ontologies, epistemologies and research cultures disappeared completely. In the same way that most research in the social sciences and humanities has a linguistic, cultural and societal dimension that the natural sciences can and do largely ignore, international comparisons require additional research skills and strategies at all stages of the inquiry to ensure that the comparative dimension is fully integrated into the research process. The divide between natural, social and human sciences may occasionally be bridged when the reasons for taking account of the sociocultural impacts of phenomena become compelling, as exemplified by research into global issues such as trade, climate change, international migration, or analysis of the ethical dilemmas surrounding technological and biomedical advances.

An optimistic assessment of the status of international comparative research in the early years of the twenty-first century is that it has most probably reached a stage in its development where international networks of researchers have available the knowledge and tools enabling them to exploit more fully and build on the array of theoretical, methodological and technological achievements of the past to enhance international understanding and knowledge of societal, cultural and scientific diversity. The risk, as in the past, is that new generations of researchers embarking on international comparisons may set about reinventing the theoretical and methodological wheel because they are insufficiently aware of the wealth of material collected by those who have observed, analysed and reflected on the theory, method and practice of international comparative research. This is a danger that the present volume is seeking to avert.

References

Adnett, N. and Hardy, S. (2005) *The European Social Model: modernisation or evolution?*, Cheltenham/Northampton, MA: Edward Elgar.

Alasuutari, P., Bickman, L. and Brannen, J. (eds) (2008) *The SAGE Handbook of Social Research Methods*, London/Thousand Oaks, CA: Sage.

Alcock, P. (2004) 'Social policy and professional practice', in S. Becker and A. Bryman (eds), *Understanding Research for Social Policy and Practice: themes, methods and approaches*, Bristol: The Policy Press, pp.4–63.

Almasy, E. (1969) 'Annotated bibliography – comparative survey analysis', in S. Rokkan, S. Verba, J. Viet and E. Almasy (eds), *Comparative Survey Analysis*, Paris/The Hague: Mouton, pp.117–343.

Almond, G.A. (ed.) (1974) *Comparative Politics Today: a world view*, Boston/Toronto: Little, Brown and Company.

Almond, G.A. and Verba, S. (1963) *The Civic Culture: political attitudes and democracy in five nations*, Princeton, NJ: Princeton University Press.

Armer, M. (1973) 'Methodological problems and possibilities in comparative research', in M. Armer and A.D. Grimshaw (eds), *Comparative Social Research: methodological problems and strategies*, London/New York: John Wiley & Sons, pp.49–79.

Armer, M. and Grimshaw, A.D. (eds) (1973) *Comparative Social Research: methodological problems and strategies*, London/New York: John Wiley & Sons.

Arminjon, P., Nolde, B. and Wolff, M. (1950, 1952) *Traité de droit comparé*, 3 vols, Paris: Pichon and Durand-Auzias.

Arve-Parès, B. (2005) 'Changing frameworks for European research policy: challenges for European social scientists', *Cross-National Research Papers*, 7 (Special Issue): 11–15.

Barbier, J-C. (2005a) 'A comparative analysis of "employment precariousness" in Europe', *Cross-National Research Papers*, 7 (Special Issue): 47–55.

Barbier, J-C. (2005b) 'When words matter: dealing anew with cross-national comparison', in J-C. Barbier and M-T. Letablier (eds), *Politiques sociales: enjeux méthodologiques et épistémologiques des comparaisons internationales; Social Policies: epistemological and methodological issues in cross-national comparison*, Brussels: P.I.E.-Peter Lang, pp.45–68.

Barbier, J-C. and Letablier, M-T. (eds) (2005) *Politiques sociales: enjeux méthodologiques et épistémologiques des comparaisons internationales; Social*

Policies: epistemological and methodological issues in cross-national comparison, Brussels: P.I.E.-Peter Lang.

Bereday, G.Z.F. (1964) *Comparative Method in Education*, New York: Holt, Rinehart & Winston.

Bernstein, B. (1971) *Class, Codes and Control*, vol. 1, *Theoretical studies towards a sociology of language*, London: Routledge & Kegan Paul.

Berry, J.W. (1969) 'On cross-cultural comparability', *International Journal of Psychology*, 4(2): 119–28.

Bertaux, D. (1990) 'Oral history approaches to an international social movement', in E. Øyen (ed.), *Comparative Methodology: theory and practice in international social research*, London/Newbury Park, CA: Sage, pp.151–71.

Berthoud R. and Iacovou, M. (2002) *Diverse Europe: mapping patterns of social change across the EU*, Report for the ESRC, Swindon: ESRC, www.esrc societytoday.ac.uk/ESRCInfoCentre/Images/diverse_europe_tcm6-5503.pdf

Berting, J. (1987) 'The significance of different types of cultural boundaries in international comparative and cooperative research in the social sciences', *Cross-National Research Papers*, 1(3): 1–13.

Bettelheim Garfin, S. (1971) 'Comparative Studies: a selective, annotated bibliography', in I. Vallier (ed.), *Comparative Methods in Sociology: essays on trends and applications*, Berkeley, CA/London: University of California Press, pp.423–67

Bloch, M. (1939, 1940) *La Société féodale*, 2 vols, Paris: Albin Michel.

Bogenschneider, K., Olson, J.R., Mills, J. and Linney, K.D. (2002) 'How can we connect research and knowledge with state policymaking? Lessons from the Wisconsin Family Impact Seminars', in K. Bogenschneider (ed.), *Family Policy Matters: how policymaking affects families and what professionals can do*, Mahwah, NJ/London: Lawrence Erlbaum, pp.187–218.

Brannen, J. (2003) 'Working qualitatively and quantitatively', in C. Cameron (ed.), *Cross-National Qualitative Methods*, EUR 20737, Luxembourg: Office for Official Publications of the European Communities, pp.15–21.

Brannen, J. (ed.) (1992) 'Combining qualitative and quantitative approaches: an overview', in J. Brannen (ed.), *Mixing Methods: qualitative and quantitative research*, Aldershot/Brookfield: Avebury, pp.3–37.

Braudel, F. (1979) *Civilisation matérielle, économie et capitalisme (XVe au XVIIIe siècle)*, 3 vols, Paris: Armand Colin.

Braun, M. (2003) 'Errors in comparative survey research: an overview', in J.A. Harkness, F.J.R. Van de Vijver and P.Ph. Mohler (eds), *Cross-Cultural Survey Methods*, Hoboken, NJ: John Wiley & Sons, pp.137–42.

Breakwell, G.M., Hammond, S. and Fife-Schaw, C. (eds) (2000) *Research Methods in Psychology*, 2nd edn, London/Thousand Oaks, CA: Sage (1st edn 1995).

British Academy (2004) '"That Full Complement of Riches": the contributions of the arts, humanities and social sciences to the nation's wealth', London: British Academy.

Brown, J. (1986) 'Cross-national and inter-country research into poverty: the case of the First European Poverty Programme', *Cross-National Research Papers*, 1(2): 41–51.

Bryman, A. (1984) 'The debate about quantitative and qualitative research: a question of method or epistemology', *British Journal of Sociology*, 35(1): 75–92.

Bryman, A. (1988) *Quantity and Quality in Social Research*, London/New York: Routledge.

Bryman, A. (2004) *Social Research Methods*, 2nd edn, Oxford: Oxford University Press (1st edn 2001).

Bryman, A. (2008) 'The end of the paradigm wars?', in P. Alasuutari, L. Bickman and J. Brannen (eds), *The SAGE Handbook of Social Research Methods*, London/Thousand Oaks, CA: Sage, pp.13–25.

Bryson, C. and Jowell, R. (2001) 'The European Social Survey (ESSIE)', in L. Hantrais (ed.), *Researching Family and Welfare from an International Comparative Perspective*, Luxembourg: Office for Official Publications of the European Communities, pp.11–15.

Büchs, M. (2007) *New Governance in European Social Policy: the open method of coordination*, Basingstoke: Palgrave Macmillan.

Büchs, M. (2008) 'The open method of coordination as a "two-level game"', *Policy & Politics*, 36(1): 21–37.

Burgess, R.G. (1984) *In the Field: an introduction to field research*, London: George Allen and Unwin.

Burnham, P., Gilland, K., Grant, W. and Layton-Henry, Z. (2004) *Research Methods in Politics*, Basingstoke/New York: Palgrave Macmillan.

Chamberlayne, P. and King, A. (2000) *Cultures of Care: biographies of carers in Britain and the two Germanies*, Bristol: The Policy Press.

Chelimsky, E. (2006) 'The purposes of evaluation in a democratic society', in I.F. Shaw, J.C. Greene and M.M. Mark (eds), *Handbook of Evaluation: policies, programs and practices*, London/Thousand Oaks, CA: Sage, pp.33–55.

Clarke, A. (2006) 'Evidence-based evaluation in different professional domains: similarities, differences and challenges', in I.F. Shaw, J.C. Greene and M.M. Mark (eds), *Handbook of Evaluation: policies, programs and practices*, London/Thousand Oaks, CA: Sage, pp.559–81.

Clasen, J. (2004) 'Defining comparative social policy', in P. Kennett (ed.), *A Handbook of Comparative Social Policy*, Cheltenham/Northampton, MA: Edward Elgar, pp.91–102.

Clasen, J. (ed.) (1999) *Comparative Social Policy: concepts, theories and methods*, Oxford/Malden, MA: Blackwell.

Collier, D. (1993) 'The comparative method', in A.W. Finifter (ed.), *Political Science: the state of the discipline*, 2nd edn, Washington, DC: American Political Science Association, pp.105–19 (1st edn 1983).

Commission of the European Communities (2000) Communication from the Commission to the Council, the European Parliament, the Economic and

Social Committee and the Committee of the Regions, 'Towards a European Research Area', COM (2000) 6, Brussels, 18 January 2000.

Commission on the Social Sciences (2003) 'Great Expectations: the social sciences in Britain', London: Commission on the Social Sciences.

Coolican, H. (1999) *Research Methods and Statistics in Psychology*, 3rd edn, London: Hodder & Stoughton (1st edn 1990).

Crow, G. (1997) *Comparative Sociology and Social Theory: beyond the three worlds*, Basingstoke: Macmillan.

Dahler-Larsen, P. (2006) 'Evaluation after enchantment? Five issues shaping the role of evaluation in society', in I.F. Shaw, J.C. Greene and M.M. Mark (eds), *Handbook of Evaluation: policies, programs and practices*, London/ Thousand Oaks, CA: Sage, pp.141–60.

Dale, A., Wathan, J. and Higgins, V. (2008) 'Secondary analysis of quantitative data sources', in P. Alasuutari, L. Bickman and J. Brannen (eds), *The SAGE Handbook of Social Research Methods*, London/Thousand Oaks, CA: Sage, pp.520–35.

Davies, H., Nutley, S. and Smith, P. (2000a) 'Introducing evidence-based policy and practice in public services', in H.T.O. Davies, S.M. Nutley and P.C. Smith (eds), *What works? Evidence-based policy and practice in public services*, Bristol: The Policy Press, pp.1–11.

Davies, H.T.O., Nutley, S.M. and Smith, P.C. (eds) (2000b) *What works? Evidence-based policy and practice in public services*, Bristol: The Policy Press.

Davies, P. (2000) 'Contributions from qualitative research', in H.T.O Davies, S.M. Nutley and P.C. Smith (eds), *What works? Evidence-based policy and practice in public services*, Bristol: The Policy Press, pp.291–316.

Davies, P., Newcomer, K. and Soydan, H. (2006) 'Government as structural context for evaluation', in I.F. Shaw, J.C. Greene and M.M. Mark (eds), *Handbook of Evaluation: policies, programs and practices*, London/Thousand Oaks, CA: Sage, pp.163–83.

Deacon, B. (1987) 'The comparative analysis of surveys of opinion about welfare policy in Britain and Hungary', *Cross-National Research Papers*, 1(4): 15–27.

De Cruz, P. (2007) *Comparative Law in a Changing World*, 3rd edn, London/ New York: Routledge–Cavendish (1st edn 1995).

Dench, S., Iphofen, R. and Huws, U. (2004) *An EU Code of Ethics for Socio-Economic Research*, Brighton: Institute for Employment Studies, www.respectproject.org/code

Denzin, N.K. (1970) *The Research Act in Sociology: a theoretical introduction to sociological methods*, London: Butterworths.

Desrosières, A. (1996) 'Statistical traditions: an obstacle to international comparisons?', in L. Hantrais and S. Mangen (eds), *Cross-National Research Methods in the Social Sciences*, London/New York: Pinter/Cassels, pp.17–27.

Deutscher, I. (1973) 'Asking questions cross-culturally: some problems of linguistic comparability', in D.P. Warwick and S. Osherson (eds),

Comparative Research Methods, Englewood Cliffs, NJ: Prentice-Hall, pp.163–86.

De Vaus, D. (2008) 'Comparative and cross-national designs', in P. Alasuutari, L. Bickman and J. Brannen (eds), *The SAGE Handbook of Social Research Methods*, London/Thousand Oaks, CA: Sage, pp.249–64.

Devine, F. and Heath, S. (1999) *Sociological Research Methods in Context*, Basingstoke/New York: Palgrave/St Martin's Press.

Dex, S. (1996) 'Quantitative methods', in L. Hantrais and S. Mangen (eds), *Cross-National Research Methods in the Social Sciences*, London/New York: Pinter/Cassels, pp.13–16.

Djelic, M-L. and Sahlin-Andersson, K. (2006) 'Introduction. A world of governance: the rise of transnational regulation', in M-L. Djelic and K. Sahlin-Andersson (eds), *Transnational Governance: institutional dynamics of regulation*, Cambridge: Cambridge University Press, pp.1–28.

Dogan, M. (1994) 'Use and misuse of statistics in comparative research. Limits to quantification in comparative politics: the gap between substance and method', in M. Dogan and A. Kazancigil (eds), *Comparing Nations: concepts, strategies, substance*, Oxford/Cambridge, MA: Blackwell, pp.35–71.

Dogan, M. (2004) 'The quantitative method in comparative research', in P. Kennett (ed.), *A Handbook of Comparative Social Policy*, Cheltenham/Northampton, MA: Edward Elgar, pp.324–38.

Dogan, M. and Kazancigil, A. (eds) (1994) *Comparing Nations: concepts, strategies, substance*, Oxford/Cambridge, MA: Blackwell.

Dogan, M. and Pelassy, D. (1990) *How to Compare Nations: strategies in comparative politics*, 2nd edn, Chatham, NJ: Chatham House (1st edn 1984).

Dolowitz, D. and Marsh, D. (1996) 'Who learns what from whom: a review of the policy transfer literature', *Political Studies*, 44(2): 343–57.

Dolowitz, D.P. and Marsh, D. (2000) 'Learning from abroad: the role of policy transfer in contemporary policy-making', *Governance: An International Journal of Policy and Administration*, 13(1): 5–24.

Dupré, M., Jacob, A., Lallement, M., Lefèvre, G. and Spurk, J. (2003) 'Les comparaisons internationales: intérêt et actualité d'une stratégie de recherche', in M. Lallement and J. Spurk (eds), *Stratégies de la comparaison internationale*, Paris: CNRS Éditions, pp.7–18.

Durkheim, É. (1938) *The Rules of Sociological Method*, S.A. Solovay and J.H. Müller (trans), G.E.G. Catlin (ed.), New York/London: University of Chicago Free Press/Collier–Macmillan (1st French edn 1895).

Durkheim, É. (1990) *Suicide: a study in sociology*, J.A. Spaulding and G. Simpson (trans), G. Simpson (ed.), London: Free Press (1st French edn 1897).

Eardley, T. (1996) 'Lessons from a study of social assistance schemes in OECD countries', in L. Hantrais and S. Mangen (eds), *Cross-National Research Methods in the Social Sciences*, London/New York: Pinter/Cassels, pp.51–62.

Elder, J.W. (1976) 'Comparative cross-national methodology', in A. Inkeles (ed.), *Annual Review of Sociology*, vol 2, Palo Alto, CA: Annual Reviews, pp.209–30.

Elster, J., Offe, C. and Preuss, U.K., with F. Boenker, U. Goetting and F.W. Rueb (1998) *Institutional Design in Post-Communist Societies: rebuilding the ship at sea*, Cambridge/New York: Cambridge University Press.

Esping-Andersen, G. (1990) *The Three Worlds of Welfare Capitalism*, Oxford: Polity Press.

Esping-Andersen, G. (ed.) (1996) *Welfare States in Transition: national adaptations in global economies*, London/Thousand Oaks, CA: Sage.

European Science Foundation (2007) 'Social Sciences in Europe: a report from the ESF Standing Committee for the Social Sciences (SCSS)', Strasbourg: European Science Foundation, www.esf.org/research-areas/social-sciences/publications.html

Ferrari, V. (1990) 'Socio-legal concepts and their comparison', in E. Øyen (ed.), *Comparative Methodology: theory and practice in international social research*, London/Newbury Park, CA: Sage, pp.63–80.

Fielding, J. and Fielding, N. (2008) 'Synergy and synthesis: integrating qualitative and quantitative data', in P. Alasuutari, L. Bickman and J. Brannen (eds), *The SAGE Handbook of Social Research Methods*, London/Thousand Oaks, CA: Sage, pp.555–71.

Flora, P. and Heidenheimer, A.J. (eds) (1982) *The Development of Welfare States in Europe and America*, New Brunswick: Transaction Books.

Galtung, J. (1982) 'On the meaning of "nation" as a variable', in M. Nießen and J. Peschar (eds), *International Comparative Research: problems of theory, methodology and organisation in Eastern and Western Europe*, Oxford/New York: Pergamon Press, pp.17–34.

Garfinkel, H. (1967) *Studies in Ethnomethodology*, Englewood Cliffs, NJ: Prentice Hall.

Geertz, C. (1973) 'Thick description: toward an interpretive theory of culture', *The Interpretation of Cultures: selected essays*, New York: Basic Books, pp.3–30.

Gillham, B. (2000) *Case Study Research Methods*, London/New York: Continuum.

Giraud, O. (2003) 'Le comparatisme contemporain en science politique: entrée en dialogue des écoles et renouvellement des questions', in M. Lallement and J. Spurk (eds), *Stratégies de la comparaison internationale*, Paris: CNRS Éditions, pp.87–106.

Glaser, B.G. and Strauss, A.L. (1967) *The Discovery of Grounded Theory: strategies for qualitative research*, 1st edn, New York: Aldine de Gruyter.

Green, N.L. (1994) 'The comparative method and poststructural structuralism – new perspective for migration studies', *Journal of American Ethnic History*, 13(4): 3–22.

Grimshaw, A.D. (1973) 'Comparative sociology: in what ways different from other sociologies?', in M. Armer and A.D. Grimshaw (eds), *Comparative*

Social Research: methodological problems and strategies, London/New York: John Wiley & Sons, pp.3–48.

Grootings, P. (1986) 'Technology and work: a topic for East–West comparison?', in P. Grootings (ed.), *Technology and Work: East–West comparison*, London: Croom Helm, pp.275–301.

Groth, A.J. (1971) *Comparative Politics: a distributive approach*, New York/London: Collier–Macmillan.

Gutteridge, H.C. (1946) *Comparative Law: an introduction to the comparative method of legal study and research*, Cambridge: Cambridge University Press.

Hall, J. (1963) *Comparative Law and Social Theory*, Baton Rouge: Louisiana State University Press.

Hammersley, M. (1992) 'Deconstructing the qualitative–quantitative divide', in J. Brannen (ed.), *Mixing Methods: qualitative and quantitative research*, Aldershot/Brookfield: Avebury, pp.39–55.

Hammersley, M. (1996) 'The relationship between qualitative and quantitative research: paradigm loyalty versus methodological eclecticism', in J.T.E. Richardson (ed.), *Handbook of Qualitative Research Methods for Psychology and the Social Sciences*, Leicester: BPS Books, pp.159–74.

Hammersley, M. (2008) 'Assessing validity in social research', in P. Alasuutari, L. Bickman and J. Brannen (eds), *The SAGE Handbook of Social Research Methods*, London/Thousand Oaks, CA: Sage, pp.42–53.

Hancock, M.D. (1983) 'Comparative public policy: an assessment', in A.W. Finifter (ed.), *Political Science: the state of the discipline*, 1st edn, Washington DC: American Political Science Association, pp.283–308.

Hans, N. (1949) *Comparative Education: a study of educational factors and traditions*, London: Routledge & Kegan Paul.

Hantrais, L. (2003) 'Cross-national comparative approaches to the analysis of family and welfare', in C. Cameron (ed.), *Cross-National Qualitative Methods*, EUR 20737, Luxembourg: Office for Official Publications of the European Communities, pp.3–14.

Hantrais, L. (2004a) *Family Policy Matters: responding to family change in Europe*, Bristol: The Policy Press.

Hantrais, L. (ed.) (2004b) *Improving Policy Responses and Outcomes to Socio-Economic Challenges: changing family structures, policy and practice (Iprosec)*, EUR 21105, Luxembourg: Office for Official Publications of the European Communities.

Hantrais, L. (2005a) 'Combining methods: a key to understanding complexity in European societies?', *European Societies*, 7(3): 399–421.

Hantrais, L. (2005b) 'Vers la mixité méthodologique en comparaisons internationales', in J-C. Barbier and M-T. Letablier (eds), *Politiques sociales: enjeux méthodologiques et épistémologiques des comparaisons internationales; Social Policies: epistemological and methodological issues in cross-national comparison*, Brussels: P.I.E.-Peter Lang, pp.271–89.

Hantrais, L. (2006a) *Family and Welfare Research*, Policy Synthesis of Research Results, series no 1, EUR 22088, Luxembourg: Office for Official

Publications of the European Communities, http://ec.europa.eu/ research/ social- sciences/newsletter/policy_reviews_en.htm

Hantrais, L. (2006b) 'Living as a family in Europe', in Council of Europe (ed.), *Population Studies*, no 49: *Policy Implications of Changing Family Formation*, Strasbourg: Council of Europe Publishing, pp.117–81.

Hantrais, L. (2006c) *Pour une meilleure évaluation de la recherche publique en sciences humaines et sociales*, vol. 2, Paris: La Documentation française.

Hantrais, L. (2007a) 'Contextualization in cross-national comparative research', in L. Hantrais and S. Mangen (eds), *Cross-National Research Methodology & Practice*, London/New York: Routledge, pp.3–18.

Hantrais, L. (2007b) *Social Policy in the European Union*, 3rd edn, Basingstoke/New York: Palgrave Macmillan (1st edn 1995).

Hantrais, L. and Ackers, P. (2005) 'Women's choice in Europe: striking the work–life balance', *European Journal of Industrial Relations*, 11(2): 197–212.

Hantrais, L. and Mangen, S. (eds) (1996) *Cross-National Research Methods in the Social Sciences*, London/New York: Pinter/Cassels.

Hantrais, L. and Mangen, S. (eds) (2007) *Cross-National Research Methodology & Practice*, London/New York: Routledge.

Hantrais, L. and Sineau, M., with B. Lust (1998) *L'administration du travail: acteur privilégié d'une politique d'égalité professionnelle entre les femmes et les hommes. Guide de bonnes pratiques*, Document no 55-1, Geneva: International Labour Office.

Harkness, J. (2003) 'Questionnaire translation', in J.A. Harkness, F.J.R. Van de Vijver and P.Ph. Mohler (eds), *Cross-Cultural Survey Methods*, Hoboken, NJ: John Wiley & Sons, pp.35–56.

Harkness, J. (2007) 'In pursuit of quality: issues for cross-national survey research', in L. Hantrais and S. Mangen (eds), *Cross-National Research Methodology & Practice*, London/New York: Routledge, pp.35–50.

Harkness, J., Mohler, P.Ph. and Van de Vijver, F.J.R. (2003) 'Comparative research', in J.A. Harkness, F.J.R. Van de Vijver and P.Ph. Mohler (eds), *Cross-Cultural Survey Methods*, Hoboken, NJ: John Wiley & Sons, pp.3–16.

Harrison, L. (2001) *Political Research: an introduction*, London/New York: Routledge.

Heclo, H. (1974) *Modern Social Politics in Britain and Sweden: from relief to income maintenance*, New Haven, CT/London: Yale University Press.

Heidenheimer, A.J., Heclo, H. and Adams, C.T. (1983) *Comparative Public Policy: the politics of social choice in America, Europe and Japan*, 2nd edn, New York: St Martin's Press (1st edn 1975).

Hetherington, R., Baistow, K., Katz, I., Mesie, J. and Trowell, J. (2002) *The Welfare of Children with a Mentally Ill Parent: learning from inter-country comparisons*, Chichester: John Wiley.

Hines, A.M. (1993) 'Linking qualitative and quantitative methods in cross-cultural survey research: techniques from cognitive science', *American Journal of Community Psychology*, 21(6): 729–46.

Holmes, B. (1981) *Comparative Education: some considerations of method*, London: Allen & Unwin.

Holy, L. (ed.) (1987) *Comparative Anthropology*, Oxford/New York: Basil Blackwell.

Hopkin, J. (2002) 'Comparative methods', in D. Marsh and G. Stoker (eds), *Theory and Methods in Political Science*, 2nd edn, Basingstoke/New York: Palgrave Macmillan (1st edn 1995), pp.249–67.

Hyman, R. (1998) 'Recherche sur les syndicats et comparaison internationale', *La Revue de l'IRES*, no 28 (Special issue): 43–61.

Hyman, R. (2005) 'Words and things: the problem of particularistic universalism', in J-C. Barbier and M-T. Letablier (eds), *Politiques sociales: enjeux méthodologiques et épistémologiques des comparaisons internationales; Social Policies: epistemological and methodological issues in cross-national comparison*, Brussels: P.I.E.-Peter Lang, pp.191–208.

Inglehart, R. (1990) *Culture Shift in Advanced Industrial Society*, Princeton, NJ: Princeton University Press.

International Encyclopedia of Comparative Law (1972–) Tübingen/The Hague/ Paris/New York: J.C.B. Mohr/Mouton/Oceana.

Iribarne, P. d' (1991) 'Culture et "effet sociétal"' *Revue française de sociologie*, 32(4): 599–614.

Jary, D. and Jary, J. (1991) *Collins Dictionary of Sociology*, Glasgow: Harper Collins.

Jessop, B. (2004) 'Hollowing out the "nation-state" and multi-level governance', in P. Kennett (ed.), *A Handbook of Comparative Social Policy*, Cheltenham/Northampton, MA: Edward Elgar, pp.11–25.

Johnson, T.P. (1998) 'Approaches to equivalence in cross-cultural and cross-national survey research', in J. Harknes (ed.), *Cross-Cultural Survey Equivalence, ZUMA-Nachrichten Spezial Band 3*, Mannheim: ZUMA, pp.1–40.

Johnson, T.P. (2003) 'Glossary', in J.A. Harkness, F.J.R. Van de Vijver and P.Ph. Mohler. (eds), *Cross-Cultural Survey Methods*, Hoboken, NJ: John Wiley & Sons, pp.347–57.

Johnson, T.P. and Van de Vijver, F.J.R. (2003) 'Social desirability in cross-cultural research', in J.A. Harkness, F.J.R. Van de Vijver and P.Ph. Mohler (eds), *Cross-Cultural Survey Methods*, Hoboken, NJ: John Wiley & Sons, pp.195–204.

Jones, C. (1985) *Patterns of Social Policy: an introduction to comparative analysis*, London: Tavistock.

Jones Finer, C. (ed.) (1999) *Transnational Social Policy*, Oxford/Malden, MA: Blackwell.

Jowell, R., Kaase, M., Fitzgerald, R. and Eva, G. (2007a) 'The European Social Survey as a measurement model', in R. Jowell, C. Roberts, R. Fitzgerald and G. Eva (eds), *Measuring Attitudes Cross-Nationally: lessons from the European Social Survey*, London/Thousand Oaks, CA: Sage, pp.1–31.

Jowell, R., Roberts, C., Fitzgerald, R. and Eva, G. (eds) (2007b) *Measuring Attitudes Cross-Nationally: lessons from the European Social Survey*, London/ Thousand Oaks, CA: Sage.

Kennett, P. (2001) *Comparative Social Policy: theory and research*, Buckingham/ Philadelphia, PA: Open University Press.

Kennett, P. (ed.) (2004) *A Handbook of Comparative Social Policy*, Cheltenham/ Northampton, MA: Edward Elgar.

Kindleberger, C.P. (2000) *Comparative Political Economy: a retrospective*, Cambridge, MA: MIT Press.

Kinnear, R. (1987) 'Interference from the researcher's background in comparisons across the ideological divide', *Cross-National Research Papers*, 1(4): 9–14.

Kohli, A., Evans, P., Katzenstein, P.J., Przeworski, A., Rudolph, S.H., Scott, J.C. and Skocpol, T. (1996) 'The role of theory in comparative politics: a symposium', *World Politics*, 48(1): 1–49.

Kohn, M.L. (ed.) (1989) *Cross-National Research in Sociology*, Newbury Park, CA/London: Sage.

Kutsar, D. (2005) 'Bridging the communications gap between research and policy in an enlarged Europe', *Cross-National Research Papers*, 7 (Special Issue): 23–6.

Kutsar, D. and Tiit, E-M. (2000), 'Comparing socio-demographic indicators in Estonia and the European Union', *Cross-National Research Papers*, 6(2): 27–34.

Lallement, M. (2003) 'Pragmatique de la comparaison', in M. Lallement and J. Spurk (eds), *Stratégies de la comparaison internationale*, Paris: CNRS Éditions, pp.297–306.

Lallement, M. and Spurk, J. (eds) (2003) *Stratégies de la comparaison internationale*, Paris: CNRS Éditions.

Lammers, C.J. and Hickson, D.J. (1979) *Organizations Alike and Unlike: international and interinstitutional studies in the sociology of organizations*, London: Routledge & Kegan Paul.

Landman, T. (2000) *Issues and Methods in Comparative Politics: an introduction*, London/New York: Routledge.

Leibfried, S. (2005) 'Social policy: left to judges and the markets?', in H. Wallace, W. Wallace and M.A. Pollack (eds), *Policy-Making in the European Union*, 5th edn, Oxford: Oxford University Press (1st edn 1996) pp.243–78.

Lesage, M. (1987) 'Comparison. Communication. Confidence', *Cross-National Research Papers*, 1(4): 1–7.

Levine, R. (1987) 'Coping with the silent language in cross-national research', *Cross-National Research Papers*, 1(3): 27–33.

Lieberson, S. (1991) 'Small N's and big conclusions: an examination of the reasoning in comparative studies based on a small number of cases', *Social Forces*, 70(2): 307–20.

Lieberson, S. (1994) 'More on the uneasy case for using Mill-type methods in Small-N comparative studies', *Social Forces*, 72(4): 1225–37.

Lijphart, A. (1971) 'Comparative politics and the comparative method', *American Political Science Review*, 65(3): 682–93.

Lipset, S.M. (1960) *Political Man: the social basis of politics*, London: Heinemann.

Lipset, S.M. and Rokkan, S. (eds) (1967) *Party Systems and Voter Alignment: cross-national perspectives*, New York/London: Free Press/Collier–Macmillan.

Liske, C., Loehr, W., McCamant, J. (eds) (1975) *Comparative Public Policy: issues, theories, and methods*, New York/London: John Wiley & Sons.

Lisle, E. (1985) 'Validation in the social sciences by international comparison', *Cross-National Research Papers*, 1(1): 11–28.

Lyons, E. and Chryssochoou, X. (2000) 'Cross-cultural research methods', in G.M. Breakwell, S. Hammond and C. Fife-Schaw (eds), *Research Methods in Psychology*, 2nd edn, London/Thousand Oaks, CA: Sage (1st edn 1995), pp.134–46.

Mabbett, D. and Bolderson, H. (1999) 'Theories and methods in comparative social policy', in J. Clasen (ed.), *Comparative Social Policy: concepts, theories and methods*, Oxford/Malden, MA: Blackwell, pp.34–56.

MacGregor, S. (2005) 'Improving the dialogue between social science research and social policy', *Cross-National Research Papers*, 7 (Special Issue): 16–22.

Mackie, T. and Marsh, D. (1995) 'The comparative method', in D. Marsh and G. Stoker (eds), *Theory and Methods in Political Science*, 1st edn, Basingstoke/New York: Macmillan/St. Martin's Press, pp.173–88.

Macridis, R.C. and Brown, B.E. (eds) (1968) *Comparative Politics: notes and readings*, 3rd edn, Homewood, IL: Dorsey Press (1st edn 1961).

Mangen, S. (2004) '"Fit for purpose?" Qualitative methods in comparative social policy', in P. Kennett (ed.), *A Handbook of Comparative Social Policy*, Cheltenham/Northampton, MA: Edward Elgar, pp.307–23.

Mangen, S. (2007) 'Qualitative research methods in cross-national settings', in L. Hantrais and S. Mangen (eds), *Cross-National Research Methodology & Practice*, London/New York: Routledge, pp.19–34.

Manning, N. and Shaw, I. (1999) 'The transferability of welfare models: a comparison of the Scandinavian and state socialist models in relation to Finland and Estonia', in C. Jones Finer (ed.), *Transnational Social Policy*, Oxford/Malden, MA: Blackwell, pp.120–38.

Mark, M.M., Greene, J.C. and Shaw, I.F. (2006) 'Introduction: the evaluation of policies, programs and practices', in I.F. Shaw, J.C. Greene and M.M. Mark (eds), *Handbook of Evaluation: policies, programs and practices*, London/Thousand Oaks, CA: Sage, pp.1–30.

Marks, G., Hooghe, L. and Blank, K. (1996) 'European integration from the 1980s: state-centric v. multi-level governance', *Journal of Common Market Studies*, 34(3): 341–78.

Marlier, E., Atkinson, A.B., Cantillon, B. and Nolan, B. (2007) *The EU and Social Inclusion: facing the challenges*, Bristol: The Policy Press.

Marsh, D. and Stoker, G. (eds) (1995) *Theory and Methods in Political Science*, 1st edn, Basingstoke/New York: Macmillan/St. Martin's Press.

Marsh, D. and Stoker, G. (eds) (2002) *Theory and Methods in Political Science*, 2nd edn, Basingstoke/New York: Palgrave Macmillan (1st edn 1995).

Marsh, R.M. (1967) *Comparative Sociology: a codification of cross-societal analysis*, New York: Harcourt, Brace & World.

Maurice, M. (1989) 'Méthode comparative et analyse sociétale: les implications théoriques des comparaisons internationales', *Sociologie du travail*, 31(2): 175–91.

May, M. (2003) 'The role of comparative study', in P. Alcock, A. Erskine and M. May (eds), *The Student's Companion to Social Policy*, 2nd edn, Malden, MA/Oxford: Blackwell (1st edn 1998), pp.17–24.

May, M. (2008) 'The role of comparative study in social policy', in P. Alcock, M. May and K. Rowlingson (eds), *The Student's Companion to Social Policy*, 3rd edn, Malden, MA/Oxford: Blackwell (1st edn 1998), pp.421–9.

McNeill, P. and Chapman, S. (2005) *Research Methods*, 3rd edn, London: Routledge (1st edn 1985).

Mill, J.S. (1973) 'Of the four methods of experimental inquiry', 'General considerations on the social science', 'Of the chemical, or experimental, method in the social science', in J.M. Robson (ed.), *Collected Works of John Stuart Mill, A System of Logic Ratiocinative and Inductive: being a connected view of the principles of evidence and the methods of scientific investigation*, vol. VII, book III, chapter viii, pp.388–406; vol. VIII, book VI, chapters vi, vii, pp. 875–8, 879–86, Toronto: University of Toronto/Routledge & Kegan Paul, (original work published 1843).

Mohler, P. (2007) 'What is being learned from the ESS?', in R. Jowell, C. Roberts, R. Fitzgerald and G. Eva (eds), *Measuring Attitudes Cross-Nationally: lessons from the European Social Survey*, London/Thousand Oaks/CA: Sage, pp.157–68.

Müller, K. (2001) 'The political economy of pension reform in eastern Europe', *International Social Security Review*, 54(2–3): 57–79.

Nadel, S.F. (1951) *The Foundations of Social Anthropology*, London: Cohen & West.

Naroll, R. (1968) 'Some thoughts on comparative method in cultural anthropology', in H.M. Blalock and A.B. Blalock (eds), *Methodology in Social Research*, New York: McGraw-Hill, pp.236–77.

Ní Bhrolcháin, M. and Dyson, T. (2007) 'On causation in demography: issues and illustrations', *Population and Development Review*, 33(1): 1–36.

Nießen, M. (1984) 'Some introductory notes on the second Vienna Centre training seminar', in M. Nießen, J. Peschar and C. Kourilsky (eds), *International Comparative Research: social structure and public institutions in Eastern and Western Europe*, Oxford/New York: Pergamon Press, pp.xiii–xvi.

Nießen, M. and Peschar, J. (1982) 'The international seminar on cross-national comparative research', in M. Nießen and J. Peschar (eds), *International Comparative Research: problems of theory, methodology and organisation in Eastern and Western Europe*, Oxford/New York: Pergamon Press, pp.xiii–xvi.

Nilsen, A. (2008) 'From questions of methods to epistemological issues: the case of biographical research', in P. Alasuutari, L. Bickman and J. Brannen (eds), *The SAGE Handbook of Social Research Methods*, London/Thousand Oaks, CA: Sage, pp.81–94.

Noah, H.J. and Eckstein, M.A. (1969) *Towards a Science of Comparative Education*, London: Collier–Macmillan.

Oksanen, T., Lehvo, A., Nuutinen, A., Kivinen, D. and Akatemia, S. (eds) (2003) *Scientific Research in Finland: a review of its quality and impact in the early 2000s*, Helsinki: Academy of Finland.

Øyen, E. (1990) 'Preface', 'The imperfections of comparisons', in E. Øyen (ed.), *Comparative Methodology: theory and practice in international social research*, London/Newbury Park, CA: Sage, pp.vii–ix, 1–18.

Øyen, E. (2004) 'Living with imperfect comparisons', in P. Kennett (ed.), *A Handbook of Comparative Social Policy*, Cheltenham/Northampton, MA: Edward Elgar, pp.276–91.

Parsons, T. (1966) *Societies: evolutionary and comparative perspectives*, Englewood Cliffs, NJ: Prentice-Hall.

Pennings, P., Keman, H. and Kleinnijenhuis, J. (1999) *Doing Research in Political Science: an introduction to comparative methods and statistics*, London/Thousand Oaks, CA: Sage.

Peters, B.G. (1998) *Comparative Politics: theory and method*, New York: New York University Press.

Portes, A. (1973) 'Perception of the U.S. sociologist and its impact on cross-national research', in M. Armer and A.D. Grimshaw (eds), *Comparative Social Research: methodological problems and strategies*, New York/London: John Wiley & Sons, pp.149–69.

Poulain, M., Perrin, N. and Singleton, A. (eds) (2006) *THESIM: towards harmonised European statistics on international migration*, Louvain: Presses Universitaires de Louvain.

Preece, R. (1994) *Starting Research: an introduction to academic research and dissertation writing*, London: Pinter.

Przeworski, A. and Teune, H. (1970) *The Logic of Comparative Social Inquiry*, 1st edn, New York/London: John Wiley & Sons.

Punch, K.F. (2006) *Developing Effective Research Proposals*, 2nd edn, London/Thousand Oaks, CA: Sage (1st edn 2000).

Ragin, C. (1987) *The Comparative Method: moving beyond qualitative and quantitative strategies*, Berkeley, CA/London: University of California Press.

Randma, T. (2001) *Civil Service Careers in Small and Large States: the cases of Estonia and the United Kingdom*, Baden-Baden: Nomos Verlagsgesellschaft (Verwaltungsorganisation, Staatsaufgaben and Öffentlicher Dienst, Band 47).

Read, M. and Marsh, D. (2002) 'Combining quantitative and qualitative methods', in D. Marsh and G. Stoker (eds), *Theory and Methods in Political Science*, 2nd edn, Basingstoke/New York: Palgrave Macmillan (1st edn 1995), pp.231–47.

Riley, M.W. (1963) 'Commentary: special problems of sociological analysis', *Sociological Research: a case approach*, vol. 1, New York: Harcourt, Brace & World, pp.700–39.

Robinson, S.W. (1950) 'Ecological correlations and behavior of individuals', *American Sociological Review*, 15(3): 351–7.

Robson, C. (2004) 'Evaluation research', in S. Becker and A. Bryman (eds), *Understanding Research for Social Policy and Practice: themes, methods and approaches*, Bristol: The Policy Press, pp.122–5.

Rodgers, B.N., Doron, A. and Jones, M. (1979) *The Study of Social Policy: a comparative approach*, London: Allen & Unwin.

Rodgers, B.N., with J. Greve and J.S. Morgan (1968) *Comparative Social Administration*, 1st edn, London: George Allen & Unwin.

Rokkan, S. (ed.) (1968) *Comparative Research across Cultures and Nations*, Paris/The Hague: Mouton.

Rokkan, S., Verba, S., Viet, J. and Almasy, E. (eds) (1969) *Comparative Survey Analysis*, Paris/The Hague: Mouton.

Rose, M. (1985) 'Universalism, culturalism and the Aix group: promise and problems of a societal approach to economic institutions', *European Sociological Review*, 1(1): 65–83.

Rose, R. (1991) 'Comparing forms of comparative analysis', *Political Studies*, 39(3): 446–62.

Rose, R. (2001) *Ten Steps in Learning Lessons from Abroad*, ESRC Future Governance Paper 1, www.hull.ac.uk/futgov/Papers/PubPapers/RRPaper 1.pdf

Rose, R. (2002) 'When all other conditions are not equal: the context for drawing lessons', *Studies in Public Policy*, no 366.

Ross, M.H. (1997) 'Culture and identity in comparative political analysis', in M.I. Lichbach and A.S. Zuckerman (eds), *Comparative Politics: rationality, culture, and structure*, Cambridge: Cambridge University Press, pp.42–80.

Rust, V.D., Soumaré, A., Pescador, O. and Shibuya, M. (1999) 'Research strategies in comparative education', *Comparative Education Review*, 43(1): 86–109.

Samuel, N. (1985) 'Is there a distinct cross-national comparative sociology, method and methodology?', *Cross-National Research Papers*, 1(1): 3–10.

Sartori, G. (1970) 'Concept misformation in comparative politics', *American Political Science Review*, 64(4): 1033–53.

Sartori, G. (1984) 'Foreword', 'Guidelines for concept analysis', in G. Sartori (ed.), *Social Science Concepts: a systematic analysis*, Beverly Hills, CA: Sage, pp.9–11, 15–85.

Sartori, G. (1991) 'Comparing and miscomparing', *Journal of Theoretical Politics*, 3(3): 243–57.

Sartori, G. (1994) 'Compare why and how: comparing, miscomparing and the comparative method', in M. Dogan and A. Kazancigil (eds), *Comparing Nations: concepts, strategies, substance*, Oxford/Cambridge, MA: Blackwell, pp.14–34.

Sartori, G. (ed.) (1984) *Social Science Concepts: a systematic analysis*, Beverly Hills, CA/London: Sage.

Savolainen, J. (1994) 'The rationality of drawing big conclusions based on small samples: in defense of Mill's methods', *Social Forces*, 72(4): 1217–24.

Scarrow, H.A. (1969) *Comparative Political Analysis: an introduction*, New York/London: Harper & Row.

Scheuch. E.K. (1989) 'Theoretical implications of comparative survey research: why the wheel of cross-cultural methodology keeps on being reinvented', *International Sociology*, 4(2): 147–67.

Scheuch, E.K. (1990) 'The development of comparative research: towards causal explanations', in E. Øyen (ed.), *Comparative Methodology: theory and practice in international social research*, London/Newbury Park, CA: Sage, pp.19–37.

Schultheis, F. (1991) 'Introduction', in F. de Singly and F. Schultheis (eds), *Affaires de familles, affaires d'État: sociologie de la famille*, Jarville-La-Malgrange: Éditions de l'Est, pp.5–22.

Shaw, I.F., Greene, J.C. and Mark, M.M. (eds) (2006) *Handbook of Evaluation: policies, programs and practices*, London/Thousand Oaks, CA: Sage.

Simmel, G. (1917) *Grundfragen der Soziologie (Individuum und Gesellschaft)*, Berlin/Leipzig: G.J. Göschen.

Singleton, A. (2007) 'Combining quantitative and qualitative research methods in the study of international migration', in L. Hantrais and S. Mangen (eds), *Cross-National Research Methodology & Practice*, London/New York: Routledge, pp.61–7.

Skocpol, T. and Somers, M. (1980) 'The uses of comparative history in macrosocial inquiry', *Comparative Studies in Society and History*, 22(2): 174–97.

Smelser, N.J. (1973) 'The methodology of comparative analysis', in D.P. Warwick and S. Osherson (eds), *Comparative Research Methods*, Englewood Cliffs, NJ: Prentice-Hall, pp.42–86.

Smelser, N.J. (1976) *Comparative Methods in the Social Sciences*, Englewood Cliffs, NJ: Prentice-Hall.

Smithson, J. (2008) 'Focus groups', in P. Alasuutari, L. Bickman and J. Brannen (eds), *The SAGE Handbook of Social Research Methods*, London/Thousand Oaks, CA: Sage, pp.357–70.

Soydan, S. (1996) 'Using the vignette method in cross-cultural comparisons', in L. Hantrais and S. Mangen (eds), *Cross-National Research Methods in the Social Sciences*, London/New York: Pinter/Cassels, pp.120–8.

Spencer, L., Ritchie, J., Lewis, J. and Dillon, L. (2003) *Quality in Qualitative Evaluation: a framework for assessing research evidence*, London: Cabinet Office Strategy Unit, www.strategy.gov.uk

Stafford, B. (2001) 'Analysing and assessing the family–welfare relationship', in L. Hantrais (ed.), *Researching Family and Welfare from an International Comparative Perspective*, EUR 20001, Luxembourg: Office for Official Publications of the European Communities, pp.85–6.

Stafford, B. (2002) 'Being more certain about random assignment in social policy evaluations', *Social Policy & Society*, 1(4): 275–84.

Stephen, S. (2001) *A Comparative Sociology of World Religions: virtuosos, priests, and popular religion*, New York: New York University Press.

Stevenson, J. and Thomas, D. (2006) 'Intellectual contexts', in I.F. Shaw, J.C. Greene and M.M. Mark (eds), *Handbook of Evaluation: policies, programs and practices*, London/Thousand Oaks, CA: Sage, pp.200–24.

Sykes, R., Palier, B. and Prior, P.M. (eds) (2001) *Globalization and European Welfare States: challenge and change*, Basingstoke/New York: Palgrave.

Szalai, A. (1977) 'The organization and execution of cross-national survey research projects', in A. Szalai and R. Petrella (eds), *Cross-National Comparative Survey Research: theory and practice*, Oxford/New York: Pergamon Press, pp.49–93.

Szalai, A. and Petrella, R. (eds) (1977) *Cross-National Comparative Survey Research: theory and practice*, Oxford/New York: Pergamon Press.

Tashakkori, A. and Treddlie, C. (eds) (2003) *Handbook of Mixed Methods in Social and Behavioral Research*, Thousand Oaks, CA/London: Sage.

Tennom, J. (1995) 'European research communities: France vs. the United Kingdom', *The Puzzle of Integration. European Yearbook on Youth Policy and Research* (CYRCE), vol. 1: 269–81.

Teune, H. (1990) 'Comparing countries: lessons learned', in E. Øyen (ed.), *Comparative Methodology: theory and practice in international social research*, London/Newbury Park, CA: Sage, pp.38–62.

Thelen, K. and Steinmo, S. (1992) 'Historical institutionalism in comparative politics', in S. Steinmo, K. Thelen and F. Longstreth (eds), *Structuring Politics: historical institutionalism in comparative analysis*, Cambridge: Cambridge University Press, pp.1–32.

Titmuss, R. (1967) 'The relationship between income maintenance and social service benefits – an overview', *International Social Security Review*, 20(1), 57–66.

Trubek, D.M. and Trubek, L.G. (2005) 'Hard and soft law in the construction of social Europe: the role of the open method of co-ordination', *European Law Journal*, 11(3): 343–64.

Turner, R.H. (1990) 'A comparative content analysis of biographies', in E. Øyen (ed.), *Comparative Methodology: theory and practice in international social research*, London/Newbury Park, CA: Sage, pp.134–50.

United Nations Economic Commission for Europe/Statistical Office of the European Communities (Eurostat) (2006) *Conference of European Statisticians: recommendations for the 2010 Censuses of Population and Housing*, New York/Geneva: United Nations.

Vallier, I. (ed.) (1971) *Comparative Methods in Sociology: essays on trends and applications*, Berkeley, CA/London: University of California Press.

Vaughan-Whitehead, D.C. (2003) *EU Enlargement versus Social Europe? The uncertain future of the European social model*, Cheltenham/Northampton, MA: Edward Elgar.

Verba, S. (1969) 'The uses of survey research in the study of comparative politics', in S. Rokkan, S. Verba, J. Viet and E. Almasy (eds), *Comparative Survey Analysis*, The Hague/Paris: Mouton, pp.56–106.

Vigour, C. (2005) *La Comparaison dans les sciences sociales: pratiques et méthodes*, Paris: La Découverte.

Walker, J.L. (1969) 'The diffusion of innovations among the American states', *American Political Science Review*, 63(3): 880–99.

Walker, R. (2000) 'Welfare policy: tendering for evidence', in H.T.O Davies, S.M. Nutley and P.C. Smith (eds), *What works? Evidence-based policy and practice in public services*, Bristol: The Policy Press, pp.141–66.

Walker, R. and Wiseman, M. (2006) 'Managing evaluations', in I.F. Shaw, J.C. Greene and M.M. Mark (eds), *Handbook of Evaluation: policies, programs and practices*, London/Thousand Oaks, CA: Sage, pp.360–83.

Wallace, C. (2003) 'Households, work and flexibility (HWF)', in L. Hantrais (ed.), *Policy Relevance of 'Family and Welfare' Research*, Luxembourg: Official Publications of the European Communities, pp.36–9.

Wallerstein, I. (1979) *The Capitalist World-Economy: essays*, Cambridge: Cambridge University Press.

Warwick, D.P. (1973) 'Survey research and participant observation: a benefit-cost analysis', in D.P. Warwick and S. Osherson (eds), *Comparative Research Methods*, Englewood Cliffs, NJ: Prentice-Hall, pp.189–203.

Warwick, D.P. and Osherson, S. (1973) 'Comparative analysis in the social sciences', in D.P. Warwick and S. Osherson (eds), *Comparative Research Methods*, Englewood Cliffs, NJ: Prentice-Hall, pp.3–41.

Weber, M. (1930) *The Protestant Ethic and the Spirit of Capitalism*, T. Parsons (trans.), 1st edn, London: Allen & Unwin (1st German edn 1904–05).

Weber, M. (1949) *The Methodology of the Social Sciences*, E.A. Shils and H.A. Finch (trans and eds), Glencoe, IL: Free Press (1st German edn 1903–17).

Wever, K.S. and Turner, L. (1995) 'A wide-angle lens for a global marketplace', in K.S. Wever and L. Turner (eds), *The Comparative Political Economy of Industrial Relations*, Madison, WI: University of Wisconsin, Industrial Relations Research Association, pp.1–7.

Wever, K.S. and Turner, L. (eds) (1995) *The Comparative Political Economy of Industrial Relations*, Madison, WI: Industrial Relations Research Association.

Whitehead, N. (2004) 'Historical methods for comparing pension policies', *Cross-National Research Papers*, 7(2), 21–9.

Wilensky, H.L. (1997) 'Social science and the public agenda: reflections on the relation of knowledge to policy in the United States and abroad', *Journal of Health Politics, Policy and Law*, 22(5): 1241–65.

Wilensky, H.L. and Lebeaux, C.N. (1958) *Industrial Society and Social Welfare: the impact of industrialization on the supply and organization of social welfare services in the United States*, New York: Russel Sage Foundation.

Wilensky, H.L., Luebbert, G.M., Reed Hahn, S. and Jamieson, A.M. (1985) *Comparative Social Policy: theories, methods, findings*, Berkeley, CA: University of California.

Williams, S. (2004) 'Observations based on experience of managing research', *Cross-National Research Papers*, 7(5), 45–9.

Zweigert, K. and Kötz, H. (1998) *Introduction to Comparative Law*, T. Weir (trans.), 3rd edn, Oxford: Clarendon Press (1st English edn 1977; 1st German edn 1969–71).

Index